Comprehensive
Emergency Management:
Evacuating Threatened
Populations

CONTEMPORARY STUDIES IN
APPLIED BEHAVIORAL SCIENCE, VOLUME 3

Editor: Louis A. Zurcher, *Ashbel Smith Professor of Social Work and Sociology,*
School of Social Work, University of Texas, Austin

CONTEMPORARY STUDIES IN APPLIED BEHAVIORAL SCIENCE

Series Editor: Louis A. Zurcher
School of Social Work, University of Texas at Austin

To Polly and Liz,
Who manage my emergencies

Comprehensive
Emergency Management:
Evacuating Threatened
Populations

by RONALD W. PERRY
Center for Public Affairs
Arizona State University

 JAI PRESS INC.

Greenwich, Connecticut   *London, England*

Library of Congress Cataloging in Publication Data

Perry, Ronald W.
  Comprehensive emergency management.

  (Contemporary studies in applied behavioral science; v. 3)
  Bibliography: p. 173
  Includes index.
  1. Assistance in emergencies—United States—Manage-
ment.   2. Disaster relief—United States—Management.
3. Evacuation of civilians—United States—Management. I. Title.   II. Series.
HV555.U6P47   1984   363.3'48'067   84-12616
ISBN 0-89232-436-8

Copyright © 1985 JAI PRESS INC.
36 Sherwood Place
Greenwich, Connecticut 06830

JAI PRESS INC.
3 Henrietta Street
London WC2E 8LU
England

ISBN: 0–89232–436–8

Library of Congress Card Number: 84–12616

Manufactured in the United States of America

CONTENTS

List of Tables

Chapter I

Chapter II

Chapter III

List of Figures

Preface

This book represents what I hope will become one of many steps toward achieving in practice the concept of comprehensive emergency management. The idea that emergency management should evolve from the status of occupation to that of profession is constructive and, I believe, it anticipates social and technological changes that are taking place in American society. The process of achieving professional status, however, will take some time and require changes both in the way emergency managers see themselves, and in the way they are viewed by the rest of our society. One of the first changes that must occur is that emergency managers must identify and take control of a body of specialized knowledge regarding the conduct of emergency management, and develop a credentialing process. There is a role for hazards researchers in this important first step; we must review the available studies and begin to consolidate existing knowledge of human performance relative to hazard management and disaster response. In this way, we can help emergency managers define the body of knowledge they need to control their profession and start to disseminate the results of our research in a form which promotes the effective conduct of emergency management. In this book I have attempted to elaborate the concept of comprehensive emergency management, to describe the present condition and the promise of the emergency management system in the United States, and to assemble, in a useable form, findings about the design and implementation of community evacuation plans in natural and man-made disasters. Some of the information reported here derives from my own research, but most of the data come from the collective research efforts of many social scientists over the past six decades. It is my hope that this book will soon become one of many which describe accumulated knowledge of different aspects of emergency management.

Books such as this one have their genesis over a period of years; consequently the author develops many debts to many individuals who should be acknowledged. The intellectual debts I have incurred are indeed far too many to allow for adequate summary in a short acknowledgment. Nonetheless, I shall attempt to mention those who have made specific contributions as well as those who have shaped my own view of the field. First among these people are my teachers. More than a decade ago, William Anderson introduced me to the idea and practice of disaster research. At the time I didn't realize that it would become my principal professional interest. There is indeed no adequate way that I can fully acknowledge the extent or importance of Bill's patient tutorage for both my personal and professional development. Also over a period of years I have been fortunate to count among my teachers three fine disaster researchers: Charles E. Fritz, Enrico L. Quarantelli and Thomas E. Drabek. Though I must assume the blame for what I may have done with it, collectively these scholars have laid the foundation and provided the building materials for my education.

My debt to my colleagues in disaster research is also great. In particular, Gary Kreps, Robert Stallings and Dennis Wenger have challenged my understanding of the substance of the field, and in so doing have forced me to clarify my own thinking and taught me much about the substance of disaster research and about what it means to be a disaster researcher. Marjorie R. Greene also merits my sincerest thanks both for her continuing help as a fellow researcher, and for helping me to better understand the "applications end" of research on natural hazards. David Gillespie and Michael Lindell have also contributed to my growth as a professional, and acted as trusted collaborators on many research adventures. Over many years, James Kerr, Roy Popkin and Forrest Wilcox, in their roles as professional emergency managers, have been my most important teachers regarding the world in which community disasters take place. I wish to acknowledge the help given me by Mrs. Adeline Dinger. Without her patient and expert guidance in translating this book from scribbled notes to a finished manuscript and her much-needed encouragement and persistent optimism, I am certain this project would never have been completed.

Finally, the data analyzed here on flood and volcano response were collected over a six-year period under two grants from the National Science Foundation (PFR-77-23697 and PFR-80-19297). The preparation of this book as supported in part by grant number CEE-81-20426 from the Civil and Environmental Engineering Division of the National Science Foundation. All of the interpretations and conclusions drawn are those of the author, however, and do not constitute official policy of the National Science Foundation.

Chapter I

An Introduction to Comprehensive Emergency Management

In recent years, natural hazards have captured the attention of the public and frequently and forcefully intruded into the lives of American citizens. The eruption of Mt. St. Helens volcano in 1980 drew attention to the reality that so-called "low-probability, high-consequence" natural events *do* indeed occur. Since then the U.S. has experienced severe and widespread floods, severe hurricanes on the Atlantic and Gulf coasts, brush fires in California, mudslides, and the apparent threat of severe earthquakes in the west. In addition to these natural events, we have also seen emergencies associated with the reactor accident at Three Mile Island, the Love Canal contamination, oil refinery explosions in Texas and exploding tank cars associated with a train derailment in Louisiana. The purpose here is not to construct an exhaustive catalog of major catastrophies in the last four years. Instead, it is to direct attention toward an apparent increase in human concern with natural and man-made disasters.

This increasing concern should not necessarily be attributed to an increase in natural and man-made disasters. There is no particularly good evidence for historical periodicity of most natural disasters, and in its absence one must assume a relatively constant rate of occurrence. In a sense, the same argument applies to man-made disasters. One might reasonably argue, of course, that with respect to technology-associated disasters advances in technology and increasing global industrialization in turn increase the opportunity for man-made disasters. While this latter point may be of value, perhaps the critical issue is not that the rate of disaster occurrence is increasing, but that due to settlement patterns and other variables, more humans are exposed to natural and man-made hazards, thereby increasing the potential for disasters to occur.

1

In this environment of vulnerability, characterized by many different threat agents, the concept of comprehensive emergency management (CEM) has begun to take shape. Comprehensive emergency management refers to the problem of developing a capacity for handling all phases of activity—mitigation, preparedness, response and recovery—in all types of disasters by coordinating the efforts and resources of many different organizations or agencies (cf. National Governors' Association, 1971, p. 11). Thus, comprehensive emergency management is distinguished from other approaches by two important characteristics. First, CEM emphasizes comprehensive management by dictating a concern with:

1. preventing (mitigating) disasters by eliminating or reducing their probability of occurrence when possible, for example, by creating breach-proof containers for transporting nuclear waste or by enforcing zoning relations to exclude building in flood plains;
2. preparing protective measures for threats less susceptable to human control, such as detection-and-warning systems for tornadoes;
3. responding to disaster events when they do happen, for example, by developing search and rescue techniques for locating victims of volcanic eruptions; and
4. restoring social systems after disaster impact, by developing, perhaps, loan programs to allow victims to rebuild homes.

The second distinguishing feature of CEM is its concern with the management of all types of emergencies whether natural or man-made. This includes such apparently diverse events as nuclear war, floods, terrorist actions, hurricanes, nuclear power plant accidents, transportation accidents involving hazardous materials, tornadoes, urban riots, and industrial explosions.

In focusing upon managing all phases of all kinds of disasters, CEM can be seen as an attempt to integrate emergency management techniques and problems by developing a management strategy effective for coping with a variety of hazard agents. CEM may be seen, therefore, as no less than revolutionary when contrasted with historical views of emergency management which partition disaster agents into discrete categories and claim that unique management techniques must be developed for each one. Furthermore, aside from the intuitive appeal of being parsimonious, many cost conscious mayors, county executives, state governors and federal officials are attracted to the more efficient use of resources promised by a comprehensive approach to emergency management.

Interestingly, with all its appeal and promise, the likely success or failure of CEM depends upon the extent to which, in practice, one may develop hazard management tools which are effective with different types of disasters. Ironically, this question is one of the least-researched topics in the field of natural and man-made hazard management. Recently however, social scientists have begun to lay the conceptual and theoretical foundations for making such cross-hazard comparisons (Kreps, 1981; Perry, 1982). A large part of this effort has involved identifying common or generic functions which must be accomplished in managing most types of emergencies—i.e., evacuation, search and rescue, warning dissemination, sheltering, rehabilitation, public information. Once identified, scholars have started to examine, based upon historical case studies, the applicability of each function across different types of disasters. In developing a capability for CEM, the logical extension of this work is to select specific functions and assemble systematic, data-based comparisons among different types of disasters. In this way, one can build a body of information which documents similarities and differences in human performance relative to specific functions for numerous disasters.

The purpose of this book is two-fold. First, I seek to examine the concept of comprehensive emergency management by developing a theoretical framework for comparing natural and man-made disasters and analyzing some data on human response to different kinds of disaster agents. The second objective, once the basic comparability of citizen response across some hazards is established, is to review principles of emergency management which generalize across a variety of disaster events. For the most part I will focus upon the utilization of a particular disaster management tool, pre-impact evacuation, and analyze its use in the larger context of warning systems for environment threats. At the outset it is also important to understand the context in which these two objectives will be pursued. This book should be seen as a three-phase effort. In the first phase, covered in this chapter and Chapter II, the *concept* of comparing citizen evacuation behavior in response to different disaster agents is reviewed. The purpose of this discussion is to establish the theoretical and logical bases upon which cross-hazard comparisons rest. The second phase, laid out in Chapter III, is to examine some *data* on citizen evacuation warning response in three different environmental threats: a volcanic eruption, a riverine flood, and a nuclear power plant accident. These data analyses are not intended to be comprehensive studies of evacuation response in each different threat. Instead, they are included as an *example* of the idea that once appropriate variations in the nature of the threat agent are accounted for, one can understand evacuation warning compliance across all three threats in similar analytic terms. Finally, the third and most important phase is represented in Chapters IV through VII. It is here that I develop a systematic framework for describing citizen emergency decision-making processes and suggest strategies and techniques for managing evacuations that are designed to be useful across any environmental threats for which movement of citizens constitutes an appropriate protective mechanism.

To begin the first phase of this work, it is necessary that I establish more precisely what is meant by comprehensive emergency management, and the basic comparability of disaster events. Thus, the remainder of this chapter is devoted to two topics. First, I will review the components and operation of the emergency management system in the United States, including a discussion of the tasks or activities which constitute "emergency management." In this way, one can begin to appreciate the challenges that face emergency managers, the tools available for manipulating the consequences of disasters, and the way different resources in the system mesh together. Following this discussion, attention is turned to the problems of how to make appropriate comparisons of human behavior in natural and man-made disasters. The focus here is upon arriving at a workable definition of what constitutes "disaster" and identifying dimensions which may be used to meaningfully compare different disaster phenomena.

THE STRUCTURE OF EMERGENCY MANAGEMENT

Some social scientists and hazard managers would say that it is presumptious to speak of an emergency management "system" in the United States. Certainly if by *system* one means an integrated collection of components with defined and agreed upon obligations and responsibilities interacting in concert to achieve a common goal, an emergency management system does not exist. The nature and philosophy of emergency management has been changing, however, and especially since the late 1970s, what can *become* a system for managing emergencies has been evolving. Much of what currently exists is still fragmented and incomplete; in particular, many emergency managers have been critical of the capability and organizational structure that exists at the federal level. However, there appears to be both a desire and certainly the rudiments of a plan on the part of some federal officials and state governments to move towards the establishment of an integrated emergency management system.

In this section I will discuss what is and what might be with respect to an emergency management system. To maintain accuracy, it is important that the reader be aware of the fact that many links among organizations described here are tenuous at best, and many functions attributed to agencies (particularly at the federal level) are minimally fulfilled, or in a few cases, completely ignored. Of course those links that do not exist are described as such, and problems are identified as appropriate throughout the discussion. Furthermore, what follows represents an attempt to describe in a very short space what is really a very complex and extensive collection of programs, agencies and interrelationships. By necessity then, many issues have been both compressed and simplified. With these caveats, then, we can turn to a description of the tasks which constitute emergency management.

Emergency Management Tasks

Comprehensive emergency management stresses that attention should be devoted to the full range of options for coping with emergencies. It is possible to describe emergency-related activities in various ways, reflecting differing levels of specificity of function and taking into account different conceptions of time phases in emergency management. Perhaps the simplest such schema groups emergency activities into four discrete but interconnected categories distinguished by time phase relative to disaster impact. Thus, *mitigation* and *preparedness* activities are generally seen as taking place before the impact of any given disaster, while *response* and *recovery* activities are seen as post-impact measures.

Mitigation activities are directed, when possible, towards eliminating the causes of disasters or significantly reducing the chance that a disaster will occur. The focus here is upon prevention; so to speak, stopping disasters before they happen. In this sense, mitigation activities have been most effectively employed in connection with technological hazards where, once the threat is identified, it is sufficiently subject to human control that steps may be taken to minimize the probability of an incident. For example, with respect to the transportation of hazardous materials by highway, one can minimize the probability of risks to public health and safety by establishing rules regarding strength and construction of containers, maintaining safety checks on transport vehicles, routing vehicles through low-density population areas, and timing shipments to coincide with low-activity periods in urban areas. Another mitigation strategy often used with natural hazards, or events over which man has little control, simply involves acknowledging the existence of the hazard and trying to manipulate human activities in a way that minimizes the consequences of periodic impact. Thus, land use management strategies to restrict residential construction in flood plains is an important mitigation measure against riverine floods. Likewise, building code requirements can be established to enable structures to better withstand hurricane force winds and/or earthquake shocks.

All of these mitigation activities have in common the characteristics of being long-range measures. They are taken well in advance, either in response to a specific disaster or after a risk has been identified, and tend to be aimed at hazard reduction or, more simply, at minimizing the chance that an incident will occur that could become a disaster. Interestingly, in the history of attempts of emergency management in the United States, the smallest proportion of resources has been traditionally devoted to mitigation activities.

Preparedness activities are those which are undertaken to protect human lives and property in conjunction with threats that cannot be manipulated via mitigation measures, or from which only partial protection may be achieved. One may think of preparedness measures as falling into two general categories: actions related to providing an alert that impact is eminent, and actions designed to enhance the effectiveness of emergency operations. Preparedness measures related to providing an alert include the development and improvement of detection and prediction technologies that allow authorities to monitor the environment to insure that they will have forewarning of environmental threats. Such technologies are evidenced in riverine flood detection systems, radar detection and tracking of severe storms, and equipment designed to detect functional and coolant irregularities in nuclear power plants used to generate electricity. Warning systems that convey information about threats from the authorities to the general public—e.g., regarding tornadoes, dam failures, hurricanes, and such—also fall into this category. Preparedness measures aimed at enhancing emergency operations encompass a variety of activities, including developing routing plans for evacuations, stockpiling medical and survival material for public shelters, assembling lists of community resources and their location for possible use in responding to a given emergency, and training cadre and conducting drills and rehearsals of emergency response plans.

Therefore, like mitigation measures, preparedness activities are conducted or undertaken in advance of any particular disaster event. They represent ways of protecting life and property when disasters do strike. It has been documented that preparedness activities historically have also received comparatively few resources relative to response and recovery. Disaster researchers have for some time documented a general cycle in which there is a great deal of interest in preparedness issues immediately following a major disaster, which declines significantly as time passes. Furthermore, because considerable time is often required to translate such concern into budget allocations and implementable programs, many preparedness strategies have simply failed to get off the ground. In developing the concept of comprehensive emergency management, a concerted effort has been made to establish the importance of both mitigation and preparedness activities. In particular, disaster researchers have argued that it is far more desirable to prevent damage in the first place than it is to try and deal with it after the fact.

Emergency response activities are conducted during and just after the period of impact and focus upon assisting the affected public, as well as minimizing damage from secondary or repeated impact. Some of the more visible response activities include securing the impact area, search and rescue, provision of emergency medical care, and sheltering evacuees and other victims. Also during the response phase, operations may be mounted to counter secondary threats, such as fighting urban fires after earthquakes, identifying contaminated water supplies or other public health threats following typhoons, identifying contaminated wildlife or fish in connection with a toxic chemical spill, or preparing for floods or mudflows following a volcanic eruption. During the response stage, emergency managers must assess damages, care for victims, coordinate and deploy converging material, and anticipate any additional short range threats. Such activities are usually accomplished through the coordinated efforts of diverse groups—some formally constituted, some volunteer—and managed via an emergency operations center (EOC). This phase of activity is marked by time pressures and a sense of urgency which is less prevalent in mitigation, preparedness and recovery. In the world of disaster response, minutes of delay can cost lives and property. Particularly since the nuclear reactor accident at Three Mile Island, there has been a renewed interest among emergency managers in developing ways to smoothly and promptly accomplish response tasks.

Recovery activities begin shortly after disaster impact and may extend for long periods of time. The objective of recovery measures is to restore the physical part of the community, as well as the quality of life to at least the same levels as before the disaster, and possibly to introduce improvements. Traditionally, recovery has been thought of in terms of short range (relief and rehabilitation) measures versus longer range (reconstruction) measures. Relief and rehabilitation activities usually include clearance of debris and restoring access to the impact area, getting affected business and industry back into operation, restoring government or community services, and developing a temporary system for caring for victims—the provision of housing, clothing and food. Reconstruction activities tend to be dominated by the rebuilding of structures—buildings, roads, bridges, dams and such—and by efforts to restore the area's economic system. In some communities, leaders may view the reconstruction phase as an opportunity to institute the community plans for change that existed before the disaster or to introduce mitigation measures into the rebuilding that would constitute an improvement upon the predisaster state. This approach to reconstruction has been documented after the great Alaska earthquake of 1964 (Anderson, 1969b), and after the eruption of Mt. Usu on the northern island of Hokaido in Japan (Perry & Hirose, 1982).

Finally, it should be pointed out that in most cases, the bulk of the resources used in the recovery phase (particularly on reconstruction) are derived from extra-community sources. In the United States, these sources tend to be private organizations and state governments, but for the most part come from the federal government. Furthermore, as Fritz (1971) has indicated, both in the U.S. and elsewhere, most of the money and resources devoted to what is here called disaster management had been directed at the recovery phase. This is consistent with the aforementioned cycle of citizen and governmental interest in disasters. Immediately after impact, the attention of both the public and community officials is captured and it becomes more feasible to appropriate resources to aid disaster victims and for the obvious necessity of physically restoring the community.

The preceding discussion has examined what might be described as the desired products of an emergency management system. That is, one would expect that a plan aimed at comprehensive management of emergencies would, as part of its provisions, promote mitigation, preparedness, and a capability for response and recovery. In summary, two points should be reiterated here. First, although the distinction among them is largely analytic, the four activities are somewhat time-phased. Mitigation and preparedness measures take place and should be planned for in advance of any specific disaster impact, while response and recovery occur during and following disaster impact. Therefore, practical problems accompany the development of mitigation and preparedness strategy because they must usually be accomplished during so-called normal times, when an environmental threat is not eminent. Historically it has been difficult to mount efforts to engage in these sorts of activities. Response and recovery take place within the context of a disaster impact—clearly non-normal times—and benefit from the operations or an emergency social system as well as from the community's cohesiveness usually promoted in the short-range aftermath (Fritz, 1961b).

The second point is that in the past, far more resources and emphasis have been given response and recovery activities than mitigation and preparedness. To a certain extent this differential emphasis has been a function of the difficulty citizens and political officials have in thinking about disasters during normal times when they apparently do not threaten. To do so requires that both citizens and leaders dwell upon what might be called negative events which may or may not occur sometime in the future—a task that is almost universally defined as undesirable. Perhaps equally important, however, particularly when expending resources is at issue, are the limitations posed by the technical state of knowledge regarding various hazards. In itself the state of technology imposes limits on the nature and type of mitigation and preparedness activities that may be undertaken. If a potential disaster event cannot be detected in advance or if the technology for doing so is crude (as in the case of predicting earthquakes, volcanic eruptions, or civil disorders), mitigation simply may be impossible or at best very imprecise. Furthermore, in the absence of a technology or detection, advance warning is not possible either. Thus, at least historically, it has sometimes seemed both expedient and logical to devote resources to response and recovery. In the future, if comprehensive emergency management is successfully implemented, the approach should be to acknowledge existing limits but at the same time to develop creative mitigation measures within these limits, while aggressively pursuing research and development designed to advance the state of technology.

Actors in the Emergency Management System

To carry out the tasks described above, there are four central actors: local governments, state governments, federal governments, and private organizations. It goes without saying that these components are extremely diverse. They tend to have different organizational structures, be of different sizes, have different resources available to them, have different political mandates, and they are accountable to different publics with different interests. For the philosophy of comprehensive emergency management to function, each component must mesh with the others and they must work together in a complimentary fashion. In the past, these components have not always fit together smoothly; indeed, they have often worked against one another either by design or by accident. At present, new barriers to cooperation are arising in connection with changes in emergency management philosophy and structure at both the state and federal levels, and budget cutbacks due to the troubled economy are introducing further strains on intergovernmental cooperation at all jurisdictional levels. Therefore, what is described below is somewhat abstracted and idealized from what actually exists. The purpose is not to ignore failures and shortcomings of organizations charged with emergency management. Instead, the idea is to communicate the *obligations* of different components and focus in a constructive fashion on what *should* be done. There are available several critiques of emergency management performance (National Academy of Sciences, 1982); such detailed reviews, however, fall outside the scope and purpose of what is written here.

In this section, I will briefly describe each of the four components of the emergency management system. Attention will be given to characterizing, for each component, its perspective on emergencies, the kinds of unique resources each brings to emergency management, and the tools (or powers) available for engaging in comprehensive emergency management. Much of this discussion draws upon capabilities and upon functions that *should be performed* by various agencies. My focus is upon the obligations of different components and the avenues available to them for fulfilling these obligations.

Local governments or localities tend to be the component closest to the problem. Indeed, it has been said that disasters, whether natural or manmade, are *local* events. That is, it is the local community that experiences the impact. The community is for the most part the place where emergency management activities must be implemented whether one is speaking of mitigation, preparedness, response or recovery. For successful emergency management, the motivation and sometimes the initiative must come from local communities. Although it sometimes has not been acknowledged by other components, the community has been and will continue to be the most important component of the emergency management system. Communities are subject directly to the harsh realities of disasters and no matter what any other components may or may not do, it is incumbent upon the locality to undertake some positive action.

It is interesting that although the locality is the component closest to the disaster, it is also the component with the smallest relative resources and with the least access to resources through its constituency. Local governments have a smaller tax base in general and are faced with a variety of local demands, some more apparently pressing than hazard management, for which their resources must be used. In this type of operating environment, a locality is often forced to allocate resources such that hazard management is not a high priority.

The kinds of actions that a locality may take with regard to managing emergencies are somewhat shaped by the issue of resource availability. A locality can pass ordinances and regulations aimed at mitigation; to some extent land use patterns may be influenced and building codes can be instituted to protect new structures. Localities can also create and sustain preparedness measures—particularly warning systems and evacuation plans—as well as response measures such as search and rescue teams and certain kinds of stockpiles. Many such activities can be accomplished through the routine operation of police and fire departments, which are normally a constant part of locality budgets. It is more difficult, and sometimes impossible, for a locality to undertake measures that require personnel with special skills—or sometimes just extra personnel. In some cases, the problems of resource shortages can be attenuated by having groups of localities band together either in county or regional structures to engage in emergency management. Under these circumstances the county or regional unit becomes the focal unit relative to other components of the emergency management system. Such alliances are becoming increasingly common in the form of mutual aid agreements, which usually link several localities within a given county.

In summary, the reality of comprehensive emergency management has been faced by communities for some time. They have not had the luxury of diversification. Often, single departments have been forced to deal with all phases of activity in all types of disaster. The available resources have also served as limiting factors in determining which types of disasters and phases of activity get the most attention.

State governments form the second component of the emergency management system, and have legislative mandates to engage in emergency management. There are two primary aspects of state government's role in emergency management relative to other components in the system. First, states directly engage in emergency management of hazards that have a very broad scope of impact. Threats associated with nuclear power plants, hazardous materials transportation, hurricanes, and some volcanic eruptions, for example, tend to affect multiple political jurisdictions requiring that emergency management be undertaken both by states and localities. The tools available to states for emergency management are largely laws and regulations. State governors can also intervene directly by using special emergency powers, usually applicable during response and recovery phases. Also, by virtue of their greater resource base, state governments should be better able to maintain personnel and programs related to mitigation and preparedness. While such programs directly apply to state emergency management issues, relevant plans and operational concepts may also be exported to localities.

The second aspect of the role of state government is that of coordination. In recent years the National Governors' Association has emphasized the importance of the state as the coordinator of interactions between the federal government and localities. The idea is that with respect to all phases of emergency management, the state can help to link localities with appropriate federal resources. Of course state government should also be expected to coordinate *within* the state, expediting both linkages among localities for mutual support and linkages between localities and the private sector, particularly during the response phase, when equipment, specialized knowledge or personnel might be needed.

Much of state government's role as a component of the emergency management system lies in promoting the effective mobilization of resources. Within the state, it has the potential to encourage emergency management on the part of localities, to build links both among localities and with private organizations that facilitate emergency management, and to provide assistance to localities when necessary management activities exceed their resources. Outside the state, it may help to connect localities with appropriate federal aid sources, as well as with national scope private organizations (e.g., Mennonite Disaster Services). The extent to which different states are currently performing this role is highly variable. While many states are moving in the direction of the model of comprehensive emergency management, and the National Governors' Association is widely disseminating information, there is still much to be done before most states are performing all of the functions described above.

The third component of the emergency management system in the United States is the federal government. Federal resources for emergency management are extensive and diverse in that they apply to all phases of activity as well as encompassing many different types of potential disaster threats. Some of these resources represent considerable technological sophistication such as the system for predicting, detecting and monitoring hurricanes operated by the National Weather Service, and the Nuclear Emergency Search Team (NEST) which maintains skilled personnel and exotic equipment used for assessing the validity of nuclear blackmail threats. Also, federal resources tend to be located in various departments and various agencies, at least to some extent because of their very specialized nature. In general, from the point of view of states and localities, federal resources for emergency management have been concealed to a certain extent and are therefore sometimes difficult to access because of this embeddedness in the massive federal bureaucracy.

The Federal Emergency Management Agency (FEMA) was established in 1978 to serve as a focal point for federal efforts in emergency management. The FEMA is designated to serve as coordinator of all federal efforts related to emergency management with regard to all types of emergencies. The agency is involved in some emergency management activities directly; for example, with regard to nuclear attack preparedness it issues planning guidance, develops model plans, and provides technical information on characteristics of the threat (cf. Perry, 1982). The FEMA is also charged with promoting emergency management activities on the part of other components of the emergency management system. This assistance may be given through information programs, planning grants, and sharing both personnel and the costs of personnel. Finally, a large part of FEMA's role is devoted to overseeing federal emergency management efforts and coordinating between states, localities and the federal government. The idea that FEMA should match state and local needs with appropriate federal resources is one of the most publicized of the organization's goals. Here it should be emphasized that even after five years in operation, FEMA is still in the process of growing into the role described above. Parts of the role are executed well, while others are completely ignored. It appears reasonable, however, to remain optimistic that FEMA will move in a positive direction. It must be remembered that FEMA was born by combining three major federal bureaucracies with several smaller ones. One would expect that any organization with such a genesis to experience problems with short range goal achievements (see Gillespie & Perry, 1976).

The federal government, through FEMA, can influence extensively the behavior of the other components of the emergency management system. FEMA's authority is based upon legislation, executive orders and regulations. It can influence other system components by establishing rules or by using its influence to get an executive order issued to promote the passage of legislation. In addition to this, the federal government is influential because it is the most important source of fiscal aid for other components in the system. It is from the federal government that preparedness-planning grants and personnel and administrative support funds are obtained, as well as specialized services, research and technical information regarding emergency management. In general, the federal government is the source of long-range recovery resources for all types of disasters. It also provides most resources for all phases of activity with respect to nuclear attack and civil disorder. Finally, the federal government sponsors a large quantity of research directed toward development of mitigation measures and is the source of much preparedness information, research and development, particularly in connection with the technology for predicting or detecting threats. Therefore, the federal component has the option (or obligation) to engage in three very broad activities: promoting emergency management among other components, coordinating among all components and providing resources for emergency management.

A summary point regarding hazard management by the three levels of government discussed above is appropriate here. Beginning with local governments, the formulation and implementation of public policy related to natural and manmade hazards is an exercise in intergovernmental relations. That is, governments at different jurisdictional levels (local, county, state and federal) have different responsibilities and different tools with which to carry out these responsibilities. It should be remembered that the development of public policy regarding any given hazard is a product of the collective actions of all the different levels of government. Sometimes, when there is agreement between levels on the agenda, the priority, and the resources to be invested, a high degree of coordination can result in effective public policy. To the extent that such agreement does not exist, intergovernmental relations may be strained and cooperation on hazards management policy may suffer. These problems of cross-jurisdictional cooperation are specifically addressed in Chapter VI, but one should bear in mind that emergency management practice is strongly influenced by the extent to which different agencies at different jurisdictional levels can work in concert toward the common goal of public protection from environmental threats.

Finally, private organizations form the fourth and probably the most diverse component of the emergency management system. It is possible to think of this component as being composed of two general types of organizations. First are organizations that exist primarily to fulfill roles in some phase of emergency management. This type of organization is represented by the Red Cross, Salvation Army Disaster Relief Program, the Mennonite Disaster Service, or local search and rescue clubs. The second type of organization is one that routinely pursues some private line of business unrelated to emergency management but has some equipment or expertise potentially useful in emergency management. For example, during the response phase of riverine floods, emergency operations personnel may have use for heavy construction equipment—bulldozers, earth movers, and such—and attempt to obtain it from local construction organizations. It should be emphasized that what is here described as the private sector includes organizations that are national in scope as well as those with regional or local focuses, ranging in size from a handful of personnel to thousands. Historically, the private sector role has focused upon the response and recovery phases and has involved providing either special materials or special skills. Specialized material tends to come from organizations not exclusively oriented to emergency management. It ranges from the above mentioned construction equipment used in floods, to radiological-detection or decontamination equipment in nuclear disasters. Special skills are usually contributed by organizations with disaster management represented in their goal structures. These skills range from those related to sheltering and feeding evacuated population, such as that provided by the Red Cross, to the identification and description of appropriate safety measures in connection with hazardous chemicals, such as that provided by CHEMTREK. Both types of organizations, as well as the general public, contribute volunteer manpower to emergency management operations.

In recent years, private organizations have become more active in mitigation and preparedness phases of emergency management. The Red Cross continues to be active in preparedness for nuclear attack, and community action and public interest groups have become involved in preparedness related to nuclear power plants, earthquakes and hurricanes. Much of this involvement is both hazard and location-specific, but it nonetheless represents both an increase in the level of private sector involvement and a departure from the tradition of involvement in post-impact activities.

In summary, the private sector performs three primary functions:

1. it identifies and publicizes citizen concerns pertaining to emergency management issues;
2. it supplies volunteer manpower in all phases of emergency management; and
3. it contributes both special material and skills to emergency management problems.

It does not appear appropriate to characterize the private sector as fulfilling a largely perfunctory support role relative to other components of this system. While it is true that private sector actions center on support activities, it must also be acknowledged that private organizations can be pro-active. For example, private organizations such as citizens groups in connection with the Love Canal contamination, can identify an emergency management need and then prod other components of the system to take action ("Love Canal residents under stress," 1980). Thus, the private sector may influence other components through lobbying activities, taking the initiative unilaterally and engaging in volunteer work for other components directed toward specific aspects of emergency management.

With this picture of the United States' emergency management system in mind, one can attend to a key assumption in the idea of comprehensive emergency management. That is, before one can develop a strategy for managing all types of disasters, it must be technically possible to compare human response across a variety of disaster agents and to apply, at least selectively, the same management tools in different disaster settings. The following sections assess the concept of the comparability of different disaster events.

COMPARING NATURAL AND MAN-MADE THREATS

To date, there have been very few attempts to make systematic comparisons of human response to different types of disaster agents. Indeed, there has been a general reluctance to apply findings about human behavior from one type of natural disaster to another; the matter of comparing natural with man-made threats did not begin to appear in the professional literature at all until the late 1970s. In part, this condition reflects the fact that historically a large component of disaster studies has been journalistic and descriptive in nature (Gillespie & Perry, 1976, p. 303). Hence, attention has often been focused upon the disaster event itself—the hurricane or the earthquake—and descriptions of specific consequences of the disaster for victims. The literature reported, then, on such things as earthquake victims crushed under rubble or burned by fires and hurricane victims drowned in the storm surge. In this context, many disaster researchers have argued that different disaster agents have different characteristics and impose different demands upon a community social system; thus, human reaction to different disasters is likely to be different. Such reasoning concentrates upon the disaster event itself and specifically focuses on the uniqueness of different events.

It is of course correct that disaster events at this level are all different; particularly in terms of the precise agent which imposes physical damage. However, this approach involves essentially a phenotypic classification system for disaster events, focusing upon the surface or visible properties of each event. Carried to its logical extreme, such an approach would conclude that even all riverine floods possess certain unique characteristics, which technically implies that they are not fully comparable with one another.

In the past decade, there has been a transition in disaster studies toward an increased concern with the development of conceptual schemes for understanding and *explaining* human response to disaster. In so doing, research attention has turned *from* describing disaster events *to* understanding the demands and stresses resulting from disaster impact and cataloguing various strategies for coping with such demands and stresses. To effect this shift from examining the event to focusing upon human response requires that (1) a more systematic means of classifying disaster events be devised to promote (2) the delineation of common functions or demands imposed upon individuals and social systems as a consequence of disaster impact.

The purpose of the classification system is to characterize disasters, not in phenotypic terms, but in terms of features which have an impact on the kinds of protective or ameliorative measures that might be used in a mitigation program. In this way, one may choose a given function—for example, population warning—and examine the ways in which the task varies across different disaster events because of different disaster characteristics—such as the presence of a technology to detect the pending threat in advance or the speed of disaster onset once detected.

The following section develops a logic for classifying disasters in terms that *facilitate* effective comparisons of human response across different disaster agents. This review draws upon the classification schemes devised by Kreps (1979) and Perry (1982) for comparing natural disasters with nuclear attack. The scheme presented here is devised by examining the definition of disaster and isolating crucial dimensions for comparison. Finally, three hazards regarding which I will examine citizen response in Chapter III—volcanoes, floods, and nuclear power plant accidents—are classified using the selected dimensions as the basis for comparison.

Classifying Disaster Events

Disasters are usually thought of as catastrophic events, frequently associated with the forces of nature: earthquakes, tornadoes, hurricanes, or volcanoes. Yet other events, such as explosions, chemical spills or industrial accidents, are also described as disasters. In establishing parameters for the social scientific study of disaster, Charles Fritz (1961a, p. 655) has advanced a definition which concentrates on important distinguishing features of disaster events. He suggests that a disaster is any event

> . . . concentrated in time and space, in which a society or a relatively self-sufficient subdivision of society, undergoes severe danger and incurs such losses to its members and physical appurtenances that the social structure is disrupted and the fulfillment of all or some of the essential functions of the society is prevented.

This classic definition stresses that disasters occur at a definite time and place and that they disrupt social intercourse for some period of time. Allen Barton (1970, p. 38) proposes a similar definition, but chooses to focus upon social systems, arguing that disasters exist "when many members of a social system fail to receive expected conditions of life from the system." Both Fritz and Barton agree that any event which results in a significant change in inputs or outputs for a given social system is accurately characterized as a disaster. The important point to be derived from inspecting these definitions is that volcanoes, hurricanes, floods, chemical spills, explosions, or nuclear power plant accidents all fit equally well into either definition. Hence, at this level of abstraction, both types of disasters may be treated under the same conceptual rubric.

Given that natural and man-made disasters may be subsumed under the same definitional umbrella, one can further specify the links between the two classes of events by comparing them in relation to known disaster characteristics in general. That is, one can specify how natural and man-made disasters compare relative to important defining characteristics of disaster events.

There has been some discussion of how natural and technological disasters differ in the early literature on human response to natural disasters. Most of this work was done at the Ohio State University Disaster Research Center between 1963 and 1972 and focused upon the problem of assessing the implications of studies of natural disaster for the problem of nuclear attack (Kreps, 1981). One study, conducted by William Anderson (1969b), examines the functioning of civil defense offices in natural disasters and applies his findings to the nuclear attack environment. In developing his analysis Anderson argued that in spite of various differences between nuclear and natural disasters:

> . . . [these differences] can be visualized as primarily ones of degree. With the exception of the specific form of secondary threat, i.e. radiation, and the probability that a wider geographic area will be involved, a nuclear [disaster] would not create essentially different problems for community response. (p. 55)

Therefore, Anderson began laying the basis of a scheme to compare one kind of man–made disaster with natural disasters by examining two important distinguishing features of all disasters: the form of secondary impacts and the scope of impact.

Allen Barton (1970) advanced a classification scheme for disasters which builds upon the two distinguishing features used by Anderson. In his attempt to characterize the nature of social system stress Barton chose four basic dimensions: scope of impact, speed of onset, duration of impact, and social preparedness (1970, pp. 40–47). Scope of impact is a geographic reference categorizing impact as involving either a small area or only a few people (narrow impact), or as encompassing a large area or number of people (widespread impact). Speed of onset refers to the suddenness of impact or to the time period between detection of a hazard and its impact on the social system. This dimension is usually classified as either sudden or gradual. Duration of the impact itself refers to the time that elapses between initial onset of impact and the point at which it subsides. This can be a few minutes (short) in the case of a tornado, or several hours (long) in the case of some riverine floods. Finally, social preparedness is used in the context of possible forewarning to indicate whether or not the current state of technology permits authorities to anticipate or predict a threatened disaster impact. Barton's typology will be given more careful attention in Chapter V when I discuss the ways in which disasters affect citizen mental health.

In addition to the dimensions discussed by Barton, I will also retain Anderson's concept of secondary impacts in my scheme. Virtually all hazards, whether natural or man-made, entail some secondary impacts; in some cases the secondary impact is even more devastating than the initial or primary impact. Riverine floods tend to deposit silt and debris over inundated areas, earthquakes involve aftershocks and often result in urban fires, tropical cyclones leave great physical destruction, often creating public health risks. Nuclear power plant accidents potentially involve radioactive atmospheric releases thereby producing a potentially lingering secondary impact in the form of residual radiation. By assembling lists of distinguishing characteristics such as these elaborated above, one can classify a range of disaster agents and be alerted to important distinctions among them. Table I.1 classifies the three agents of interest in this book relative to these five important defining characteristics.

It is interesting to note at the outset that volcanoes and nuclear power plant accidents are identically classified on all five dimensions for comparison. Both hazards involve a variable scope of impact, with volcanoes' negative effects usually extending a maximum of a few miles from the crater, and plume inhalation hazards associated with power plant accidents extending to an approximate 10–mile radius from the plant (cf. U.S. Nuclear Regulatory Commission, 1981). Under special conditions, however, the scope of impact may be considerably greater. The May 18, 1980 eruption of the Mt. St. Helens volcano spread volcanic ash over a three state area and a "worst-case" reactor accident involving a core melt could affect an entire region of the United States. The speed of

Table I.1

Disaster Agents Classified by Selected Defining Characteristics

Defining Characteristics	*Disaster Agent*		
	Riverine Floods	*Volcanoes*	*Nuclear Power Plant Accident*
Scope of impact	variable	variable	variable
Speed of onset	gradual	sudden	sudden
Duration of impact	long	long	long
Secondary impacts	yes: public health problems; physical damage	yes: physical damage and public health	yes: public health (radiation)
Social preparedness (Predictability)	yes	detect but not predict	detect but not predict

onset for volcanoes and power plant accidents is sudden, with no long period of threat before the initial impact. For both cases, the duration of impact tends to be long. A volcanic eruptive sequence usually involves multiple eruptive events sometimes extending over a period of 5 to 20 years (MacDonald, 1972). The duration of impact for power plant accidents is highly variable, but could involve several days; at TMI, which was an "emergency" rather than a disaster, the danger period extended about 6 days. In absolute time, this is shorter than a volcanic eruption sequence, but both are of long duration compared to other hazards such as tornadoes, hurricanes, explosions, or tsunamis.

Both volcanic eruptions and power plant accidents generate secondary impacts. Human settlements near a volcano may experience lasting physical damage from any of several agents—lava flows, mud flows, large tephra, ash fall, or flooding—and the aftermath of this type of damage can create public health hazards due to polluted water supplies, waste disposal, or continuing flood threats. Power plant accidents which involve atmospheric releases of radiation produce potential secondary hazards associated with human inhalation and possible entry of radiation into the food chain via animal ingestion.

Finally, with regard to social preparedness or predictability, the present state of technology is such that neither volcanic eruptions nor power plant accidents may be forecast in advance. There is, in both cases however, a technology for detecting and monitoring events once they have occurred. In the case of some volcanoes, once an eruptive sequence has begun, either seismic or geochemical clues may be used to make approximate forecasts of eruptive events. With nuclear power plants, available technology is designed to detect minor aberrations early in the hope of taking correction action before more serious difficulties develop. Thus, while strictly speaking one cannot predict power plant accidents, the nature of the detection function is such that by detecting malfunctions early, subsequent malfunctions which may eventually result in a serious atmospheric release may be anticipated (and perhaps prevented).

Riverine floods differ from volcanoes and power plant accidents primarily in terms of two of the defining characteristics: riverine floods are predictable, usually some time in advance, and speed of onset is gradual, requiring 6 hours or more to reach a flood crest (Owen, 1977). Also, another general point of distinction is that floods occur more frequently than either volcanic eruptions or nuclear power plant accidents. Thus, from the standpoint of both the authorities and the public, riverine floods are a relatively familiar hazard, which can be predicted in advance, and that develops at a slow pace.

Like volcanic eruptions and power plant accidents, floods have a variable scope of impact, usually affecting only a few square miles, but potentially a much larger area. Riverine floods are characterized by a long duration of impact, usually a few days. Secondary impacts associated with riverine floods include physical damage to dwellings, damage to arable land due to silt and sand deposits, and associated public health hazards, such as contamination of public water supplies.

It has been argued above that one can appropriately examine a variety of disasters—specifically riverine floods, volcanoes and nuclear power plant accidents—within the same conceptual and analytic framework. The same basic definition subsumes all of the events, and they may be described using a single scheme for defining characteristics of disasters. Thus, a careful examination of the problem reveals no significant *conceptual* reason for treating natural and man-made hazards as fundamentally different such that they must be separated and examined using different frameworks in social scientific analysis.

Unique Aspects of Disaster Events

The preceding discussion was meant to demonstrate that logical and appropriate comparisons can be made among natural and man-made threats. Analytically, in terms of the present state of disaster research, there is no justification for isolating man-made disasters in a class by themselves. This is not to say, however, that all hazards do not involve some *unique* characteristics.

In conducting a comparative analysis, one should consider the implications of unique hazard characteristics for the human response variables of interest. With regard to the preceding comparisons, it can be acknowledged that citizen perceptions of a reactor accident are likely to differ from natural threats, due to the nuclear component of the former phenomenon. The following paragraphs briefly highlight several unique aspects of the nuclear hazard by noting specific qualifiers which need to be taken into account when making comparisons with natural hazards.

As a disaster event, the most unique aspect of a nuclear power plant accident is that a *nuclear* component is involved. Thus, some attention is necessary because, in terms of the way people perceive the situation, such circumstances are different from those which accompany other disaster agents. Research indicates that some of the public views nuclear energy, and most applications of it, as a particularly threatening hazard with the potential for extraordinarily long-term negative effects—literally the power to irreversibly destroy generations (Lindell, Earle, Hebert, & Perry, 1978). Of course, the idea that people have a different "mind set" for nuclear disasters certainly does not preclude comparisons with nonnuclear disasters. Instead it only requires that this "emotional" dimension be acknowledged and that the necessary qualifications be made when such perceptual differences may have some bearing upon human performance.

Two aspects of this emotional dimension should be mentioned here: risk perception and experience. The primary agent of threat to the human population in a nuclear power plant accident is nuclear radiation. In contemporary American society, this agent is a high fear-generating mechanism regarding which the public at large is poorly informed (Kaplan, 1978; Rankin et al., 1978). Furthermore, surveys indicate that much of the information that the public does hold about nuclear power plants is technically incorrect (Earle, 1981). This situation produces an environment where some people have potentially exaggerated conceptions of the destructive potential of an accident, while others may believe that negative consequences are of less concern. Also, there is widespread disagreement among citizens regarding what constitutes a source of acceptable ("accurate") information about nuclear hazards, particularly power plants (Martin, 1980). Thus, public perception of danger associated with nuclear power plants is highly variable, and there are few sources of information perceived to be acceptable which might serve to promote a more homogeneous definition of threat. That is, through selective choice of information, individuals with extreme attitudes, whether exaggerating or minimizing risks, can locate sources which reinforce their point of view. Such circumstances tend to exacerbate the problems associated with emergency planning and response.

The second aspect of the emotional response to nuclear disasters is that most citizens lack a reference point in their experience for such events. Only one reactor accident involving potential threat to offsite populations has occurred in the United States, and this involved an area of comparatively small size around Harrisburg, Pennsylvania. While the media coverage was extensive, the majority of the United States population has at best only vicariously experienced the power plant accident. Consequently, unlike the situation which prevails with natural disasters, one cannot expect people's "prior experience" with nuclear disasters to help them arrive at a definition of threat associated with a given nuclear hazard.

Indeed, the effects of the accident at Three Mile Island upon public perception of risks associated with nuclear power plant accidents are unclear. Three Mile

Island was a localized threat, characterized by apparent confusion of all parties involved, a shortage of visible, strong official leadership and shrouded in conflicting accounts in the mass media (cf. Chenault, Hilbert, & Reichlin, 1979; Sandman & Paden, 1979). In the short run, the incident produced two general consequences: (1) it resulted in intensive dissemination of a variety of information (some technically accurate and some not) regarding nuclear power plant safety; and (2) the apparent confusion and slow action initially on the part of officials raised doubts among the public about the capability of authorities to handle nuclear disasters. On the other hand, in spite of the attention given the incident and whatever its seriousness may have been, no documented negative health effects have been observed in the local population.

In closing this section on the unique aspects of hazards, it is important to point out that, from the public's point of view, volcanoes share some of the emergency response problems associated with nuclear power plant accidents. Volcanic eruptions are not common, particularly in the continental United States, and public experience with them is almost nil. Furthermore, public knowledge of the risks associated with volcanoes is limited and sometimes technically inaccurate (Perry, Lindell, & Greene, 1980a,e). In the case of volcanoes, however, there is an identifiable body of *publicly accepted* sources of information about the hazard. Thus, there is an available source of threat-relevant data which the public may use in devising or arriving at situational definitions of threat.

Finally, the purpose of this discussion has been to document special aspects of hazards which may be helpful in interpreting human response data. As it was pointed out, the simple presence of some unique characteristics does not justify separating the analysis of natural and man–made disasters. Instead, such distinguishing features should be acknowledged and treated as factors deserving special attention in the context of comparing human response to man-made and natural disasters.

PLAN OF THE BOOK

Up to this point, I have considered the meaning of emergency management, examined the system through which it is carried out, and reviewed the theoretical bases upon which one can base comparisons of human response to natural versus man-made threats. The remainder of this book is built around six chapters. The two which follow are empirically oriented and focus upon a data-based examination of the theoretically developed hypothesis of comparability across man-made and natural disaster events. Chapter II lays the groundwork for selecting one generic function for analysis—population evacuation—and describes human response to three emergency situations: the nuclear reactor accident at Three Mile Island, the May 18, 1980 eruption of Mt. St. Helens volcano, and a riverine flood. Three studies serve as primary sources of information regarding the reactor accident:

1. a telephone survey of Harrisburg-area residents sponsored by the Nuclear Regulatory Commission (Flynn, 1979);
2. a mailed survey sponsored by Rutgers University and conducted by that institution's geography department (Barnes, Brosius, Cutter, & Mitchell, 1979); and
3. a mailed survey sponsored and conducted by the Department of Geography at Michigan State University (Zeigler, Brunn, & Johnson, 1981).

Each of these studies is based upon a probability sample of citizens living within a specified radius of the Three Mile Island Nuclear Reactor. The data on volcano response are drawn from a study of evacuations in a community threatened by Mt. St. Helens in Washington State (Perry, et al., 1980a; Perry & Greene, 1982), and the flood data are from a larger study of flood evacuation planning in the Western United States (Perry, Lindell, & Greene, 1980b, 1981b). Both the natural disaster data sets are based on personal interviews with random samples of community residents.

Chapter III focuses upon citizen response comparisons among the three disaster events. In particular, attention is devoted to comparing: (1) the source and credibility of evacuation warnings, and (2) citizen evacuation decisions. This involves comparing citizens' source of first warning, the relative utility of warning information, and the perceived reliability of different warning sources. In examining evacuation decisions, cross-disaster comparisons are made among the total number of citizens who evacuate, reasons given for compliance with an evacuation warning, and reasons for ignoring warnings. This chapter also summarizes the implications of the data analyses for the problem of implementing comprehensive emergency management.

The last four chapters of the book are designed to address topics relevant to the problem of practicing comprehensive emergency management. More specifically, retaining the focus upon evacuation warning behavior, these chapters are directed toward supplying an emergency manager with the social scientific data on how citizens make decisions in emergencies, social-psychological responses to emergencies, the context of evacuation planning in hazard management and strategies for enhancing citizen compliance with evacuation warnings. The emphasis in each of these chapters is upon relating research findings which are applicable across a number of disaster agents. Thus, a concerted effort is made to provide a perspective on the design and implementation of evacuation warning systems, which is compatible with the philosophy of comprehensive emergency management.

Chapter II

Generic Functions in Disasters

In Chapter I, I mentioned that part of the promise of comprehensive emergency management was the idea that disaster management tools could be developed which would be useful in a variety of disasters. Such tools have been called *generic functions* because, presumably, they represent tasks which are general enough to be necessary in many, if not most, disaster situations without regard to whether the agent is natural or man-made. Generic functions include such activities as providing emergency medical care to victims, finding and rescuing people trapped during impact, and sheltering those in need. To promote a more detailed discussion of emergency management, this book focuses upon one such generic function: population evacuation.

This generic function is by far the most broadly generalizable of all the generic functions. Indeed, for certain hazards—floods, nuclear power plant accidents, hurricanes, some hazardous materials incidents, some terrorist incidents, volcanic eruptions, tsunamis—evacuation of the threatened population is an important, and sometimes the only, management option for protecting citizens. Thus, in many cases, voluntary preimpact evacuation constitutes an important management tool for minimizing the catastrophic consequences of natural and man-made disasters in an orderly way. A properly implemented evacuation program reduces initial loss of life from the impact of a hazard agent. Moreover, fewer people are left in the impact area, a circumstance that significantly enhances the operation of emergency services. In general, the greater the number of residents who can be removed from the scene, the more likely it is that post-impact activities can be shifted *away from* recovering bodies, administering medical aid, and transporting survivors, and *concentrated upon* the prevention of further destruction. Furthermore, in addition to preserving life and property, evacuations can strengthen the public impression that authorities recognize the problem and are maintaining at least a modicum of control over the situation; thus serving to moderate the negative psychological impacts of disaster upon public morale (Perry, 1982).

23

Hence, successful evacuation programs can not only directly save lives but also serve to reduce loss of property and disruption of social networks, and consequently may enable communities to reach equilibrium more quickly and smoothly.

The remainder of this chapter is directed toward two primary objectives. First, I will carefully examine evacuation as a generic function, paying particular attention to the problem of understanding the history, meaning and different uses of evacuation. The second part of the chapter is devoted to providing a description of each of the mass emergencies from which data will be analyzed in Chapter III. The purpose of these descriptions is twofold: to provide an overview of the event and to convey general information which will make interpretations of between-event comparisons more meaningful.

EVACUATION AS A GENERIC FUNCTION

Evacuation has a very long history as a technique for protecting people threatened by disaster. As early as the fifth century, B.C., the Greek historian Herodotus described the annual evacuations undertaken by Egyptians in an attempt to cope with seasonal flooding of the Nile River (Rawlinson, 1880, pp. 28–67). In the Southwest Pacific, records describe German attempts to evacuate a typhoon threatened atoll important to it at the turn of the twentieth century (Reichstag, 1908, p. 4122). Furthermore, if one considers man-made threats, the history of warfare is in itself a history of population movements, many of which began as evacuations aimed at protecting or preserving indigenous peoples. Similarly, the study of epidemiology—especially during the middle ages in Europe—reveals evacuations from towns, cities and even regions to escape epidemic disease in general, and the Black Death in particular. Indeed, evacuation is a concept which pervades the journalistic, popular and professional literature on disaster; it has done so for centuries.

In spite of its apparent ubiquity, however, social scientists have devoted little effort to specifying the features—both social organizational and social psychological—of evacuation and to classifying its different uses. This has contributed to considerable confusion in discussions of evacuation both among laymen and professionals. As we have seen, historically evacuation is a multi-faceted concept which has meant different things to different people. Therefore, in an effort to more carefully specify the many possible meanings of evacuation, a rudimentary classification scheme will be developed which is based upon two critical dimensions of the process. After outlining the basic scheme, I will briefly discuss other aspects of social policy which relate to different types of evacuation.

A Typology of Evacuations

Although numerous social scientists have proposed classification schemes for disasters (cf. Anderson, 1969b; Barton, 1970; Carr, 1932), until recently only one systematic classification scheme for evacuations has been advanced (Iklé and Kincaid, 1956). Furthermore, this classification is unidimensional—based upon different time periods—and is oriented to describing wartime evacuation of cities, rather than elaborating evacuations as means of *coping* with either man-made or natural disaster.

A review of the disaster literature suggests that two factors have a major impact upon the nature and conduct of evacuation, as well as the way the public reacts to it. These factors are the timing of evacuation relative to disaster impact and the amount of time it is expected that evacuees will spend away from their homes. Whether or not mobilization for evacuation is instituted prior to or following the impact of a natural disaster depends to a large degree upon whether the hazard is detected in time to disseminate a warning. This dimension is of course correlated with the type of hazard involved and with the society's level of technological sophistication, which controls threat detection and prediction. If there was no effective flood detection technology, pre-impact evacuation would not be possible. It may be noted that, although progress is being made, the United States still lacks an effective technology for predicting earthquake occurrence (cf. Mileti, 1975, p. 10; National Academy of Sciences, 1975, pp. 24–31), and as a result pre-impact protective actions are very restricted.

Assuming that forewarning is possible, there are substantial differences in purpose between pre and post-impact evacuations. Pre-impact evacuation is generally aimed at *minimizing* potential damage by removing people and their property from a high-threat area. Most empirical studies of warning response which include evacuation have focused upon the pre-impact period (cf. Drabek, 1969; Drabek & Boggs, 1968; Drabek & Stevenson, 1971; Mileti, 1974; Mileti, Drabek, & Haas, 1975; Windham, Posey, Ross, & Spencer, 1977). Pre-impact evacuation then, is a means of manipulating the severity of the impact of a natural or man-made disaster and as such represents what might be called a *preventive* intervention.

Post-impact evacuation, on the other hand, is generally treated under the rubric of reconstruction or rehabilitation rather than warning response. It can involve such tasks as removing the dead and injured, or relocating surviving victims to a safer place while attempts are made to restore a devastated community. There are only a few studies of the reconstruction phase of disaster to begin with (Mileti et al., 1975, p. 13), and the research on evacuation during this phase is particularly sparse. A recent study of large-scale post-impact evacuation was conducted in connection with the 1974 cyclone disaster of Darwin, Australia (Haas, Cochrane, & Eddy, 1976). This evacuation was made necessary by poor public health conditions which developed subsequent to (and as a function of) disaster impact. Other post-impact evacuations have been necessitated by massive destruction of housing (cf. Haas & Ayre, 1970; Kates, Haas, Amaral, Olson, Ramos, & Olson, 1973), heavy destruction of the natural environment

(Kirkby, 1974; Lessa, 1964), high human death tolls (Haas, 1977; Hersey, 1946).

It is important to recognize that pre- and post-impact evacuations can, and usually do, occur together in the course of a single disaster event. In some cases, evacuation is begun before disaster impact, is continued during the period of impact and may be completed post-impact. For example, when a flash flood ravaged Thompson Canyon, Colorado, warnings to evacuate were begun in the communities at the canyon mouth before the flood impact. The personnel involved in issuing face-to-face warnings moved up the canyon (toward the coming flood crest) as they warned households and campgrounds. After a short time these personnel met the "high water" and were in effect warning people during the time of impact; a circumstance which cost the life of at least one law officer (cf. Gruntfest, 1977; Judkins, 1976). Evacuation of residents and visitors to the canyon continued for several days after the flood impact (cf. Gruntfest, 1977). In this case the extended period of evacuation—before, during and after impact—may be seen as a function of the extremely short period for forewarning.

The second major dimension of evacuation important in the present classification scheme focuses upon the period of time that evacuees are absent from the evacuated area. Short-term evacuations can be distinguished from longer-term evacuations by the unique logistical problems which they pose, as well as the magnitude of social impact. Even when many people are involved, short-term evacuations can pose fewer logistical difficulties, especially relative to provision of food, shelter, medical and public health facilities to evacuees (American National Red Cross, 1975b, p. 8; Davis, 1974, pp. 23–40; Hans and Sell, 1974). Such short-term evacuations usually involve temporary relocation of two weeks or less (cf. Iklé, 1959, p. 78; Iklé & Kincaid, 1956, p. 5).

Long-term evacuations tend not to rely on public shelters, require attention to issues such as complicated planning for sustained provision of supplies, transportation, billeting, elaborate security and social control provisions (e.g., keeping evacuees from returning to cleared areas), which do not arise substantially in short-term evacuations. Long-term evacuations may also have serious consequences for the social and economic stability of communities and regions (Bernert & Iklé, 1952; Iklé, 1950, p. 131; Iklé, 1951, p. 383; Lammers, 1955; Titmuss, 1950). It should be mentioned, too, that while routine social services—education, health care, fire and police protection, local governing and administration, etc.—can be suspended or minimized in short-term evacuations, they must be addressed in longer-term settings. Therefore, long-term evacuation involves dismantling a community and *either* reassembling it at another location or dispersing it within a second community.

In general, when dealing with natural disasters, the amount of time evacuees spend away from their home area is related to the *severity* and the *nature* of disaster impact. All other things equal, the more intense and physically destructive the impact, the longer the necessary period of evacuation. There are exceptions of course when disaster impact, although brief and not particularly intense, can create significant threats to the public health; such is the case periodically with minor floods (White, 1975) or chemical releases (Finkel, 1974) which contaminate regional or local water supplies, or airborne pollutants which may temporarily threaten communities.

By cross-classifying these two important dimensions of evacuations, one may generate a tentative classification format for distinguishing four kinds of evacuations: preventive, protective, rescue and reconstructive (see Table II.1). Each of these "types" may be seen as resulting from a different protective strategy, creating different demands upon the emergency social system, and producing different consequences for individuals, organizations and communities.

Preventive evacuation refers to short-term, pre-impact evacuations designed to minimize losses of life and property by clearing an area before disaster strikes. Most empirical studies of evacuation in natural disasters have focused upon preventive evacuation. With regard to this type of evacuation, the threat is anticipated or detected, forewarning is possible, and the primary objective is to remove the inhabitants of an area during impact, after which they may return. Preventive evacuation constitutes an *interruption* of routine social life. Except, of course, for damage which evacuees return to in the evacuated area, the "interruption" aspect itself may even be minimized through high levels of community disaster preparedness. With respect to man-made disasters, preventive evacuation is essentially the same as what civil defense planners in the 1950s called "tactical evacuation"—the short notice removal of people from a city threatened with conventional warfare (cf. Davis, 1974; Iklé, 1959; Iklé & Kincaid, 1956).

Protective evacuation is also a process which occurs prior to impact, but is distinguished by the fact that evacuees must remain clear of the area for longer periods of time. In the United States, civil defense planners have devoted consid-

Table II.1
A Classification Scheme Based Upon The
Timing And Duration of Evacuation

	Period of Evacuation	
Timing of Evacuation	*Short-Term*	*Long-Term*
Pre-impact	Preventive	Protective
Post-impact	Rescue	Reconstructive

erable attention to protective evacuation (Baker & Cottrell, 1962; Garrett, 1962; Office of Civil Defense, 1968). Early civil defense evacuation planning (cf. Davis, 1974), whereby people are resettled to safe areas from attack-prone or attached areas, is an example. The presently promoted crisis relocation plan to protect citizens in the event of a nuclear attack also falls within this category of evacuations. Pre-impact, long-term evacuation is not often the subject of natural hazards research. The only recent discussion of this type of evacuation has been in connection with the consequences of long-range earthquake prediction (Haas & Mileti, 1976; National Academy of Sciences, 1975; Working Group on Earthquake Hazards Reduction, 1978) with concern focused upon the public policy, as well as social and economic impacts, of such evacuations.

Rescue evacuations involve recovery operations concentrated upon short-term removal of victims after the impact of a disaster agent. Generally discussed under the rubric of search and rescue (cf. Drabek, 1968; Olson, 1973, p. 216), such post-impact evacuations are undertaken in connection with most disaster events, and take on particular significance with hazards where speed of onset and how predictability allow little or no time for warning.

It should be noted here that rescue evacuations conceptually do not include operations for the recovery of bodies (cf. Hershiser & Quarantelli, 1976; Kastenbaum, 1974). The purpose of rescue evacuation is the removal, after disaster impact, of injured or uninjured persons to a place of relative safety. Thus, the massive search for known dead following the Skopje (Poland) earthquake (Ciborowski, 1967) should not be classified as rescue evacuation, while attempts to recovery trapped miners (Beach & Lucas, 1960) is correctly so classified. Traditionally, research under the conceptual umbrella of "search and rescue" has not distinguished consistently among recovery of dead, injured and uninjured victims.

Reconstructive evacuation involves post-impact removal of victims for a long period of time to permit rehabilitation and reconstruction of an area that has become largely uninhabitable due to the impact of some disaster agent. Haas et al. (1976) have recently described such an evacuation in an Australian community which experienced severe public health problems as a result of a Christmas 1974 cyclone. Reconstructive evacuations have also occurred in connection with wartime devastations. The evacuation of Hiroshima following the atomic bomb explosion is the most notable example in the open literature (Hersey, 1946; United States Strategic Bombing Survey, 1947b).

It is interesting to note that with regard to natural hazards, longterm evacuations have been relatively rare and almost exclusively associated with post-impact activities. That is, people have been removed from an area (with the intention of keeping them away for some time) only *after* great destruction has been experienced or at least *after* a threat has been identified and publicized (as was the case with the aforementioned public health threats). Thus, in connection with reconstructive evacuation, the *reason* for the evacuation is usually obvious. This circumstance permits attention to be focused upon the logistics of evacuating the population rather than upon means of *motivating* individuals to comply with the planned evacuation. In particular, recent studies by Haas (1977) and Haas et al. (1977) which suggest that post-impact populations are very cooperative with planned evacuations tend to support this contention. This potential to shift emphasis *away* from concern with motivation is a major distinguishing feature of reconstructive evacuation which sets it apart from the other three types of evacuation where it is not possible to minimize attention to the problem of motivating individuals to cooperate.

Voluntary versus Coercive Compliance

The typology developed above permits the classification of evacuation along two important dimensions—timing and duration. Another dimension of evacuation also requires brief mention: the degree of coercion involved. Although not often resorted to in the United States, there are legal bases for enforcing evacuation in most states (cf. Olson, 1973, p. 272). Hence, compliance with the call for evacuation may be either forced or voluntary. Forced evacuation involves removal of people from a force if necessary (cf. Haas et al., 1976, pp. 17–26). Many states in the United States have legal provisions for forcing people to leave an endangered area, and enforced evacuation is often used outside the United States. For example, Robinson (1959, p. 150) reports that in connection with a flood in Piedras Negras, Mexico, the military evacuated threatened residents and when necessary "used gun butts and bayonets to make people stir." There are rather obvious political and sometimes not so obvious practical reasons that enforced evacuations would be undesirable in the United States. Perhaps the most important reason that enforced evacuation can be problematic centers upon the relative inefficiency of the procedure.

Robert Olson (1973) indicates that during the Van Norman dam evacuation, where the California penal code permitted forced removal of threatened residents, cooperation with the evacuation order was secured through an emphasis upon persuasion rather than through threats and arrests. Indeed, forced evacuation is considerably less efficient than voluntary evacuation because the basis of forced evacuation is simply to arrest and forcibly remove people who do not comply with the evacuation order. Such mass arrests would have the undesirable effect of bringing more personnel (e.g., law officers and equipment, transport vehicles, holding areas), as well as increasing the traffic in the impact area (i.e, arrestees must still be removed). The successful Van Norman dam evacuation required the efforts of 238 police officers; a rigidly enforced evacuation would have involved considerably more officers, much more time and, hence, a higher dollar cost (cf. Olson, 1973, p. 273).

Voluntary evacuations, on the other hand, involve efforts on the part of authorities to coax people to leave an endangered area, but such efforts stop short of formal enforcement. In general, hazard warning systems in the United States rely upon voluntary evacuation. When a voluntary evacuation strategy is successful, it is particularly efficient since official energies can be directed toward overseeing the exodus from the threatened area and by providing security, rather than spent coercing residents to leave.

The major "cost" associated with voluntary evacuation is that authorities must motivate or somehow persuade residents to comply. It is interesting to note that while reliance is usually placed upon traditional measures for motivation—constructing a warning message which is convincing—some local authorities have attempted various innovations. During the Van Norman dam evacuation warning period, for example, mass media broadcast pictures of the crumbling and damaged dams. Given the relatively long period of forewarning and the broadcast of pictures within the context of responsible reporting, this approach was particularly effective (cf. Murphy, 1973, pp. 293–294). In Chapter V, we will address at some length this concept of providing motivations—incentives—to comply with evacuation warnings and its implications for the design and operation of hazard warning systems.

While the distinction between voluntary and forced compliance may seem trivial at first glance, it has important theoretical and practical implications. When interest focuses upon evacuation as a *dependent* variable, the goal is to isolate other variables which explain variance or differences in evacuation behavior (e.g., evacuated immediately, evacuated after a long wait, did not evacuate). In the case of *forced* evacuation, departure is mandatory; hence, there is no variance to be explained. One might describe factors which appear to contribute to people's decisions to leave after the authorities' *first* warning as opposed to subsequent requests, but in the end everyone evacuates, by definition.

EVACUATION IN THREE COMMUNITIES

As a starting point for understanding how citizen response to evacuation warnings can be compared across different disaster agents, Chapter III will be devoted to examining evacuations conducted in response to a volcanic eruption, a riverine flood, and a nuclear power plant accident. The basic characteristics of each of these threats were discussed in Chapter I, and it was demonstrated that each could be classified relative to the five defining characteristics of scope of impact, speed of onset, duration of impact, secondary impacts and social preparedness. When comparisons of *evacuation response* are to be made across these three threats, one might initially hesitate because the flood and volcanic eruption involved both the threat and actual *impact,* while the reactor accident was a threat but didn't actually involve what is normally conceived of as an impact—particularly in terms of physical destruction. When interested in evacuation behavior, however, this difference does not constitute a significant problem. To compare citizen response to a *pre-impact* evacuation warning across different threats, they need only possess two characteristics in common: sufficient lead time before impact must exist for a warning to be issued, and there must be sufficient response time before impact for citizens to engage in evacuation as a response to the warning. Our interest in studying pre-impact evacuation is in whether citizens comply with a warning issued by authorities, not in the impact itself. Social psychologically, we are interested in citizens' beliefs about the threat—which may or may not be technically accurate—and the consequences of these beliefs for the way in which citizens act after being warned. All three events described below are characterized by the issuance of danger signals to the public in the form of explicit warnings and the presence of sufficient time for the public to engage in some response before the *anticipated* impact time. The key here is the idea of anticipated impact or threat. In one case people were evacuated because a flood was *believed* to be imminent. In another people were evacuated because volcanic mudflows were *believed* to be imminent. In the nuclear power plant accident, evacuation was advised because it was *believed* that a radiation danger might develop. In each case the data analyzed in Chapter III deal with citizen response in connection with an anticipated threat; evacuation decisions were made both by authorities and citizens in advance of impact. In this case—and many other evacuations—the objective is to move people before impact and decisions are made upon the basis of beliefs about a pending threat rather than upon actual impact. The distinction here is the difference between preventive and rescue evacuations discussed in Chapter I, the following descriptions provide an overview of the environmental threat in each community.

Volcanic Eruption

Late in March, 1980, Mt. St. Helens, Washington, resumed volcanic activity after 123 years of dormancy. In general the public responded with excitement and curiosity to this activity. News media devoted much attention to the small steam and ash eruptions. As it became apparent that the volcano was not going to settle quietly back into dormancy, public officials in the surrounding counties and in several federal agencies developed or strengthened existing emergency plans. Scientists, particularly those from the U.S. Geological Survey, provided information to the media and officials concerning likely scenarios of future volcanic activity. The Cowlitz County Sheriff's Office prepared a pamphlet describing their warning system and distributed it to residents along the Toutle and Lewis River drainage areas (Greene, Perry, & Lindell, 1981).

The public maintained a high level of interest throughout this six-week period from initial activity to the cataclysmic eruption, fostered in part by the media's attention on the volcano. While there is some evidence that citizens in the vicinity of the mountain were concerned that specific contingency plans be developed and that officials be prepared for a major eruption (Perkins, 1980), there is also evidence that the public felt officials were too restrictive in their policies concerning access to the volcano. Cougar residents, for example, were reported as being angry by the roadblocks which cut their town off from a "booming" volcano business (The Columbian, 1980, p. 20).

The cataclysmic eruption began when an earthquake of approximately magnitude 4.9 was recorded at 8:32 a.m. on Sunday, May 18th (Rosenfeld, 1980, p. 498). This earthquake apparently triggered a tremendous landslide on the north side of the volcano which led immediately to the explosion (Geophysics Program, 1980, p. 530). A member of the U.S. Geological Survey volcano team described the eruption in detail, writing that this avalanche was, within seconds, overtaken by a large laterally directed blast that exploded out, with hurricane force winds, more than twenty kilometers from the volcano's summit (Christiansen, 1980, p. 532). The avalanche then formed a debris flow that turned and flowed down the valley of the North Fork of the Toutle River for 18 kilometers. The displaced water of Spirit Lake, the melting blocks of ice from the former glaciers on the volcano's north flank, water from the displaced river bed, and melting snow and ice on the volcano's remaining slopes produced mudflows that flooded the debris flow and generated floods all the way down the Toutle River, the Cowlitz River and eventually the Columbia River (cf. Christiansen, 1980, p. 532). These mudflows and floods destroyed bridges, roads and romes and filled the channel of the Columbia River, temporarily stranding ocean-going ships upstream in the Port of Portland.

The effects of the eruption were tremendous. The once symmetrical 9,671–foot peak now has a rim that reaches a reported 8,400 feet at its highest point. The north flank opening to the crater is now at about the 4,400 foot elevation (Korosec, Rigby, & Stoffell, 1980, p. 16). The blast destroyed 150 square miles of forest, killing vegetation and wildlife. Sixty-eight people have been listed as killed or missing. Three billion board feet of timber valued at approximately $400,000,000 were damaged or destroyed (U.S. Senate Hearings, 1980, p. 151), 169 lakes were either moderately damaged or destroyed, and over 3,000 miles of streams are either marginally damaged or destroyed (U.S. Senate Hearings, 1980, p. 139). In total, after the first two major eruptions (May 18 and May 25) it was estimated that damages totaled more than $1.8 billion in property and crops; this included damages in the vicinity of the volcano as well as those areas that suffered from the ash fall (U.S. Senate Hearings, 1980, p. 18).

Toutle and Silverlake, Washington, constitute adjacent unincorporated areas in Cowlitz County approximately 25 miles northwest of Mt. St. Helens, situated along the Spirit Lake Highway. Year-round area residents are for the most part involved in some aspect of the logging industry. The other mainstay of the local economy is tourism. Toutle and Silverlake are located just north of the point at which the north and south forks of the Toutle River join. The area's population is relatively small, approximately 1,500.

Few people in the Toutle/Silverlake area reported hearing any noise from the initial eruption on the morning of May 18. For many, the first evidence of the eruption was the high mushroom-shaped ash cloud which filled the horizon to the south. Residents reported feeling a dramatic increase in temperature; with it came the sounds of trees and automobile windshields cracking from the heat. The area also experienced light ash fall; the ash cloud reached Silverlake about one and a half hours after the eruption (Korosec et al., 1980, p. 14). The most serious threat, however, was from mudflows and flooding.

After the blast, the water temperature in the Toutle River rose above 80 degrees farenheit; these temperatures and the mudflows contributed to the destruction of most of the anadramous fish in the river. The mudflows and floods caused the river to rise well above its banks. Seven state highway bridges and numerous county and private bridges over the Toutle were destroyed, as well as almost 300 homes in low-lying areas nearby the river. Fortunately, most of the communities of Toutle and Silverlake lie on the slopes above the Toutle River and were minimally affected by the midflows and floods.

Official concern about flood danger along the Toutle remained high for the several days immediately following the eruption. The eruption had raised and reshaped Spirit Lake which fed into the north fork of the Toutle River. Down valley from Spirit Lake, a large debris flow raised the valley floor of the South Fork Toutle River by several hundred feet for a distance of about 14 miles. At first the massive debris flow was thought to be only marginally stable, but a study of the deposit by soils engineers concluded that there was virtually no possibility that it would become remobilized and move on down valley.

Most residents were alerted by Cowlitz County Sheriff's officials of the initial eruption. The deputies drove predesignated routes, using their high-low sirens and their public address systems. A telephone ring-down system was also implemented, again in predesignated areas that had a high probability of flooding. Although the Toutle Fire Department did not receive official notification of the eruption from the County Sheriff's Office, as had been arranged in pre-eruption planning meetings, once there was physical evidence of the eruption Fire Department volunteers assisted in the warning. They also helped man the roadblocks to keep sightseers out of the area. A large proportion of the residents evacuated, a process which was facilitated by unfounded rumors that a cloud of poison gas was moving toward Toutle and Silverlake.

Flood Event

Fillmore is a Western community of about 8,500. The citrus and railroad industry are major local employers. The community is located near the Santa

Clara River, where it is joined by a tributary, Sespe Creek. The Sespe has flooded at least six times since 1962, the greatest damage being inflicted in 1969. Although flood control plans for the Sespe are currently being considered, at the time of the flood no man-made levees existed in the area around Fillmore.

Early on the morning of March 4, 1978, the Sespe, swollen by nearly nine inches of rain in a 24-hour period, began to overbank. As the banks began to fail, the Sespe in effect was diverted through the west end of Fillmore. To make matters worse, Highway 126, which connects Fillmore with nearby towns, is a raised highway. Debris accumulating under the bridge dammed the Sespe, creating a lake in the low-lying areas. When the highway was bulldozed to stop the formation of the lake, at least one main phone line was severed, considerably increasing the extent of Fillmore's isolation.

Flood damages in Fillmore exceeded six million dollars. Nearly 200 homes sustained major structural damage and approximately 1,200 people evacuated from their homes. Most of the damage and half of the evacuations occurred in the extreme west end of town. One man was killed when his home collapsed due to water erosion.

Warnings to evacuate in Fillmore were delivered by police and fire department personnel both door-to-door and by public address systems from patrol cars and helicopters. The process of warning residents began at approximately 6:00 a.m. on March 4; the flood waters reached a peak at about 2:00 p.m. the same day. Most evacuees were directed to a Red Cross shelter located in a nearby school gymnasium. By the evening of March 4, police cordoned off the flooded area to maintain security, and evacuees were prevented from returning to their homes until the following day.

Nuclear Power Plant Accident

The reactor accident at Three Mile Island (TMI) is probably best described as an extremely complex event which has been the subject of volumes of description in the print and broadcast media, as well as a number of technical and scientific studies (cf. Kemeny, 1979; Martin, 1980). Technically, of course, TMI was not a disaster; the major environmental release of radiation which would constitute a disaster was precluded. The situation may be technically characterized as an emergency, however, and the evacuations which occurred in connection with the nuclear *threat* may be compared with evacuations in the face of other threats. To attempt a brief overview of the event itself is a difficult undertaking, and by necessity must focus upon a few milestones rather than trying to portray each facet of the incident. This overview concentrates on milestones associated with three general human response issues: the nature of warning information disseminated; the communication system for dealing with the public; and the outcomes of the incident itself.

The accident at Unit Two of TMI began at approximately 4 a.m. on March 28, 1979, with a malfunction which disabled the reactor's pneumatic control system. The accompanying heat and pressure, coupled with a mechanical failure, resulted in hundreds of thousands of gallons of radioactive water being pumped into the containment building, and then into an adjacent auxiliary building. The ventilation system in this auxiliary building pumped some of the highly radioactive gases which accompanied the water into the atmosphere. At approximately 6:50 a.m. radiation alarms sounded and reactor operators declared a site emergency.

After the site emergency was declared, the notification process was initiated and contacts were made with local, county and Pennsylvania State authorities, as well as regional and headquarters offices of various federal agencies: the Nuclear Regulatory Commission (NRC), Department of Energy, Defense Civil Preparedness Agency, Environmental Protection Agency and Food and Drug Administration.

For the rest of the day, Wednesday and Thursday, contacts and information exchanges involving many conflicting and garbled messages took place among Metropolitan Edison officials, reactor operators, county, state and federal agencies and the Governor's Office (cf. Martin, 1980, pp. 47–130). Representatives of the national and international mass media converged on the site (Sandman & Paden, 1979). Pennsylvania Emergency Management Agency and county officials were advised of a possible need for evacuation of civilians and began preparing for such an eventuality. Although "reactor technicians suggested that the machine was under control and slowly returning to normal," some local residents began to leave the area (Chenault, 1979, p. 5).

On Friday morning at approximately 8:00 a.m., a significant release of radiation was detected and a general emergency was declared at the site (Donnelly & Kramer, 1979, p. 23). This release was apparently "uncontrolled" and further uncontrolled releases were believed to be possible. Information was released to the NRC regarding the presence of a hydrogen gas bubble in the reactor which was growing in volume and making the task of cooling the core more difficult (Martin, 1980, p. 229). At approximately noon, Governor Richard Thornburgh issues an advisory that pregnant women and small children living within 5 miles of TMI evacuate and people living within a 10–mile radius should stay indoors (American Nuclear Society, 1979, p. 4). Following this Friday evacuation advisory, approximately 12,180 persons living within 5 miles of TMI and 31,360 persons living within a 5– to 10–mile ring evacuated (Flynn, 1979, p. 16). These figures represent 35% of the total population within 5 miles and 25% of the total population of the 5– to 10–mile ring. The number of representatives of federal agencies at the site continued to grow and by Friday evening 83 NRC personnel were either on site or in the area (Donnelly & Kramer, 1979, p. 23).

By Saturday official concern about the hydrogen bubble was increasing. At approximately 2:30 p.m. Chairman Joseph Hendrie of the NRC held a news conference and announced that the hydrogen bubble could potentially explode. Federal and state officials discussed the possibility of extending the plans for potential evacuation to a 20–mile radius around the reactor site. The spontaneous (that is, not officially ordered) evacuation of citizens living near the power plant continued. By late afternoon, NRC staff determined that the hydrogen bubble could not explode. NRC representatives Harold Denton and Governor Thornburgh held an 11:00 p.m. news conference to announce this and President Carter's visit on Sunday (cf. Martin, 1980, p. 230).

By Sunday, April 1, it was determined that the hydrogen bubble was shrinking and that the reactor appeared to be stable (Donnelly & Kramer, 1979, p. 22). President Carter made a well publicized visit to the reactor site. Evacuation readiness preparations were continued in nearby counties.

On Monday it was announced that the hydrogen bubble had shrunk to 150 cubic feed and was still diminishing (Martin, 1980, p. 231). Civil Defense officials noted that large numbers of citizens had already evacuated the area and absenteeism was creating labor difficulties in Harrisburg (Donnelly & Kramer, 1979, p. 22). County and state authorities continued to formalize plans for possible evacuations and the Food and Drug Administration recommended that potassium iodide tablets be distributed. Late Monday evening the situation at the reactor had stabilized enough that the NRC agreed to let Metropolitan Edison allow the reactor to cool without depressurization.

By Tuesday, the crisis had begun to subside. The hydrogen bubble had significantly reduced in size, thereby reducing the likelihood that any evacuation of the general population would be necessary. Schools located near the TMI site were reopened on Wednesday. People who had left the area began to return home. It is estimated that 144,000 people—approximately 39% of the total population (Flynn, 1979, p. 14)—living within a 15–mile radius evacuated their homes at some point between March 28 and April 3. On April 9, Governor Thornburgh advised pregnant women and young children to return to their homes.

The precise severity and consequences of the reactor accident are difficult to assess, even 2 years after the event. While the potential for human deaths and environmental contamination is very high in reactor accidents, there were no deaths at TMI and comparatively little environmental contamination. It was estimated that, as a function of atmospheric releases, (1) persons living within a 50-mile radius of TMI received an average radiation dose equal to about one percent of the annual background radiation level, and (2) persons living within 5 miles received an average dose of about ten percent of the annual background level (Kemeny, 1979, p. 34). Even allowing for errors in measurement, these doses are so small that the President's Commission on the accident reported that there will be no detectable physical health effects. Three TMI employees received larger doses during the course of the accident, but even these doses were not major. Transient mental health disorders were believed to be "the major health effect" due to the accident (Kemeny, 1979, p. 35). No evacuations were officially "ordered", i.e., an advisory was issued for pregnant women and school children. While physical damage to the TMI reactor was extensive, the major consequences of the accident appear to be related to identifying specific improvements necessary in the capability to respond to power plant emergencies at all levels.

Chapter III

Evacuation Behavior in Natural and Man-Made Threats

In this chapter I will explore empirically the kinds of conceptual hypotheses about the comparability of natural and man–made emergencies as discussed in Chapter I, where I laid out the basic characteristics of each of three types of disasters: volcanic eruptions, floods, and nuclear power plant accidents. All three events were found to be basically comparable in terms of human response, with the qualifier that the nuclear component of the last named event will require some special attention to perceived risk in analysis. With the descriptions given in Chapter II as background, this chapter focuses upon making empirical comparisons of human response to each of the three emergencies. This is accomplished in the first two sections. The first section examines the warning aspect of each emergency: the first warning source and warning source credibility. The second section looks at citizen evacuation performance, including reasons given for warning compliance, reasons given for not evacuating and an examination of the overall evacuation response in each community. The third section of this chapter summarizes the findings and recounts the implications of the data for emergency management.

COMPARISONS OF WARNING SOURCE AND CREDIBILITY

It is sometimes difficult to separate warning source from communication channel. The concept of warning source concentrates upon the person or agency that presumably construct and delivers the warning message. Communication channel or warning mode refers to the mechanism through which a message is disseminated. Emergency management authorities, police, fire fighters, friends, neighbors, relatives and political authorities are all clearly warning *sources*. The warning message developed by these sources may be delivered via a variety of warning *modes,* including face-to-face verbal contact, a mobile loudspeaker, telephone, radio or television. The distinction between source and mode is clear analytically speaking, but very unclear in practice. Indeed, certain modes are commonly used, or even exclusively used, by certain sources. A warning from a friend, relative or neighbor is likely to come face-to-face or via telephone. Emergency authorities may transmit warning messages via mobile loudspeakers, radio, television, or face-to-face. In the context of warning source, mass media may be conceived as either mode or source.

At one level the mass media, represented by radio, television and newspapers, are *channels* through which information passes. In the context of environmental threats, an emergency manager might formulate a warning message and then chose to ''send'' it to the public by asking radio, television or newspapers to reproduce the message. More direct dissemination may be achieved by activating the Emergency Broadcast System, whereby an emergency manager can read a message that is transmitted via cooperating media. In both the preceding examples the media are channels rather than sources.

Mass media can be warning *sources* as well as channels, however. This is particularly true in the case of multiple impact disasters or environmental threats where the period of forewarning is *long*. In such cases, the mass media fulfill their ''normal'' news function regarding the environmental threat. A quantity of information from multiple sources is gathered by reporters, assembled, interpreted and disseminated to the public. Such information may include specific information attributed to emergency managers, but it is also likely to include descriptive information about the current threat derived from different sources, as well as coverage of past and/or related threats. In this situation, the medium becomes a source: it gathers information about the threat and interprets the information for the public. In our analyses here we are concerned with the mass media as sources, not channels. In all three events studied here, particularly the Three Mile Island emergency and the eruption of Mt. St. Helens, the media had time and did engage in information gathering and dissemination to the public, both in conjunction with and independent of emergency authorities. Thus, in answer to the question of from what source did you first hear about the environmental threat, respondents in each of the three communities could meaningfully respond ''the mass media'' (or more likely designate a specific medium).

The sources from which citizens receive information regarding the disaster event and their assessment of these sources are important in understanding patterns of evacuation behavior. Disaster research in general has shown that the source from which disaster warning information is received is related to how the warning and the hazard are evaluated and what immediate reaction is undertaken (McLuckie, 1970, p. 38; Mileti and Harvey, 1977, p. 5; Perry et al., 1980a, p. 73; Windham et al., 1977, p. 39). Furthermore, the importance of a warning source shows up in a variety of contexts. For example, knowing the source from which individuals first received information regarding a disaster event can be used to draw inferences about (1) the response capacity of the emergency preparedness systems, and (2) the relative speed with which different communication channels to the public operate.

Also, research shows that a first step toward getting citizens to evacuate is accomplished when the individual receives a warning message from a source perceived to be credible (Anderson, 1969b, p. 299; Janis, 1962, p. 59; Mileti, 1975, p. 210; Perry, 1979a; Williams, 1964, p. 94). Studies of the differential credibility of warning sources provide feedback regarding whether or not the official emergency response system itself is credible, whether the way in which a particular warning was handled affected credibility, and to what extent other sources already viewed as highly credible might be incorporated into the emergency response system. Understanding the differential credibility of sources also allows authorities to evaluate which ones are most useful for delivering immediate warning information regarding a disaster in progress and which ones are most effective for communicating information about ways of planning for and coping with a hazard or risk on a longer range basis. In this section we will compare source of first disaster information and source credibility among one man-made and two natural environmental threats.

Source of First Information

Table III.1 shows the source from which residents nearby the reactor at Three Mile Island first learned of the accident. The majority of respondents—69%—cited the mass media as first source, with most of these mentioning radio as the specific source. Virtually all other respondents—29%—first heard about the accident from a social contact, primarily friends, neighbors, relatives or job

Table III.1
First Source of Information:
Three Mile Island*

Source	N	%
Radio	186	52.0
Television	50	14.0
Newspaper	11	3.0
Radio truck (Authority)	7	2.0
Friends/Neighbors	46	13.0
Job colleagues/Employer	18	5.0
Other (Relatives, etc.)	41	11.0

Source: *Adapted from Barnes et al. (1979, p. 13).

colleagues. Interestingly, almost no one reported that they first heard of the accident from an "official source"—that is, from a contact with emergency management personnel or a responsible local or state governmental official. At TMI, then, the mass media provided initial information to the largest proportion of citizens and social network contacts accounted for most of the remainder. In performing a "notification" or "news" function, the news media broadcast routine notification to the public. Hence the first announcement made by Lt. Governor William Scranton in effect simply informed the *media* of the accident, without describing the role to be played by state or local emergency response professionals.

Table III.2 shows source of first information for the two natural disasters: the May 18, 1980 eruption of Mt. St. Helens volcano and the flood. These data show a very different pattern by which citizens first heard of the disaster events. In each event, most respondents—nearly half—first heard of the threat from local emergency response authorities. The next largest proportion of citizens, again in both disaster events, cited social networks (neighbors, friends or relatives) as the first source of information. The mass media accounted for only a small proportion of the first contacts. These findings represent a reasonably common pattern of first source contacts in natural disasters (Perry et al., 1981a): emergency response authorities constitute the first and primary sources of information, supplemented by informal contacts in overlapping social networks. The pattern sometimes varies with higher dependence on social networks when the disaster occurs with no forewarning. In natural disasters, however, comparatively little forewarning rarely results in heavy dependence on mass media.

To a certain extent, the differences in patterns of first warning source between TMI, the flood and the volcanic eruption may be understood in terms of the forewarning issue. However, the differences point to an important control distinction in the pattern of the emergency response to the two types of environmen-

Table III.2
First Source of Information in Natural Disasters

Source	Volcano[1]		Flood[2]	
	N	%	N	%
Neighbor/Friend	21	23.3	33	25.0
Relative	13	14.4	11	8.4
Local emergency authorities	38	42.2	64	48.5
Mass media	9	10.0	6	4.5
State or other authorities	3	3.3	0	0.0
Saw eruption or high water	6	6.7	18	13.6

Sources: [1] Adapted from Perry et al. (1980a).
[2] Adapted from Perry et al. (1980b).

tal threat. In natural disasters, control and communication tend to remain with local authorities and the mass media play a less distinct role during the emergency time phase. Even in the case of brief forewarning when authorities may not be highly visible initially, they tend to assume generally undisputed control of communications and disaster operations early in the emergency period. Two important factors in this control are that in natural disasters: (1) technical status reports on the disaster go from experts to emergency response authorities who incorporate the information into their plan and interpret the data for the public, and (2) emergency response authorities are *traditionally* visible to and recognized by the public as being responsible for protecting the citizenry. The consequences of having visible emergency response authorities in control is that it enables the public to define the disaster as an event which can be managed to an acceptable outcome. This is a function of the fact that the public sees familiar authorities, performing their expected role as emergency responders, who communicate disaster relevant information via traditional emergency communication channels.

In contrast, from the public's point of view, there was considerable question throughout the accident regarding exactly which agency was fully in control at TMI. Interestingly, the finding that most people first heard about the accident from the mass media (as a source) foreshadowed the subsequent reliance on the mass media as a communication *channel* to the public by virtually all parties. As Chenault et al. (1979, p. 124) note:

> There is little to suggest . . . that the Public Information Office position was an especially prominent one in the activities of any county [Emergency Management Office]. The media–contact . . . was taken up by the Governor's and Lieutenant Governor's offices, by the Public Information Officer of PEMA, and by County Commissioners and the County Coordinators.

Of course, many factors influenced public perceptions of the emergency response efforts at TMI, including high visibility of political figures coupled with lower relative visibility of traditional emergency response personnel, and real conflict among responder agencies. The use of the media, however, as a main communication channel to the public probably exacerbated (and no doubt sometimes exaggerated) problems of control.

When the mass media were chosen by political officials as a communications channel, they were in effect spotlighted for the public as a source of information. The problem which arises here is that, when emergency response information is involved, mass media are a communication channel with a considerable amount of "built-in noise." That is, in the context of conveying the official message, the media can be expected to comment on it editorially. That is, the media serve both a "notification function" and pass on information, but the media also serve a "journalistic function" *vis-à-vis* the public.

When officials attempt to communicate disaster relevant information largely through press conferences, they appear (to the public) to be officially sanctioning the mass media. It must be remembered that while the media do disseminate the official message, they are also likely (even obligated) to run a variety of related stories at the same time. Such related stories may or may not be consistent with the official message and may or may not be technically correct. The impact of these circumstances is that the public is confronted with many messages, possibly conflicting, all presumably from knowledgeable sources. The public does not get, in straightforward form, the official message which is presumably based upon the authorities' plan for an integrated response to the emergency. In effect, the public is confronted with many spokesmen who have many messages and it is difficult for citizens to determine just what response is desired of them.

Source Credibility

Use of the mass media as a primary channel for communicating emergency response information to the public also has an effect upon the perceived credibility and usefulness of all information sources. Table III.3 shows citizen evaluations of the usefulness of the information disseminated from eleven sources. Respondents were asked to classify the utility of each source into four categories: "extremely useful or useful;" "of some use;" "totally useless;" or "don't know about the source."

Table III.3
Utility of Information From Sources: Three Mile Island*

	Percent of Respondents Answering			
Source	Extremely Useful or Useful	Of Some Use	Totally Useless	Don't Know
Governor's Office	57.0	27.0	13.0	4.0
Nuclear Regulatory Commission	57.0	25.0	11.0	8.0
State Emergency Agencies	40.0	27.0	22.0	11.0
Local Government	36.0	27.0	27.0	11.0
Metropolitan Edison	11.0	18.0	60.0	11.0
Newspapers	50.0	31.0	14.0	6.0
Local Television	67.0	20.0	9.0	6.0
Radio	67.0	20.0	7.0	7.0
Friends	30.0	27.0	38.0	5.0
Relatives	30.0	21.0	40.0	8.0
Network Television	55.0	25.0	15.0	5.0

Source: *Adapted from Flynn (1979, pp. 23–26).

The ratings given these sources group them into four categories. Local television and radio were rated highest, with 67% of the respondents rating each source as extremely useful or useful. The second highest utility rating went to the Governor's office, network television, newspapers, and the NRC. The Governor's office and the NRC were rated as extremely useful or useful by 57% of the respondents, network television was given this rating by 55% and newspapers by 50%. It should be noted that for all 6 of these sources, most citizen ratings are at least as high as "of some use;" Very few people rated any of these sources as useless.

There is considerably more variance in ratings for the two lowest rated groups. State emergency agencies and local government were rated as extremely useful or useful by 40 and 36% of the respondents, respectively. This indicates that the public rated these sources as moderately useful. One must balance this positive judgment, however, by acknowledging that 33% (emergency agencies) and 38% (local government) of the respondents rated these sources as either totally useless or "don't know the agency." Hence, roughly equal proportions of citizens saw these sources as being on opposite ends of the utility scale.

The next lowest rated grouping is composed of friends, neighbors and relatives. An inspection of the row percentages in Table III.3 shows that the modal rating for these sources is the category "totally useless." While in each case about 30% of the respondents saw these sources as useful, there is a definite skew in the direction of being perceived as of less use than the other sources. This is not a particularly surprising finding for two reasons: (1) the highly technical nature of the emergency was such that one would not expect most citizens to have special information; and (2) friends and relatives were not useful in suggesting new interpretations or providing new information because the mass media was already doing so on a frequent basis and very thoroughly.

Finally, the lowest rating was given to Metropolitan Edison. This source was rated as totally useless by 60% of the respondents. An additional 11% of the respondents claimed not to have enough information to even rate the utility.

To summarize this discussion, the mass media are rated as the most useful sources of information. Local television and radio received the highest ratings, followed by network television, newspapers, the Governor and NRC. Substantially below this high grouping of 6 sources, we find the state and local authorities. Social network contacts (i.e., friends and relatives) rated lowest among the four groupings of sources, and Metropolitan Edison received by far the lowest utility rating.

Given the consistently high utility ratings assigned the mass media, it is difficult to judge the relative perceived usefulness of the other sources. Table III.4 shows citizens' selections of a single most reliable source from all three emergencies. The list for TMI did not include mass media. When Harrisburg area residents were asked to chose among non-media sources, 58% of the re-

Table III.4
Most Reliable Source of Threat Information

Source	Volcano[1] N	Volcano[1] %	Flood[2] N	Flood[2] %	Three Mile Island[3] N	Three Mile Island[3] %
Neighbor, friend, relative	7	7.8	55	34.7	8	2.0
Local emergency response authorities	33	36.7	71	45.0	7	2.0
State/County emergency authorities*	1	1.1	9	5.7	69	19.0
Federal authorities**	11	12.2	0	0.0	207	58.0
Mass media	20	22.2	5	3.2	—	—
Personal judgment	18	20.0	18	11.4	—	—
Metropolitan Edison	—	—	—	—	6	2.0
No reliable information	—	—	—	—	31	9.0
No answer/Other	—	—	—	—	31	9.0

Sources: [1]Adapted from Perry et al. (1980a).
       [2]Adapted from Perry et al. (1980b).
       [3]Adapted from Barnes et al. (1979, p. 14).
Notes: *For TMI data, this category refers to Governor Thornberg.
       **For TMI data this category refers to Harold Denton.

spondents selected the Nuclear Regulatory Commission spokesman, Mr. Harold Denton, as the most reliable source of information. This rating sets the NRC clearly apart from all other sources which received negligible endorsements except for Governor Thornburgh, who was seen as most reliable by 19% of the respondents. It is interesting that when given this list of sources, 9% of the people answered that there was no source of reliable information. Respondents also rated local emergency response authorities very low as reliable sources, putting them in essentially the same category as Metropolitan Edison and friends or neighbors.

The first two columns in Table III.4 show the most reliable source chosen by citizens involved in the two natural disasters. In both types of disaster, the source most frequently selected as having greatest reliability is local emergency response authorities. Indeed, more than one-third of those in the volcanic eruption and more than one-half of the flood victims placed their highest confidence in local authorities. For the lower reliability ratings there is a slightly different pattern between volcanoes and floods.

For the volcanic eruption, after local authorities, people listed most reliable sources (in order of descending confidence) as: mass media (22.2%), personal judgment (20%), federal authorities (12.2%), and social networks (7.8%). This particular pattern of public confidence in different sources is probably best understood in terms of citizen perception of who controlled current and accurate information about the volcano. In these data, mass media refers largely to local radio. The fact that this source received the second highest confidence rating is a function of two circumstances: numerous volcano status bulletins were issued on the radio daily, and the emergency plan disseminated to the public by the County Sheriff's office urged citizens to monitor radio broadcasts. Under these circumstances, radio was seen by the public as having a defined role in an eruption response and could be perceived as an extension of local authorities. Personal judgment is rated as the third most reliable source. This degree of confidence in one's own judgment reflects the fact that volcanic eruptions were a very unfamiliar hazard; Mt. St. Helens had been dormant for 123 years. Respondents argued that the decision to leave their homes was a personal one, which they felt had to be based somewhat on their own interpretation of the risk information given them by authorities (cf. Perry et al., 1980a, p. 21).

In the case of flood victims, most of whom placed highest confidence in local authorities, the second most reliable source cited was social networks. Friends, neighbors, or relatives were chosen as the most reliable source by 34.7% of the respondents. As Table III.4 shows, those rating social networks and local authorities as most reliable account for virtually all of the respondents; a few selected state or county authorities, mass media, or personal judgment as most reliable, but these proportions are relatively small. The relatively high levels of confidence in social network contacts is probably related to citizens' perceived importance of past experience as a basis for responding effectively to floods. In the United States, floods are the most widespread geophysical hazard (White, 1975), and consequently many citizens have been exposed to this hazard at one time or another. Hence, many private citizens, particularly those who have lived in an area for some time, can claim to have special knowledge of flood patterns. Many times, this type of information is passed around social networks in the form of advice about the threatening flood based upon a person's knowledge of previous floods. Frequently flood coping information acquired in this fashion is useful and information recipients develop confidence in the source.

Summary

In comparisons of public confidence in information sources, the important finding is that at TMI the public perceived the mass media as the most reliable source, while in the natural disasters the public placed highest confidence in local emergency response authorities. Furthermore, for both types of natural disasters, the proportions of people who chose local authorities as most reliable was considerably higher than the proportions choosing any other source. Local authorities were clearly the preferred reliable source.

With respect to the nuclear accident at TMI, it is possible to explain the observed pattern of public confidence in different sources by carefully examining events during the emergency period. Several factors are important in the high levels of confidence ascribed to the mass media. First, it was via the mass media that most people initially heard about the accident, and virtually all parties involved, particularly political officials, continued throughout the emergency to communicate with the public via mass media. Hence, with this official sanctioning, the public attended to the media and came to expect threat information from this source. Second, TMI presented citizens with a threatening event that they had not previously experienced, which was complex and not easy to understand, and about which there was not a great deal of information available. In such situations, when no other source dominates or controls the scene, the mass media are attractive to the public because they make available a variety of information from different sources, all presumably with some special expertise. Third, the mass media, particularly radio and television, are available to the public on an almost continuous basis and therefore are presumed to have very current information. Finally, after the emergency when citizens try retrospectively to decide which source provided what turned out to best fit what happened, mass media have an advantage. This is because the media ran many stories and accounts of the incident, and thereby have a greater likelihood of being correct just by chance. (If enough predictions are made, one of them is apt to be right.) Although this requires some selective recall on the part of citizens, it is not an unheard of phenomenon.

The problem of Metropolitan Edison's very low public confidence rating as a source of information is interesting, especially since the company was probably the single source with the most technical expertise and special knowledge of the continuing status of the reactor. Probably the major contributor to the low confidence rating was the press conference held at 4:30 p.m. on the first day of the accident in which Lt. Governor William Scranton disassociated his office with the utility and stated that the utility was disseminating conflicting and misleading information about the accident (Kemeny, 1979, p. 109). This public rebuke of Metropolitan Edison was undertaken by the state because it had evidence that Metropolitan Edison officials were misrepresenting the condition of the reactor and the resultant risks to the general public (Martin, 1980, pp. 107–108). As the President's Commission concludes: "Met Ed's handling of information during the first three days of the accident resulted in loss of its credibility . . ." (Kemeny, 1979, p. 57).

Finally, we can address the question of why local emergency authorities at TMI were perceived as highly reliable by such a relatively small proportion of the public. Three general circumstances seem to contribute to this perception. First, apparently due to the active involvement of so many agencies and particularly political officials, local emergency response personnel played a relatively less visible public information role in the emergency. They were infrequently represented at press conferences and apparently appeared, at least to the public, to be performing support functions rather than a primary management function. Unfortunately, much of the massive planning efforts for 5, 10, and 20 mile evacuations by the counties were "invisible" to the general public. Second, there were very few *direct* communications between local authorities and the public. Counties did maintain rumor control centers and some distributed evacuation information to risk area residents; and if an evacuation had been ordered, provisions were made by locals for dissemination of the order and monitoring the exodus. As it was, however, there were no provisions by political leaders of federal agencies to routinely channel accident information intended for the public through local emergency personnel. Third, and largely because of the above described communication patterns, the public did not see local authorities as possessing any *special* access to technical information about the TMI event. Finally, based upon experience in managing natural disasters, it is likely that by not assigning local emergency officials a more *visible* role, political authorities inadvertently limited their credibility and contributed to the public perception that the accident was being poorly handled.

EVACUATION DECISION-MAKING

After examining citizens' sources of information about the threats and their beliefs about the utility of these sources, it is important to consider how people acted upon the information available to them. Here we are concerned with one type of action: evacuation or relocation to an ostensibly safer place. This section reviews citizen answers to some general inquiries about why they did or did not evacuate in response to each of the three threats. In this way, one can gain perspective on the way citizens evaluated the threat through examining their beliefs about what made them act. The analysis is structured around three topics: reasons given for evacuating; reasons given for not leaving; and a discussion of the overall evacuation response.

Reasons for Evacuating

Table III.5 shows reasons given for evacuating by people who left their homes in response to the reactor accident at TMI. In this case, respondents were read a list of possible reasons for leaving and asked, for each reason, whether it was important in their decision to evacuate. These data show that people's perception of danger by far dominated the reasons given for leaving. Situational danger was cited by 91% of the respondents as an important factor in the evacuation decision; this perception of danger is probably also a concern for the 61% who mentioned a need to protect children and the 8% who cited concerns about pregnancy. Confusing information about the threat was cited as a reason for leaving by 83% of the respondents. This confusion on the part of the public was

Table III.5
Reasons for Evacuating: Three Mile Island*

Reason	Percent
Situation seemed dangerous	91
Information on situation was confusing	83
To protect children	61
To protect pregnancy	8
To avoid the confusion or danger of a forced evacuation	76
Pressure from someone outside family (friend/neighbor)	28
Trip planned before incident	5

Source: *Adapted from Flynn (1979, p. 18).

no doubt related to the fact that different groups of presumed experts were disagreeing about the dangers involved and even the basic condition of the reactor. When the public lacks the technical skills to evaluate the disaster itself, and those who have the technical skills disagree, it tends to create relatively high levels of anticipatory fear, causing people to try to minimize their total potential losses. In this case, evacuation was seen as a prime path to minimization. The third reason for evacuating cited by a substantial proportion (76%) of the people was to avoid the confusion associated with a forced evacuation. In this case, people were endorsing the belief that the situation was getting worse—it was only a matter of time until everyone would be told to go—and it seemed best to get "a jump on the situation" by leaving before exit routes became congested. Interestingly, relatively fewer people (28%) said that pressure from social network contacts contributed to their decision to evacuate.

Overall, the major concerns cited by evacuees focused upon the danger involved, the difficulty associated with obtaining clear, accurate information about the threat, and the likely problems of forced evacuation. To narrow this field down and assess the relative importance of different reasons, one can examine the single most important reason for leaving. Table III.6 shows respondents' choice of a single, critical piece of information used in deciding to evacuate. These data show that concerns about situational danger were indeed paramount in the decision to evacuate: the largest proportion of evacuees (30%) said that the danger implied by the formation of a hydrogen bubble in the reactor was critical in their decision to leave. This factor is followed in relative importance by conflicting reports about the threat (19%), the Governor's evacuation advisory (14%), and concerns with a forced evacuation (14%). News bulletins from the mass media and urging from social network contacts were least frequently chosen as a most important reason for evacuating. Finally, it should be noted that

Table III.6
Critical Information in Decision to
Evacuate: Three Mile Island*

Information	Percent
Hydrogen Bubble	30
Conflicting Reports	19
Governor's Advice to Leave	14
Threat of Forced Evacuation	14
News Bulletins	9
Urging of Relative	6
No Single Reason	25

Source: *Adapted from Flynn (1979, p. 22).

for many citizens the presence of danger, conflicting information, an evacuation advisory, threat of forced evacuation, and other events had an *additive* effect: 25% of the respondents said it was a combination of factors rather than a single piece of information which was critical.

When the question of the most important reason for evacuating in natural disasters is considered, one sees a slightly different pattern. Table III.7 shows volcano and flood victims' choices for the critical factor in the decision to leave. For the volcano and the flood, the two reasons cited by the largest proportions of respondents as most important are (1) seeing evidence of the threat, and (2) being advised by officials to leave. The ability to see physical evidence of a threat in effect clarifies many questions a citizen may have about his susceptability. Indeed, when one can experience first-hand such environmental cues, part of the problem of evaluating personal risk is transferred from technical experts to a

Table III.7
Most Important Reason for Evacuating: Natural Disasters

Reason for Evacuating	Volcano[1]		Flood[2]	
	N	%	N	%
Neighbors/Relatives left	12	15.2	16	13.8
Media warnings	5	6.3	0	0.0
Officials urged departure	21	26.6	27	23.3
Relatives urged departure	16	20.3	6	5.2
Past experience	2	2.5	3	2.6
Saw eruption/high water	23	29.1	64	55.2

Sources: [1]Adapted from Perry et al. (1980a).
[2]Adapted from Perry et al. (1980b).

citizen. He feels able to look at the situation and make a personal judgment about whether the threat is likely to affect him or his family and decide what protective action seems warranted. Research on natural disaster has shown that visibility of a threat is positively correlated with undertaking protective actions (Perry et al., 1980a, 1980b). Gruntfest, Dowing, and White (1978) have documented, for example, that flash flood warnings issued in the absence of any visably threatening environmental conditions sometimes go completely unheeded. In effect, seeing environmental cues allows people to quickly arrive at a definition of the situation as dangerous and requiring special attention. Thus, if we group (as it seems reasonable to do) "seeing the threat" with belief that the situation is dangerous, one sees that perceived danger was cited as the most important reason for evacuating by those involved in both the TMI emergency and the natural disasters.

The second most frequently cited reason for evacuation, again in both the volcano and flood data, was that the respondent was urged by officials to depart. These data reflect citizen confidence in officials as (1) having access to special hazard-relevant information, and (2) assuming responsibility for managing the emergency response efforts which involve the public. Under these conditions, citizens can define emergency officials as important sources whose advice constitutes information which should be acted upon. Although the proportions of respondents citing official advice as a reason for leaving are higher in the natural disasters, the official advisory from the Governor was the third most prominent reason for evacuating given in the TMI data.

For the natural disasters, the next most frequently cited reasons for evacuating relate to social network contacts: either the respondent witnessed neighbors and relatives evacuating or was urged by relatives to depart. In both natural disasters, media warnings and past experience were infrequently given as most important reasons for leaving.

In summary, situational danger and advisories from officials were cited most frequently as critical reasons for evacuating in all three environmental threats. Indeed, these two reasons alone account for more than 55% of the volcano evacuees, 78% of the flood evacuees, and nearly 45% of the TMI evacuees. Also, media warnings were infrequently chosen as the most important reason for evacuating across all three threat agents. It was found, however, that social network contacts were relatively more important to evacuation decision-making in the two natural disasters than at Three Mile Island.

Reasons for Not Evacuating

Having reviewed reasons given as important in deciding to evacuate, we can now examine the reasons given for staying by people who chose not to evacuate. Table III.8 shows the proportion of respondents at TMI endorsing each of twelve

Table III.8

Reasons for Not Evacuating: Three Mile Island*

Reason for not Evacuating	Percent of Respondents Endorsing
Not ordered to evacuate	62
Too many conflicting reports	42
No real danger existed	38
Home safe distance away	31
Fear of looting	24
No children involved	23
Could not leave job	21
Neighbors did not evacuate	16
Must care for farm	6
No place to go	5
Too old to leave	3
Handicapped	2

Source: *Adapted from Zeigler et al. (1981, p. 6).

reasons for not leaving; note that respondents were allowed to select more than one reason for not evacuating. A fairly substantial number of respondents (62%) said that one reason they didn't evacuate was that they were not ordered to do so. Presumably, many of those who did not evacuate were waiting for an unambiguous directive from an authority. This is no doubt related to the fact that 42% of the respondents also said that the many conflicting reports about the threat were relevant to their decision to stay.

The data in Table III.8 suggest, however, that the most pervasive reason for not evacuating was the belief that no real danger existed. No fewer than 5 of the most frequently endorsed reasons make a reference to low levels of perceived danger. These are: no real danger existed, 38%; my home is a safe distance away, 31%; no children were involved (implying no danger to adults), 23%; and my neighbors didn't leave (thereby also believing the danger to be low, 16%. Finally, although not prominent, fear of looting was cited by 24% of the respondents as a factor in choosing not to evacuate. Various logistical difficulties—job responsibilities, farm care responsibilities, no place to go, age, handicap—were also endorsed by a few respondents.

Table III.9 shows the most important *single* reason given for not evacuating by volcano and flood victims. It will be noticed immediately that virtually all respondents in the volcanic eruption evacuated: only 10 people chose to stay in their homes. Thus, some care is required in interpreting these data. Confidence in the volcano data is enhanced, however, by the fact that the relative ranking of reasons for not evacuating *matches* the rankings in the flood data. As we found in the TMI data, the most prominent reason for not evacuating was the belief that no

Table III.9

Most Important Reason For Not Evacuating: Natural Disasters

Reason for not Evacuating	Volcano[1]		Flood[2]	
	N	%	N	%
No evacuation order	0	0.0	2	4.9
Did not believe real danger existed	7	70.0	22	53.7
Feared looting	0	0.0	0	0.0
Stayed to help others	0	0.0	5	12.2
Family not together	0	0.0	2	4.9
Stayed to protect house	3	30.0	9	22.0
High water blocked exit	0	0.0	1	2.4

Sources: [1]Adapted from Perry et al. (1980a).
[2]Adapted from Perry et al. (1980b).

real danger existed. This reason accounts for 70% of the Mt. St. Helens non-evacuees and 53.7% of those who didn't evacuate in response to floods. The second most frequently cited reason for staying, which together with no danger, accounts for all of the volcano nonevacuees and more than 75% of the flood nonevacuees is "stayed to protect house." In this case, reference is made to protecting the house from the environmental threat, not from a threat due to looters. The problem of looting is generally rare in natural disasters (Quarantelli & Dynes, 1970, p. 168; Dynes, Quarantelli, & Kreps, 1972, p. 33), and was not perceived as a reason not to evacuate in the data at hand.

In summary, one should remember that the reasons discussed above are those given only by people who chose not to evacuate. In their decision-making calculus, these factors were sufficient to make them believe that leaving was unnecessary. For both TMI and the natural disasters, most of those who didn't evacuate chose not to because they did not believe that real danger existed. Among nonevacuees at TMI, the presence of conflicting messages and the absence of an official evacuation order were frequently cited reasons for staying. In the natural disasters people also reported that they chose to stay so that they could protect their homes from the environmental threat. Unlike the natural disasters, fear of looting was given as a reason for not evacuating at TMI.

The Overall Evacuation Response

After reviewing reasons given by evacuees for leaving and by nonevacuees for staying, to gain perspective on the process of evacuation one can consider the overall public response. In general, particularly in natural disasters, getting people to evacuate is a difficult problem. Many people refuse to leave even when ordered to do so (Quarantelli, 1981, pp. 15–20; Quarantelli & Dynes, 1972;

Quarantelli & Dynes, 1977; Quarantelli & Taylor, 1977). In the volcanic eruption studied here, 11.1% of the citizens at risk failed to evacuate. For natural
disasters this is a low proportion of nonevacuees and has been explained in terms
of the uniqueness of the threat and the high level of emergency preparedness in
the affected community. The more commonly seen figure is that for the flood
communities where 48.6% of those who received a warning failed to evacuate.
At TMI, where only an evacuation advisory for pregnant women and young
children was issued, it is estimated that 144,000 people, 39% of the total population within 15 miles of the reactor, evacuated. This relatively high proportion of
evacuees contrasts with the general situation in natural disasters and requires that
one assess the probable reasons for this response at TMI.

The answer to the question of why so many people evacuated at TMI lies in an
examination of two general categories of reasons: (1) largely circumstantial
factors related to the way in which the emergency was managed; and (2) factors
related to the public's perception of the risks involved in nuclear accidents.

With regard to managing the emergency, the situation at TMI was characterized by three elements. First, the public was faced with an unfamiliar risk
which was difficult to understand. In the entire history of the United States
nuclear program, prior to TMI only three times have there been equally serious
reactor accidents and none of these involved radiation releases off-site (Donnelly
& Kramer, 1979, p. 3). Thus not only the public, but emergency management
officials too, were not attuned to the problems of response to this kind of risk.
Second, especially for the first three days of the emergency period, there appeared to the public to be confusion among officials and many contradictory
messages about the accident—its seriousness and the risks to the public—were
disseminated. Therefore, the public was facing an unfamiliar hazard regarding
which there were many conflicting assessments of danger. Third, however, there
was one thing upon which most experts did seem to agree (which also made
intuitive sense to the public): safety was correlated with increasing distance from
TMI. Furthermore, this distance idea came up in the form of public discussions
of evacuation by officials and experts a number of times during the emergency
period. On the morning of the second day (Thursday), a physician being interviewed on Harrisburg radio recommended evacuation (Martin, 1980, p. 125).
Friday morning the Emergency Management Director of Dauphin County warned that an evacuation may be needed very soon; he also described things people
should take with them and where they should go (Martin, 1980, p. 144). Although this evacuation ''advisory'' was not made ''official,'' that afternoon
Governor Thornburgh did advise that pregnant women and small children evacuate. Also, in Dauphin, York, Lebanon, and Perry counties information packets
(or instruction sheets) on evacuating—what to take, how to leave, where to go—
were prepared and distributed directly to the general population (Chenault, 1979,
pp. 124–129). To summarize, people were confronted with an unfamiliar risk,

regarding which it was difficult to get information, but were told that evacuation was a definite path to safety. Put this way, it is less difficult to understand why a person seeking to minimize potential negative consequences would evacuate. While it is correct that an evacuation was never officially ordered, evacuation was sanctioned by experts as a protective action. Indeed, while experts argued about whether the situation was so serious that people *should* evacuate, they agreed that evacuation *would* substantially reduce the danger. One would expect that these circumstances would encourage evacuations independent of the nature of the hazard involved, whether nuclear or nonnuclear.

The second category of reasons for evacuation at TMI, the public perception of the threat, depends largely upon what have previously been described as "unique" aspects of nuclear threats. Although empirical assessments of perceived threat from nuclear disasters are virtually nonexistent, social scientists have argued that citizens have a distinct view of nuclear hazards as constituting a special threat different from other man-made and natural hazards (Perry et al., 1980c). This view stems from public beliefs about the characteristics of radiation as hazard. Of interest here are two general types of belief patterns that relate to the problem of detection and the concept of dose.

In the case of natural hazards, such as tornadoes, floods, or volcanoes, people have a sense of what constitutes danger—wind, water, mudflows, ash, etc. These agents may not exactly be familiar, but neither are they completely outside the citizens' realm of experience or imagination. Also, these risks are spatially defined in the sense that they are "visible" and finite; one can feel the wind or see the water or mud. A citizen, relying upon his senses—sight, touch, hearing, etc.—can reliably detect the presence or absence of such risks in the environment and, if need be, generate some protective strategy on his own, perhaps by seeking high ground or some special shelter. Hence, these types of risks can be perceived by citizens as identifiable, understandable, and as threats from which it is possible to protect oneself. Interestingly, this view of natural hazards has been cited as one of the reasons that citizens are slower to respond to disaster warnings than authorities deem appropriate.

On the other hand, studies show that the public views radiation risks as "involuntary, unknown to those exposed and to science, uncontrollable, unfamiliar, potentially catastrophic, likely to be fatal rather than injurious, and dreaded" (Slovic, Lichtenstein, & Fischhoff, 1980, p. 5). As a hazard, then, almost opposite qualities or characteristics are attributed to radiation than are attributed to natural disasters. Radiation tends to be viewed as an invisible, lethal threat that radiates in all directions from a source, against which protection is difficult or impossible to achieve. Hence, radiation is an unfamiliar danger which the citizen cannot see, hear, smell, feel, or taste (Grinspoon, 1964, p. 120) without special equipment. The idea that a hazard, perceived to be very lethal, is for the most part undetectable distinctly sets it apart from other hazards.

With regard to dangers from the not easily detected hazard of nuclear radiation, most citizens are familiar with the rather dire nature of the consequences of exposure. The public has seen many discussions of death from radiation exposure, and studies indicate that people tend to associate death—either immediately, or within a few weeks due to radiation sickness, or in years due to cancer—as a consequence of such exposure (cf. Lifton, 1967, pp. 48–52; Kiyoshi, 1967, pp. 93–98; Slovic et al., 1980, pp. 8–12). There are, of course, many hazards in which exposure appears to result in death. With respect to radiation, however, the concept of dose or the extent of exposure is very important in determining the extent of negative consequences. In fact, radiation is present in much of the human environment; sensitive detection instruments must even be calibrated so that background levels are accounted for in measurements. Humans are constantly bombarded by radiation—it is only when these levels of exposure become high that health consequences seem to accrue. The idea of dose does not appear to be fully appreciated by the public in that many people seem to equate any level of exposure with death, the most serious consequence.

It is very likely that people do not appropriately distinguish radiation from nuclear power plants from radiation associated with nuclear bombs. Indeed, when asked to describe health consequences of radiation exposure, people tend to mention symptoms common in exposure only to very high doses, such as one would experience if exposed to a nuclear bomb explosion. Parenthetically, dose levels as well as types of radiation are considerably different for nuclear power plant accidents than for weapons. The point of this discussion, however, is that the public in general sees radiation as a difficult to detect threat which produces very negative consequences in those exposed. This sets it apart from other disasters, particularly natural disasters, both in the way people think about it and in the way they react to possible exposure. As our data show the level of threat attributed to nuclear disasters is much higher than for the nonnuclear disasters. This heightened threat associated with the nuclear disaster is also no doubt related to the frequently cited "fear reactions" to nuclear disaster (Glass, 1956, p. 630; Lifton, 1964, p. 152); that such fear characterized citizens during the TMI incident was documented (as "demoralization") by the Report of the Public Health and Safety Task Force (Fabrikant, 1979, p. 275) of the Presidents' Commission.

IMPLICATIONS FOR EVACUATION PLANNING

The analyses presented in this chapter exclusively focus upon two issues: (1) warning source credibility and (2) evacuation decisionmaking as seen by the public. These particular foci were chosen largely because analyses were confined to published data on the Three Mile Island accident. Regretably, no TMI data bases were available for a thorough secondary analysis.

The empirical comparisons which were possible, however, have important implications for evacuation planning procedures for nuclear threats. The importance of these implications lies not so much in the TMI findings themselves, but in the extent to which findings about special issues in natural disaster evacuations are applicable to the man-made threat. The following sections summarize a number of conclusions which may be drawn from the comparative analyses undertaken in this chapter. These conclusions are discussed in terms of two general categories: implications of the comparisons of source credibility and implications of the study of evacuation decision-making.

Implications Arising from Source Credibility

During the course of a nuclear reactor emergency, local emergency response officials should be integrated into the public information system and should constitute the public's primary source of official accident-relevant information. In the eyes of the public this enhances the authority and credibility of the local emergency response officials who will ultimately be responsible for the operations involved in getting the public-at-risk to undertake some protective action—whether it is evacuation or some other measure. By highlighting the role of local authorities, confidence in them is increased among the public-at-risk, which in turn promotes public compliance with emergency measures. Of course this does not mean that local officials should be the only information disseminators; it does require, however, careful coordination and cooperation among emergency response personnel at all levels—city, county, state, federal—and between emergency response officials and political officials at all levels. At TMI political officials initially assumed and retained the majority of the public information task.

When an emergency—either man-made or related to a natural threat—is in progress, the mass media should not be relied upon as a primary communication channel to the public. The mass media constitute a communication channel characterized by considerable "noise"; juxtaposing "official" messages with other related messages (sometimes conflicting) promotes confusion in the mind of the public regarding exactly what response is required of them. In natural disasters, the media have been effectively used as a supplementary source of information particularly when, as part of an established emergency plan, officials instruct citizens to monitor radio or television broadcasts for status reports regarding a hazard. In this case the role of the mass media is to provide the public with information about the immediate status of the hazard which allows the public to determine whether specific provisions of a community evacuation plan should be implemented. As part of the emergency plan for responding to the volcanic activity at Mt. St. Helens, for example, the public was instructed to monitor radio bulletins on the volcano's status (Perry et al., 1980a), and to evacuate specified areas in the event of an eruption alert.

When an emergency is in progress, officials should distinguish the function of providing public information about the emergency from the function of sending messages which direct some emergency response. This helps the public to understand when they are expected to take an action and when they are not. As part of a public information function, officials can provide updates regarding changing conditions regarding the event, or describe a range of potentially useful measures where the decision to implement is left to the public. Although ideally such matters are addressed before a given disaster as part of a general community preparedness plan, public information during an incident might also include a description of what constitutes a warning signal and what should be done when such a signal is received. It is important, however, to separate such public information clearly from an emergency response directive. This latter message is one which instructs the population-at-risk to begin a planned (and presumably coordinated) protective response; it is intended to evoke full participation rather than being an option for which the public is left to make a decision regarding implementation. When these two types of messages are not carefully distinguished, particularly in the case of evacuations, the public can be expected to undertake a range of protective actions (some possibly substantially differing from the actions desired by officials) according to widely differing time schedules.

In all disasters, particularly technological disasters, rumor control is a critically important function. In general problems associated with rumor control will increase to the extent that the disaster or hazard is less familiar to the public. In the case of natural disasters, officials are usually concerned with dispelling popular myths or technically inaccurate conventional wisdom regarding the event. In dealing with technological disasters (particularly those with a radiological component) the problem is even more pronounced, due to the general unfamiliarity of the public with such threats. The importance of rumor control is underscored by the reported high utilization of public information telephone lines during the Three Mile Island incident.

The public education function is a particularly important component of emergency response plans for dealing with nuclear power plant accidents. The time to explain the nature and specific dangers involved with a given hazard is before a crisis occurs. Official attentions during the crisis should be devoted to achieving protection for the public; this function is unnecessarily complicated if the nature of the risks in general as well as those specifically involved in the immediate incident must be described. By attempting to run a "mini" hazard awareness campaign during an incident, authorities force the public into a general information gathering posture rather than allowing the public to assimilate and prepare to respond to a specific emergency management strategy. It is likely that much of what was described as confusion on the part of the public during the TMI accident was related to the fact that public education was being conducted simultaneously with crisis management. In Chapter VI I discuss several examples of public education strategies.

Evacuation Decision-Making

Citizen evacuation response during technological emergencies may be understood in terms of the same variables which explain evacuation in natural disasters. Several researchers have pointed to the relatively high levels of spontaneous evacuations at TMI and argued that because of this there must be something about nuclear disasters that makes people more responsive. The implication here is that there is some unspecified basic difference between nuclear threats and other man-made and natural disasters. The evidence marshalled in the present study suggests that the difference is the fear or dread characteristics associated with nuclear disasters. The effect of apparent "heightened fear" appears to be reflected in higher citizen perceptions of personal risk or danger. In turn, much research has shown that higher levels of perceived risk are associated with higher levels of citizen compliance with evacuation warnings (Perry et al., 1981b). Thus, citizens evacuate when four conditions are met: (1) they have accounted for the safety of their immediate household; (2) they have been given—by authorities—or have personally developed a plan for protective action; (3) they believe that a threat does exist in the environment; and (4) they perceive that upon impact this threat could result in some level of damage to their person and/or property (see Perry, 1979a; Perry et al., 1980a, 1980b). At Three Mile Island the nuclear nature of the threat appears to have produced high levels of perceived personal risk (cf. Zeigler, 1981).

The high level of spontaneous evacuations around TMI appears to be related to the above described elevated perception of personal risk (threat) by the public. The perceived negative consequences associated with failing to undertake some protective action or doing so too late were extremely high. In planning to manage nuclear threats, one must be sensitive to the effects of elevated perceptions of risk, particularly since high levels of spontaneous or unsupervised evacuation are not necessarily desirable. Furthermore the presence of citizen beliefs that nuclear—radiation—threats pose very high risks suggests four logistical and procedural implications for managing an evacuation:

1. If authorities issue an evacuation route and destination to the public early in an incident with instructions to wait until officially advised before leaving, citizens are likely to ignore the instructions and depart before being told to do so.
2. Evacuation shadow effects will be multiplied. That is, when an evacuation is announced for a specific geographic area, it should be expected that residents who are nearby but still outside this area will also evacuate.

3. Graded or group-specific evacuation orders—for example, for pregnant women and children under five years—will generate evacuations by others as well. In general, such orders that would otherwise divide families will be needed at least by all members of a given family.
4. Planning attention needs to be devoted to the problems associated with getting evacuees back to an area after they have been evacuated. Although not the case at TMI, if a significant radioactive release had caused citizens to evacuate it is not obvious that they would respond readily to an "all clear" signal. A study should be made of how one should structure and disseminate a message that an area once threatened by radiation is now safe.

Summary

Although not directly derivable from the specific data presented here, an additional general conclusion may be *inferred* based upon the overall analysis. Inter-organizational and inter-agency coordination and preparedness for ordering and overseeing a mass evacuation are crucial problems in both nuclear and nonnuclear disasters. As Quarantelli (1980, p. 149) has pointed out, at almost all jurisdictional levels such preparedness is poor, and the data examined here on TMI serve to further support this hypothesis. It is particularly interesting that in the face of poor coordination among and guidance from authorities, the public seems to some extent to be able to take care of itself. Remember that 39% of the population within fifteen miles of TMI managed to evacuate successfully with a minimum of guidance from authorities. This should not be interpreted, however, as evidence that in all disasters the public will survive with a minimum of help from authorities. Instead, it indicates that even in the absence of official coordination, the public is not reduced to panic flight or a total breakdown of reason (cf. Quarantelli, 1960a). There is no guarantee that the remaining 61% of the population around TMI could have evacuated without some coordinated official intervention.

To describe the event accurately, it must be acknowledged that inter-organizational coordination did improve over time during the TMI incident. It seems apparent that some evacuations can proceed with a minimum of coordination by officials; this has been true for years in the relatively small and short-term evacuations associated with natural disasters in the United States. As the number of people involved and the time outside the risk area increases, however, it is less likely that mass evacuations can be smoothly executed without high levels of inter-organizational preparedness and coordination. It is likely that the number of spontaneous evacuees at TMI approaches the upper limit of the size of mass evacuation which can be accomplished in the face of relatively low levels of inter-organizational coordination.

In closing this chapter, it is interesting to realize that most of the conclusions and implications discussed above are neither striking nor absolutely unique in the social science literature on human behavior in disasters. In many cases, they reflect suggestions made in connection with research on a variety of disaster agents over the years. It is of course important to document empirically cross-disaster agent applicability of planning and citizen response principles, as we did here. However, given that much information is available from research on how people can be expected to respond to evacuation orders, how public information should be handled during disasters, and how to issue and structure evacuation advisories and warnings, one cannot help expressing surprise that apparently so little of this available information was utilized in the management of the TMI accident. Often planners and policy-makers read the conclusions of research reports and respond by saying, "I already knew that." The experience at TMI, which also occurs periodically in connection with natural disasters, where various emergency management problems arose in spite of the availability of research-based planning and response principles that bear upon the issues, causes one to look askance at such claims. More importantly, though, it raises questions about how research results are disseminated from researchers to planners and policy-makers, as well as how these latter actors evaluate and incorporate research information into the emergency management process. Clearly, much information regarding emergency response performance of citizens that was available before TMI was not used in managing that incident. It may be that the research was not used because relevant officials were not aware of it, because it was not in a form which could be implemented, because it was not in a form which could be understood, or because the research was perceived to be irrelevant to the problems. The point is that to date little attention has been devoted to examining the channels through which research findings reach those people at different jurisdictions (local, state or federal) who would use them, and how feedback travels from users back to the research community. Understanding and perhaps formalizing such communication channels would seem to be one way to insure that research is relevant to planning and operational concerns and is presented in a fashion which lends itself to evaluation and utilization by policy-makers and implementers.

The remaining chapters of this book represent an effort to bring together and summarize in a single place the bulk of social scientific information currently available on the design and implementation of community evacuation plans. In one sense these chapters are meant to elaborate upon and provide documentation for the implications of the data on evacuation behavior presented in this chapter. More broadly conceived, the subsequent chapters are intended to provide a comprehensive guide for emergency managers who use evacuation as a management tool in their work. The topics reviewed reflect the philosophy of comprehensive emergency management in that they deal with evacuations in connection with man-made and natural threats, and in that consideration is given to evacuation planning conducted as emergency *preparedness* and evacuation operations conducted during *response* and *recovery* phases. These chapters begin with an examination of the way in which citizens make decisions during emergencies, continue with a review of social psychological factors in emergency management, present an analysis of the administration of emergency management, and conclude with consideration of the factors important in enhancing citizen compliance with evacuation warnings.

Chapter IV

The Structure of Citizen Emergency Decision–Making

Chapter III was devoted to examining the outcomes of citizen decisions made during two natural disasters and the technological emergency at Three Mile Island's nuclear reactor. Among other things, these data were interpreted to demonstrate that citizen *evacuation performance* does not significantly differ among the three types of threats. More specifically, the data suggest that response variations among evacuations in response to floods, volcanoes and nuclear power plant emergencies can be explained in terms of differences in the theoretical dimensions of citizen perception of the threat and the structure of the warning process. One need not attribute differences in citizen response patterns to the fact that the threat agents themselves differ. The data show that there are some common response patterns across the three events and in so doing demand that analytic dimensions or a theoretical framework be developed in which human response to natural and man–made emergencies may be understood. The purpose of this chapter is to focus upon such analytic dimensions while carefully examining the question of how citizens make decisions in emergencies.

In the process of responding to a disaster, emergency managers call upon citizens to make a number of decisions. In effect, one "asks" citizens to "decide" to comply with requests to be vigilant and listen to local radio for instructions, to evacuate some given area, to avoid entering some other area, or perhaps to go to a specified place for shelter. These, as well as many similar types of official "requests," are processed by citizens who must decide whether or not to comply. It is possible, by examining the social science literature, to specify reasonably carefully the likely elements of this decision-making process. The utilty of such an operation lies in the idea that if emergency managers understand the citizens' reasoning process, then messages conveyed during the disaster response period can be tailored to the process, thereby increasing the likelihood of compliance and decreasing the time necessary for the decision-making process.

This chapter is devoted to two major topics: (1) describing the emergency decision-making process and (2) laying out a model of the variables important in decisions to comply with disaster warnings. In connection with the first task, attention will be given to reviewing the relevant literature on warning response, particularly focusing upon pre-impact evacuation of threatened populations, and sorting out those findings which are relevant to developing a framework for understanding the process through which individuals make decisions to comply with evacuation warning messages. For the most part this involves a review of the literature on citizen decision-making in emergencies. In pursuing the second topic, using the framework describing the emergency decision-making process, additional studies of human response to disaster warnings will be reviewed and a model describing factors relevant to warning compliance will be elaborated. The last section of the chapter examines the implications of the warning response model for managing emergencies.

EMERGENCY DECISION-MAKING PROCESSES

To understand emergency decision-making, one must understand the calculus used by individuals to determine both the meaning of the warning message and what action is necessary as a function of message receipt. It should be recalled that any effective warning message does two things: it alerts one that an environmental danger is present and it suggests an appropriate action to counter the danger. Thus, traditionally the study of warning response has focused upon actions taken by warning recipients. While it is important to document what people do in response to a warning, it is equally important to understand why they do it. In understanding why—or what factors are involved in—a given warning response, attention must be devoted to the process through which individuals make emergency decisions. The purpose of this section is to briefly examine current perspectives on emergency decision-making and to outline, based upon an integration of theoretical and empirical studies, a model of the emergency decision-making process.

A prominent sociological theoretical perspective on warning response is based upon an adaptation of the "emergent norm" approach to collective behavior to the disaster setting (Gillespie & Perry, 1976; Turner and Killian, 1972). An emergent norm perspective focuses upon the development of situational norms and expectations which arise when some crisis or change in the social or physical environment renders traditional norms inappropriate guides for behavior (Perry, 1979a; Perry et al., 1981a; Tierney, 1978; Weller & Quarantelli, 1973). Drabek (1968, p. 143) has succinctly summarized the emergent norm orientation to disaster behavior:

Societies are composed of individuals interacting in accordance with an immense multidue of norms, i.e., ideas about how individuals *ought* to behave . . . Our position is that activities of individuals . . . are guided by a normative structure in disaster just as in any other situation . . . In disaster, these actions are governed by *emergent* rather than established norms, but norms nevertheless.

Thus, human behavior in disaster can be conceptualized as nontraditional behavior in response to a changing or changed environment. The emergent norm perspective is concerned with the *process* which begins with a change in the stimulus environment that requires individuals to "re-examine" their behavior *vis-à-vis* the environment; a process referred to as arriving at a new or different "definition of the situation." Broadly speaking, the purpose of most disaster warnings is to "cause" individuals to redefine the situation *from* one in which the environment is threatening. The process of defining the situation concludes with the individuals' decision either to undertake or not undertake some protective action.

The emergent norm perspective highlights, with respect to individuals, the reasoning process which takes place after warning receipt. It is the warning itself in this case which signals that a pending change in the environment could produce the need for nontraditional or nonroutine behavior; perhaps going to a basement to protect oneself from a tornado or leaving the area in the event of a flood. It is argued, however, that the decision to adopt a nonroutine behavior is a function of the individual's definition of the situation following receipt of a warning message.

Thus, whether or not a person undertakes a protective action is dependent upon the outcome of the process of redefining the situation. In this connection, four components of the process of reaching a post-warning definition of the situation have been identified (Perry et al., 1981a, pp. 27–28). First, the individual focuses upon *confirming* the warning. This involves gathering information regarding the message, such as contacting another person or agency to verify that a warning intended for you was in fact issued. A second component relates to developing a "warning belief," or determining that a "real" environmental threat exists. At this stage individuals might, among other things, check the environment to see if there are signs of a disaster—heavy rain in connection with floods, or threatening clouds in the event of tornados. Third, assuming development of a warning belief, individuals attempt to define the level of personal risk posed by the threat. This usually takes the form of determining one's *proximity* to the expected impact area, and deciding just how *certain* it is that impact will occur, and just how *severe* the consequences are likely to be. Finally, if the person believes both warning and threat to be real, and assesses personal risk as high, he/she is expected to conclude that some protective response (i.e., nonroutine behavior) is necessary and begins to consider the practical aspects of making such a response.

As the above outline suggests, an emergent norm approach typically emphasizes the processes which occur early in the emergency decision-making process. That is, the greatest attention is given to the problem of *interpreting* the warning; confirming the message, arriving at a warning believ, assessing personal risk. These are the elements of developing a definition of the situation as one which is potentially dangerous and that requires some nonroutine action. Emergent norm thinking is less directed toward understanding *which* protective action the individual is likely to adopt.

Particularly in recent years, geographers have devoted much attention to the problem of what factors are involved in individuals' decisions to adopt particular protective actions (Burton & Kates, 1964; Burton, Kates, & White, 1978; McPherson & Saarinen, 1977; Oliver, 1978; Saarinen, 1979; Slovic, Kunreuther, & White, 1974; Waterstone, 1978; White, 1974). This work has tended to focus upon what might be called the "latter end" of the emergency decision-making process, highlighting those events which occur for the most part after an individual has arrived at a situational definition of potential danger. Although most of this research has dealt with decisions to adopt some protective action as a preparatory measure well in advance of a specific disaster, the same general model can be applied to the problem of warning response (Perry, 1981a, pp. 5–6).

Underlying most models of adoption decisions is the idea of maximization of expected utility under conditions of uncertainty (cf. Slovic et al., 1974, p. 188). That is, when faced with an uncertain outcome, people tend to adopt the behavior which is believed likely to produce the least negative outcome. Such utility theories have great intuitive appeal but involve at least two troublesome assumptions. They assume a rational approach where the individual is familiar with the full range of options open to him, as well as the likely outcomes associated with each option. As Burton et al. (1978, p. 86) point out,

> People are rarely aware of all the alternatives open to them . . . they differ greatly in the way they judge the consequences of particular actions even on the rare occasions when the physical outcomes are known accurately. The comparison of many different consequences is a highly complex operation [even] for a decision analyst.

For some time, decision theorists have sought to refine the basic maximization hypothesis so that a more adequate description of observed human reasoning is achieved. Toward this end, Herbert Simon has introduced what is called the theory of bounded rationality:

> . . . which asserts that cognitive limitations of the decisionmaker force him to construct a simplified model of the world to deal with it. The key principle of bounded rationality is the notion of "satisficing", whereby an organism strives to attain some satisfactory, though not necessarily maximal, level of achievement [or outcome] (Slovic et al., 1974, p. 189).

Thus, from this perspective one no longer need assume that the individual knows and enumerates all possible outcomes, associates a level of negativeness or positiveness with each, and chooses the option leading objectively to the most positive outcome. Instead, it is hypothesized that individuals probably survey those options which they are aware of, subjectively rate the outcomes they believe likely, and choose the one they perceive to have the most desirable outcome (cf. Kates, 1971; Slovic et al., 1974; White, 1972). Burton et al. (1978, p. 87) translates the bounded rationality model, in applying it to decisions to undertake protective actions in natural disasters, into four decision elements wherein "the individual (1) appraises the probability and magnitude of extreme events, (2) canvases the range of possible alternative actions, and after (3) evaluating the consequences of selected actions, (4) chooses one or a combination of actions." Studies suggest that the first two steps in this process are somewhat interdependent, and that when considering alternative actions people deal with them sequentially rather than simultaneously (Burton et al., 1978; Kunreuther, 1974).

The bounded rationality approach, then, focuses upon the process through which people go about deciding to undertake a protective action. Like the emergent norm approach, it postulates that a series of interdependent steps compose the process. Furthermore, because emergent norm thinking focuses upon the problem of arriving at a definition of the situation, the two frameworks can be seen as complimentary; addressing two aspects of the same process. By synthesizing elements of each approach, one can obtain a more complete perspective on the components of the emergency decision-making process.

With regard to decision-making in the warning response setting, the analyst faces one general problem. Given that the warning both alerts people to a danger and suggests a protective action, what reasoning process operates between message receipt and the adoption of either the recommended action or some other behavior? It is argued here that, taken together, emergent norm thinking and the bounded rationality approach go far toward providing an answer to this question.

To provide an ordering structure for this decision analysis, one can begin by noting that there are three milestones in the process of decision-making under conditions of uncertainty (Rowe, 1977, p. 25): risk identification, risk assessment, and risk reduction. Risk identification in the general sense involves the "reduction of descriptive uncertainty" through such activities as research, screening, and monitoring (Kates, 1976). In the case of warning response, the message informs the individual of the risk—minimizing the need for research or screening behavior—and risk identification involves those behaviors which lead to an individual's "awareness" of the threat. More simply, risk identification involves answering the question: is the threat described in the warning really there? Risk assessment, in the context of disaster warnings, refers to the process of determining the likely consequences of the risk specified in the message

(Otway, 1973; Perry, 1979a). Finally, risk reduction involves determining not how to eliminate risk, but instead what can be done to reduce risk to some "acceptable" level (Rowe, 1977).

In the context of these three milestones, the following discussion attempts to define the kinds of questions which individuals must resolve in making emergency decisions. This presentation draws upon the basic tenets of emergent norm thinking and the bounded rationality approach. It is assumed that the emergency decision-making process is composed of a series of inter-related questions which, taken together, address progressively the issues of risk identification, assessment, and reduction. Also, in addition to identifying relevant questions, an attempt is made to isolate factors which affect the way the individual answers the question. In this way, we sketch out not only the emergency decision-making process, but include reference to some of the variables which empirical studies document as having an effect on the outcome of the process.

Risk Identification

When dealing with disaster warning response the problem of risk identification is somewhat simplified. The warning itself serves to identify the risk or threat and direct the individuals' attention to it. The individual must interpret the message and in so doing, answer the question "does the threat really exist?" It will be recalled that, with regard to emergent norm theory, answering this question marks the initial phase in arriving at a definition of the situation. Research has consistently shown that for an individual to begin thinking about making any type of response, the threat described in the disaster warning must be perceived as *real*. That is, unless the warning recipient believes that the threat is genuine, he is not likely to undertake any protective action (Janis, 1962, pp. 59–66; Mileti, 1975, pp. 21–23; Perry et al., 1980b, p. 45; Williams, 1964, p. 94).

With regard to the process of interpreting the message, studies indicate that individuals consider the credibility of the authorities who issue the warning, try to verify the warning by checking for environmental cues, and/or attempt to confirm a warning with multiple sources which may include authorities as well as friends, neighbors or relatives (social contacts). When individuals receive a warning from what they perceive to be a very credible source, they are more likely to believe the threat exists (Drabek & Boggs, 1968, p. 445; Perry, Lindell, & Greene, 1980d, pp. 19–21), and more likely act on the warning without engaging in a lengthy confirmation process (Perry et al., 1980b, pp. 47–49). It is also known that warning recipients more readily develop a warning belief if some environmental cues are present which indicate that disaster impact is imminent. Gruntfest et al. (1978) have reported that during the Thompson Canyon, Colorado flood which was caused by heavy rains in the mountains, citizens living in the mouth of the canyon hesitated to evacuate when warned, citing the fact that the skies were clear and it had not rained all day. Under the same circumstances, citizens who were incorrectly told that a dam break had precipitated the flooding believed the warning at once. In the latter case, the warning message was consistent with the environmental cues available to warning recipients. Finally, most detailed message interpretation probably occurs within the context of warning confirmation, during which warning recipients attempt to verify a message or gain further information about the threat from various sources (Drabek, 1969; Drabek & Stephenson, 1971, p. 195; Mileti, 1974; Perry, Lindell & Greene, 1980e, p. 442), including community authorities, mass media, or social contacts.

Risk Assessment

In assessing citizen perceptions of personal risk, concern centers upon the individual's beliefs about potential damage to his person or property which would accrue from disaster impact (Perry, 1979a; Perry et al., 1981a). In discussing the likelihood that people will respond to knowledge of a threat, Withey (1962, pp. 104–107) emphasizes the importance of the individual's beliefs about "the probability of he impending event occuring and the severity, to the individual, of such a development." Thus, the process of risk assessment is represented in the individual's search for an answer to the question, "assuming the threat is real, what specific consequences does it have for me?" Empirical studies have shown that perceived personal risk is positively correlated with the adoption of protective measures (Perry et al., 1980b, p. 259; Williams & Fritz, 1957, p. 46; Withey, 1964, p. 86).

Research also indicates that at least three factors bear upon the way in which individuals make decisions about personal risk. The first of these is the credibility of the authorities from which the warning was received. The higher the credibility of the message sender, the more likely the individual is to believe that he is at risk simply on the word of the authority (Mogil & Groper, 1977; Perry et al., 1980b, 1980d). Second, the warning message itself is an important source of risk relevant information for the individual, particularly regarding where, when, and the probable force of disaster impact (Moore, Bates, Lyman, & Parenton, 1963, pp. 31–33; Williams, 1957, pp, 15–19). Information obtained during warning confirmation in addition to original message content may also be used by individuals in determining the extent of personal risk (Perry, Lindell, & Greene, 1981b). Third, the individual's past experience with the disaster agent also forms a basis for assessing risk (Drabek & Boggs, 1968, p. 446; Wallace, 1956a, p. 31; Windham et al., 1977, p. 49). Perry et al. (1980b, p. 113) point out that "a warning message provides current information on the threat and available adaptive behaviors, while past experience affords similar information based on the individual's history of experience."

Risk Reduction

With regard to the issue of risk reduction, the problem facing the individual is to determine what to do about a risk. Assuming that the threat is real and some unacceptable level of personal risk exists, the individual must resolve several issues in deciding whether to adopt some recommended protective action or to devise some alternative strategy for protection or simply to do nothing. In examining the components of this decision, we accept the basic premises of the founded rationality approach; namely that the individual must operate within the limits of the range of alternatives of which he/she is aware and that judgments of relative consequences of different choice outcomes are approximate. Given this qualification, the following discussion is structured around four questions which the individual must answer in connection with the issue of risk reduction.

The first question facing the individual is simply, "Is protection possible?" Put another way, one must determine if any action on the part of the individual will serve to reduce the negative consequences associated with disaster impact. Fortunately, with regard to most natural and technological disasters the answer to this question is yes; at a minimum, some level of protection can be obtained through the expedient of evacuation—putting distance between oneself and the threat (Perry, 1981b, p. 17). Whether or not the individual answers this query in the affirmative, however, depends upon his/her perceptions of the threat as much as upon the technical state of knowledge. In making this determination, individuals may be expected to draw upon: (1) past experience with the threat—e.g., has any action taken in the past reduced negative outcomes, and (2) their knowledge of the threat itself—sometimes subsumed under the topic of hazard awareness.

Once it has been determined that protection is possible, the individual must deal with a second query: *Can* a protective action be undertaken? Unlike the first question, the issue here is largely one of logistics in that the person must decide, *in the present circumstances,* if a protective action may feasibly be undertaken. Studies have shown that at least three factors impinge upon this decision. First, the timing of the warning must be such that the individual has time to act before disaster impact (Perry, 1979b, p. 443). In connection with floods, for example, if a warning is received only seconds prior to impact or simultaneously with impact, it greatly complicates the process of protecting oneself. Second, the family context in which warning is received bears upon the feasibility of undertaking protective measures in that families hesitate to engage in some actions until the safety of all family members is established (Drabek & Boggs, 1968; Haas, Cochrane, & Eddy, 1977; Killian, 1952; Perry, 1979a). In general it is known that families faced with disaster seek to account for the safety of all members and perform as units when undertaking any protective behavior (Quarantelli, 1960b). Particularly when evacuations are involved, a family may delay departure or simply not leave a threatened area at all if even a single household member is not accounted for or cannot be located. Finally, it is known that possession of an emergency plan, assembled in advance, facilitates individuals' decisions to undertake protective actions (Perry, 1979b; Hamilton, Taylor, & Rice, 1955, p. 120; Windham et al., 1977, p. 15). That is, if the individual has given enough thought to the hazard (i.e., the potential risk) to have developed some plan for coping with it, then he/she has in hand knowledge of at least one protective action that can reasonably be undertaken. In the case of flood evacuations, for example, individuals who have a family emergency plan specifying safe routes out of the area and high ground destinations, are more likely to comply with an evacuation order and to successfully relocate.

Assuming that the logistics are such that a protective action can be undertaken, the individual must decide whether undertaking a protective action will *significantly* reduce the negative consequences of impact. The idea here is that individuals must compare the consequences of doing nothing with those judged to be likely if a protective action is undertaken. Unless the difference between the subjectively assessed outcomes is perceived to be both meaningful and in favor of taking protective action, the individual will do nothing (Janis & Mann, 1977, p. 38), but is likely to experience anxiety or psychological distress. When an individual assesses just how much protection is achieved by engaging in a protective action, the ultimate decision is related both to past experience and socio-cultural beliefs about the hazard. The extent to which cultural beliefs can interfere with the adoption of protective actions has been demonstrated in connection with various types of disasters (Anderson, 1968; Clifford, 1956). Lachman and Bonk (1960, p. 1095), in studying response to volcanic eruptions, found that some rural Hawaiians believed that the performance of rituals to a volcano Goddess constituted an effective protective action. Other research has indicated a degree of fatalism—apparently connected to ethnic or cultural factors—can result in individuals tending to fail to undertake suggested protective actions and that the consequences are reflected in higher death and injury rates (Sims & Baumann, 1972, p. 1386).

Finally, if the individual resolves that adopting a protective action does reduce negative consequences, then he/she must determine whether different actions yield different levels of protection and select a course of action. This is the point at which, following Burton et al. (1978, p. 43), the individual must survey the alternatives open to him and determine which one results in the most desirable outcome. In the case of warning response, the warning message usually carries a suggested protective action; one which authorities want members of the threatened population to adopt. Thus, in such situations, the problem confronting the warning recipient is to determine whether he should adopt the suggested action or devise some alternative.

It is hypothesized here that this choice is governed by the individual's subjective assessment of the likely consequences accruing from the suggested action versus any alternatives under consideration. If the individual believes that a relatively higher level of protection is achieved with the suggested action, he/she is apt to adopt that behavior. If one believes that the protection is the same or lower with the suggested action, the behavior finally adopted will depend upon the individual's rating of the outcomes associated with the alternatives. In making these comparisons or ratings, field studies suggest that the individual will consider: (1) conventional wisdom regarding appropriate responses to the threat (Perry & Lindell, 1978, p. 105); (2) the types of actions adopted or recommended by kin or friendship groups (Drabek & Boggs, 1968; Drabek, 1969); and (3) the types of actions adopted by neighbors (Perry et al., 1980b). Therefore, this decision process is governed both by the individual's subjective projection of likely consequences and a social influence process.

Figure IV.1 summarizes in flow chart form the emergency decision-making process described above. The chart reflects basic tenets of both emergent norm thinking and a bounded rationality approach to decision-making. The purpose here is to begin to describe the reasoning that takes place between the individual's receipt of a warning message and the decision to undertake a given protective action. The decision-making process is presented as a series of questions that the individual answers with regard to assessing threat and the level of personal risk, determining if protection is possible and feasible, and deciding what actions should be taken. The elements of the process (or the questions) are interdependent in that the answer to each question controls whether or not the following question will be addressed. This figure offers in summary form a picture of the emergency decision-making process in natural disasters and specifies variables which have been shown empirically to impinge upon the elements of the process.

A MODEL OF EVACUATION WARNING RESPONSE

In the preceding section we identified three general variables which are crucial in citizens' evacuation decision-making processes:

1. the definition of the threat as real (that is, the development of a belief in the warning);
2. the level of perceived personal risk (beliefs about the personal consequences of disaster impact); and
3. the presence of an adaptive plan (being acquainted with a means of protection).

In addition to these variables which are important as primary components of the decision-making process, research on evacuation performance in natural hazards

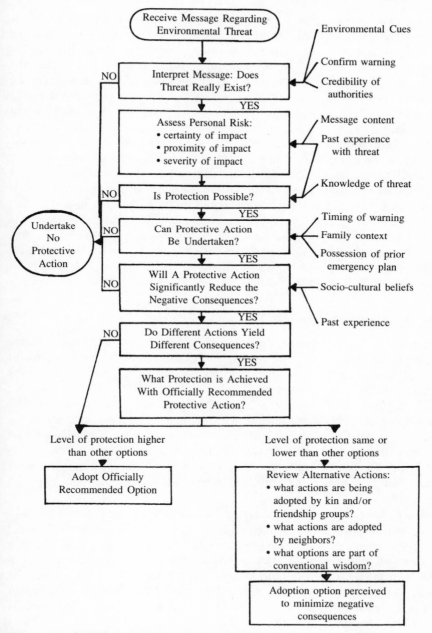

Figure IV.1. Flow model of emergency decision-making process in natural disasters.

suggests four social variables: the family context in which the warning is received, the network of kin relationships in which the family is enmeshed, the level of community involvement, ethnic group membership, and the individual's beliefs about his locus of control. Using these variables as a starting point, the remainder of this chapter reviews pertinent research findings, identifies other relevant variables antecedent to these, and assesses the interrelationships among all of the variables. In so doing, we will assemble a framework or model which specifies the variables important in individual decisions to relocate or evacuate. It should also be emphasized that this model should apply equally well to evacuation decision-making in the event of natural or technological disasters or in the case of a warning to relocate under a civil defense plan. The variables considered here are those which research suggests are important in people's decisions to leave. In a few cases qualifications would be necessary because of special features of different hazard agents, but in general the framework to be developed is not hazard specific. In developing the basis for a warning response model, this review will consider studies of citizen response to natural and technological disasters, and where possible will integrate information on civil defense planning, where nuclear attack is defined as an environmental threat.

Perception of Threat as Real

For *any* protective response—particularly evacuation—to be defined as necessary, the individual must perceive the threat described in the hazard warning to be real. Hence, unless the warning is believed to be valid, no action (protective measure) is likely to be undertaken (Anderson, 1968, pp. 299–304; Janis, 1962; Janis & Mann, 1977; Mileti, 1975, pp. 21–23; Williams, 1964, p. 94). The importance of establishing a situational definition of real threat is underscored by the existence of a large empirical literature detailing the ways in which people go about *confirming* warnings in the case of natural disasters (Drabek, 1969, p. 344; Drabek & Stephenson, 1971, p. 195). In general, the empirical literature indicates that the greater the perceived threat the greater the probability of evacuation.

Three factors important in producing a warning belief or enhancing the individual's perception of threat may be derived from existing research findings: warning content, prior education or training, and the warning source. Warning content and prior experience with, or education about disasters are important in that each affords information to the individual upon which an assessment of threat is made (Lachman, Tatsuoka, & Bonk, 1961, p. 1409). A warning that contains precise information about the hazard and its probable consequences is more likely to create the "reflexive fear" which contributes to the individual's belief that the warning is to be taken seriously (Janis, 1962, pp. 59–66; Levine & Scotch, 1970, p. 314). Anderson (1969b, p. 100) has also pointed out that individuals who have recently experienced a natural hazard are more sensitive to warnings and are more likely to attempt some adaptive response. Indeed, a study of people who left their homes in response to what turned out to be a false warning reports that "few of the evacuees complained about being misled by the false alarm: the vast majority said that they would evacuate again under the same circumstances" (Janis, 1962, p. 85). Assuming that a warning is confirmed, it can be argued that previous experience with disaster (even with false alarms) enhances warning belief and the probability of an *adaptive* (as opposed to non-adaptive) response.

A recent study of evacuation in response to hurricanes on the Gulf coast would seem to contradict this contention by reporting that a large proportion of people who failed to evacuate were long-time residents of the area who presumably had previously experienced hurricanes (Windham et al., 1977). Two qualifiers must be considered in the interpretation of this finding. First, the data are *not* unequivocal; two communities were studied and in one of them, the proportion of people with prior experience is nearly the same among both "stayers" and "leavers." Secondly, hurricanes on the Gulf coast are a recurrent disaster threat, with possibly *several impacts* in a single season. Although empirical studies are not available, it is possible to speculate that under such conditions prior experience becomes a "constant" with *no* relationship to evacuation. This is another possible interpretation of the Windham et al., (1977, p. 29) study. A more cautious interpretation of the data, however, would suggest that recent experience with a valid warning contributes positively to the development of a warning belief.

Of course one substitute for prior experience that can have an influence upon citizens development of a warning belief is prior education and training. This applies equally well to natural and technological hazards, since in both cases the training would convey information which would allow the individual to understand the threat and its potential consequences. In the last chapter of this book, considerable attention will be devoted to the problem of educating the population with regard to emergency measures for coping with environmental hazards.

Finally, research indicates that the more credible the source from which one receives a warning, the more likely one is to believe that the threat is real. Drabek and Boggs (1968, p. 445), in a study of flood warning response, report that "families were warned through three distinct processes: (1) authorities, (2) peers, (3) mass media . . . those warned by an authority were less likely to be skeptical of the warning." The warning confirmation literature generally supports this contention, suggesting that people more often seek other sources for confirmation when they receive warnings from peers or media than when the source is an authority or kinsman.

The utility of this research finding has been demonstrated in connection with civil defense plans in the U.S. where authorities have attempted to enhance the establishment of a warning belief by using a warning source with an anticipated high level of credibility. They argue that in a situation where the President of the United States announces the warning to relocate and newspapers publish full page evacuation instructions (State of Idaho, 1979), the warning source will be seen as unimpeachable and would contribute positively to citizen's definition of the threat as real. While in this case the reasoning is sound, it should be remembered that unless carefully implemented, significant problems can arise. For example, during the nuclear power plant accident at Three Mile Island, Pennsylvania, warning messages or other communications which were often contradictory were issued by a variety of presumably authoritative officials and the result was general public confusion (Nuclear News, 1979, pp. 1–6; Martin, 1980). For the warning source to have the desired effect of enhancing warning belief, the source must be perceived as reliable and the warning message must be clear and apparently logical in any action it suggests.

Perceived Personal Risk

In assessing personal risk, concern centers upon the individual's perception of the chance that impact of the hazard agent will result in great damage or destruction to his person or property (cf. Diggory, 1956; Fritz & Marks, 1954, pp. 29–21). Withey (1962, pp. 104–107), in developing a series of stages of reaction to threat, emphasizes the importance of the individual's perception of "the probability of the impending event occurring [and] the severity, to the individual, of such a development." Put differently, personal risk may be thought of in terms of an individual's conception of his proximity to impact and the certainty and likely severity of the impact. Studies have shown that the perception of personal risk has a direct affect on the nature of the individual's response to a warning (Menninger, 1952, p. 129; Williams & Fritz, 1957, pp. 46–50; Withey, 1964, p. 86).

Glass (1970, pp. 64–67) in discussing "contingency responses" to threat points out that unless a person is convinced that impact is certain and that he is within the danger area, there is general reluctance to cooperate with emergency plans. Menninger (1952, p. 129), in reporting evacuation problems during the floods in Kansas during the summer of 1951 found that:

> . . . an amazing number of people refused to believe that the flood would hit them . . . [and] . . . would not move themselves or their belongings out of their homes.

Similar findings have been reported by Tyhurst (1957b, p. 43) and Danzig, Thayer, and Galanter (1958, pp. 51–53). Thus, the literature indicates that a direct and positive relationship exists between the individuals' perceived level of personal risk and the probability of evacuation.

In the study of natural disasters, warning content and prior experience and education have been shown to be closely related to the individual's level of perceived personal risk. It is fairly routine that warning messages of an impending natural disaster contain information on place, time, and the probable force of disaster impact (Mogil & Groper, 1977; Moore et al., 1963, pp. 31–33; Williams, 1957, pp. 15–19). Furthermore, the individual's prior experience or training, as well as his reading of environmental cues, contributes to the perception of the degree of personal risk (Drabek & Boggs, 1968, pp. 445–447; Windham et al., 1977, p. 49).

In the case of technological disasters or a nuclear attack environment, citizen's assessment of personal risk is not a particularly well-studied phenomenon. As the data from the emergency at Three Mile Island showed, citizen perception of risk associated with radiation hazard appears to be high relative to risk perception in some natural disasters. In Chapter III it was pointed out that this may be due to the media attention given nuclear risks, or to people's tendency to see radiation in primarily a destructive sense, or to citizens' generally low levels of accurate information regarding radiation hazards. Indeed, rather than being a property of nuclear threats themselves, public perception of high risk associated with such hazards is likely to be a function of some combination of the factors just listed. In a similar vein, American civil defense plans, or specifically Crisis Relocation plans, are based on the idea that the population-at-risk can be evacuated in advance of a nuclear attack. Based upon social surveys and some opinion poll data, it is assumed that the population as a whole probably overestimates the destructive potential of a nuclear attack, and would tend to define personal risk as very high. From a planning and response perspective, however, it is not appropriate to depend upon citizens to correctly define personal risk as high because of widespread misinformation. In the case of technological hazards, such as liquid natural gas, gasoline, or chlorine, where the public is either generally unaware of the precise nature of the threat or treats the dangerous substance as an ''ordinary'' part of everyday life, the ''error'' of misinformation may result in failure to define personal risk as high enough to merit attention to the instructions of emergency managers. In the end, an appropriate emergency management strategy must rely upon devising education and training programs which convey correct risk assessment information to the public.

Adaptive Plan

Studies of evacuation in natural disaster sometimes overlook the fact that in order to effectively clear an area, residents must either have prior knowledge of some standing evacuation plan or be informed of such a plan by officials. Hamilton et al. (1955, p. 120) interviewed a disaster victim who reported:

We couldn't decide where to go or what to do. So we grabbed our children and stuff and were just starting to move outside. Where if it had just been ourselves, we might have taken out. But we didn't want to risk it with the children.

This family received a warning to evacuate, but had no plan which identified safe routes for exit or appropriate destinations. Thus, even if one wants to evacuate, the absence of a plan for so doing is sufficient to hinder any adaptive response.

The problem of families *not* evacuating (or evacuating to an even more dangerous location) when evacuation routes and destinations are not well known or well publicized has been widely documented with a variety of types of natural hazard (cf. Windham et al., 1977, p. 15). Although not universally implemented, most manuals for community predisaster preparation encourage the planning and dissemination of evacuation routes (cf. Healy, 1969; Leonard, 1973). Therefore, the possession of an adaptive plan, at a very minimum a route and safe destination, is positively related to the probability of evacuation.

Research indicates that individuals' knowledge of an adaptive plan depends largely upon two factors: warning content and prior experience. Williams (1964, pp. 91–93) has pointed out that the most effective warning messages are clear, specific, consistent, and if possible, contain instructions for an appropriate protective response. The warning message itself, whether delivered via official channels or through kin and friendship networks, is one source of an adaptive plan. With respect to natural disasters and conventional warfare, it has also been reported that the *experience* of warning and/or evacuation provides the individual with a potential adaptive plan for future hazards, simply by replicating his past behavior (Bernert & Iklé, 1952, pp. 133–135).

Family Context

As Killian (1952) has indicated, the study of human behavior in disaster must take into account the network of community and family roles in which the individual is immersed. Furthermore, research to date suggests that in the event of conflicting responsibilities among various roles, "the majority of persons involved in such dilemmas resolve them in favor of loyalty to the family . . ." (Killian, 1952, p. 311). In particular, we know that families faced with disaster seek to protect members (Quarantelli, 1960) and generally perform as units when undertaking any protective behavior. Studies of evacuation have revealed that "when they did evacuate, families left as units . . . these data provide additional support for the hypothesis that families move as units and remain together, even at the cost of overriding dissenting opinions" (Drabek & Boggs, 1968, p. 446). Support for the contention that families evacuate as a group may also be drawn from studies of the bombing of London during World War II (Bernert & Iklé, 1952, pp. 133–135; Titmuss, 1950, p. 172). The primary consequence of these findings is to introduce an additional constraint on evacuation: unless the family is together or missing members are safely accounted for, evacuation will not occur. Thus, family context is positively related to the probability of evacuation.

Ethnicity and age indirectly affect family context. Family structure as well as kin relations, vary among ethnic groups. Staples (1976, p. 123), for example, reports that ". . . the Black kinship network is more extensive and cohesive than kinship bonds among the White population . . . a larger proportion of Black families take relatives into their households." As indicated above, the structure of the household is important in defining family context. Age of the head of household is important for family context in two ways. In general, age correlates with the life-cycle position of the family, and especially among minorities, with the generational depth of the extended family household (Lansing & Kish, 1957, p. 512). Furthermore, the presence of aged persons in a household (or a household composed of aged people), has been cited by disaster researchers as a factor which complicates family evacuation by increasing the complexity of family role responsibilities. Thus, Ellemers (1955, p. 421) points out that "old and sick people were unable to leave their homes at the time of the flood warning." Hill and Hansen (1962, p. 186) have also observed that the "extended family is poorly organized to meet threats and hardships, for its very young and very old members are often ill-equipped to meet such sudden challenges." In terms of our knowledge of family tendencies to adapt to disaster as a unit, it becomes clear that such "deficiencies" of individual family members reflect upon the performance of the group.

The tendency of families to evacuate as a unit is most problematic from a planning standpoint when forewarning—lead time before disaster impact—is very short. In such cases, pre-impact evacuation of a threatened area may be greatly slowed by families who attempt to assemble at home before evacuating. In natural disasters, this problem can be minimized by encouraging families, as part of a community preparedness plan, to select a safe rendezvous point away from home where the family could assemble in an emergency (Perry et al., 1981b).

Kinship Relations

Kin relationships are here conceived in terms of people's interaction and exchange patterns with their kinsmen. Several studies of communities in disaster have pointed out that very close kin relationships promote post–disaster recovery success among victims (Bolin, 1976, p. 268; Drabek & Key, 1976, p. 90; Drabek, Key, Erickson, & Crowe, 1975, p. 486). Although less often studied, kin relationships also play an important role in the warning dissemination process and, consequently, in the promotion of successful adaptation to disaster warning (Clifford, 1956, pp. 113–124). In particular, one's interaction patterns with kin have an impact upon the content, and source of the warnings an individual receives.

Drabek and Stephenson (1971, p. 199) report that "extended family relationships were crucial as warning message and confirmation sources . . . telephone conversations with relatives during the warning period were usually a key factor." Official warning messages broadcast via mass media are sometimes vague, often not heard by all the potential victims, and are usually confirmed via some other source (Bates, Fogelman, Parenton, Pittman, & Tracy, 1963, pp. 11–13; Drabek, 1969, p. 341; Mileti & Beck, 1975). Thus, kinsmen can supply both additional information (i.e., warning content), and serve as confirmation sources for hazard warning. It has also been found that people who hear disaster warnings relay the information to kinsmen who reside within the probable impact area (Drabek & Boggs, 1968, pp. 445–447). This has the immediate effect of *increasing* the number of warning messages received by potential victims. Even under crisis relocation planning, where a warning message would be widely disseminated, the operation of such contacts to afford social and psychological support increases the chance of adaptive reactions to warning. Hence, kin serve as supportive "sources" of warning and also provide information regarding warning content.

Studies have shown that the nature and frequency of relationships with primary kin are very much affected by ethnicity and age (cf. Litwak and Szelenski, 1969, p. 465; Sussman & Burchinal, 1968, 1962). In general, Anglo-American elderly are relatively more socially isolated (Bennett, 1973, p. 179), and exhibit greater variation in income and wealth accumulation than minority elderly (Terrell, 1971, p. 363). Aged Blacks, in contrast, tend to be more uniformly poor but are also more actively involved in kin networks (cf. Babchuk & Ballweg, 1971; Jackson, 1971; Kent, 1971). McLuckie (1970, p. 38) indicates that ". . . different classes or ethnic groups have varying conceptions of what constitutes adaptation to a threat, or credibility of community organizations which might be involved in issuing warning messages." Hence, what might be perceived as appropriate protective behavior by Blacks or Indians may not at all be related to the adaptive behavior promoted by some official agency in its warning message. Studies also show that aged people tend to more often be affected with chronic illnesses which make them less mobile and thus able to comply with a warning for evacuation (Friedsam, 1962, pp. 155–157).

Community Involvement

Community involvement refers to the individual's patterns of interaction with friends (neighbors), and his participation in voluntary associations and other community organizations. Barton (1970, pp. 63–124) has pointed out that the extent of people's integration into the community affects the content, source, and number of warnings received in much the same way as kin relationships. The greater one's social contacts, the more likely one is to receive more information regarding a potential hazard. It is generally agreed that when both kin and community contacts are available, kin relationships are more important in evacuation decision-making (Drabek & Boggs, 1968). The reason for including community involvement, however, is that when kin bonds are weak or absent, ties to the community can serve a similar function as far as response to evacuation warning is concerned.

As with kin relationships, community involvement varies with age and ethnicity. Blacks, in particular, are cited as relatively more involved in voluntary and formal organizations than Whites or other minority groups (Babchuk & Thompson, 1962; Oram, 1966; Renzi, 1966). Tomeh (1973, p. 99) points out that, with respect to membership in voluntary associations, "studies . . . show higher participation rates for Blacks at all social class levels, especially lower class." Previous research which did not control for social class erroneously reported Black participation rates lower than White rates (Wright & Hyman, 1966, p. 32).

Although it is generally argued that social isolation—shrinking friendship networks and decreased affiliations with organizations (Watson & Maxwell, 1977, pp. 59–66)—characterizes most aged people, it has recently been acknowledged that the variance along this dimension is greater than previously believed" (Cottrell, 1974, pp. 49–57). Broadly defined, however, community involvement tends to decline with increasing age of the head of household (Harry, 1970).

Community involvement also has special relevance to the development of a capacity for community emergency management. It is generally acknowledged that to maintain optimal effectiveness, some quantity of emergency preparedness information should be disseminated to the public in a standardized form. We devote particular attention to techniques of information dissemination in Chapter VI. In the past, and to some extent now, such information has been communicated via training or review classes sponsored by community organizations— e.g., Boy Scouts, Girl Scouts, Kiawanis, Jaycees. Presumably similar programs, designed to familiarize the public with particular hazards or even nuclear attack, could be revitalized and implemented at a local community level. Under such circumstances, the higher one's level of community involvement, the more likely it would be that he will have some prior education or training in connection with emergency management.

Ethnicity

For the purposes of this review, an ethnic group is composed of "people who conceive of themselves as being alike by virtue of common ancestry, real or factitious, and are so regarded by others" (Shibutani & Kwan, 1965, p. 31). This is similar to the concept of social race, "a group that is socially defined but on the basis of physical criteria'' (Van den Berghe, 1967), except that it is broader in the sense that social factors rather than physical characteristics are emphasized as the basis for group membership. We embrace Rose's (1973, pp. 262–263) contention that ethnicity reflects the extent to which an individual feels, or is made to feel, a member of some ethnic group.

Given this definition of ethnicity, how can we expect that it will impinge upon emergency decision-making in general, and specifically upon variables in an evacuation warning response model. There are basically two ways in which ethnicity effects existing models of warning response behavior: (1) by directly impacting some variables that have already been discussed, and (2) by affecting other factors not mentioned yet. The following paragraphs address these two concerns.

Existing research results suggest that ethnicity has a direct effect upon three variables in the warning response model—perceived personal risk, kin relationships, and community involvement—and an indirect effect upon family context through kin relationships. While there have been very few studies dealing with risk assessments among ethnic minorities faced with disaster, there is some general evidence that American minority groups define danger from the environment in different ways (Sims & Baumann, 1972). Moore (1958, pp. 150–151) in his studies of tornado response indicates that Black families reported "less emotional stress and concern," before impact, about the tornado danger than White families. He attributes this difference to the idea that Black families in the Texas towns studied were very poor and immersed in the problems of economic survival on a day-to-day basis; the struggle for economic viability was immediate and continuing, and in comparison, warnings about threats from the environment seemed to pose less relative danger. Hence, although the data from empirical studies is sparse, there does seem to be enough consistent evidence to argue that ethnicity does have a direct effect upon individual's conceptions of personal risk. That is, membership in an ethnic minority group structures the individual's world view, both in general and specifically in the way in which threats from natural disasters are conceived.

Ethnicity has a very pronounced effect upon the individual's relationship to kin, particularly in the context of disaster. In his study of a Mexican community during a flood of the Rio Grande, Clifford (1956, pp. 116–120) observed that in preparing to evacuate "Mexican towns-people were oriented so strongly toward the extended family that they almost completely neglected neighbors and friends." Similarly, Staples (1976, p. 123) reports that ". . . the Black kinship network is more extensive and cohesive than kinship bonds among the White population . . . a larger proportion of Black families take relatives into their households." Perry and Perry (1959, pp. 45–59) have also commented upon the relatively greater cohesion among relatives in Black as opposed to White communities facing tornado disasters. These findings are consistent with the recent research of minority scholars who, in trying to sort out accurate descriptive data from population myths about minority family structure, report that ties among members of ethnic minority families in general are stronger than traditionally described. It is argued that the problem with many earlier studies of the minority family as an institution lies in a failure to appreciate the exigencies imposed upon minority families as a function of adapting to the majority milieu, and consequently the different functions the family must serve for members (Staples & Mirande, 1980).

Furthermore, ethnicity not only affects the nature and frequency of relationships with primary kin, but also, through this variable, affects what is described in the warning response model as family context. That is, family structure and role responsibilities vary both among minority groups and between minority and majority groups (Bianchi and Farley, 1979). For example, it is known that minority family households are more likely to be extended families, to involve multi-generational depth, and to have more than a single family in the same household. These conditions affect the number of relevant kinsmen to be accounted for in connection with undertaking protective actions in response to disaster warnings, and can complicate the accounting process itself. Hill and Hansen (1962, p. 186) argue that the extended "family is poorly organized to meet threats and hardships" associated with disaster warning response; it is possible that this accounts for at least some of the variance in warning response by minority families. To date, however, no studies have specifically examined the impact of extended family structure, among minorities or nonminorities, upon the logistics of warning response. It is certainly true that response among extended family households is more complicated, but it is yet to be determined if this hinders or promotes warning response.

Finally, ethnic group membership has also been found to have a direct impact upon levels of community involvement. For example, Blacks in particular are cited as relatively more involved in religious organizations than Whites or other minority groups. Olsen (1970, p. 682) reports that with regard to voluntary associations and voting behavior, "the general tendency for Blacks to be more active than Whites [when socio-economic status and age are controlled] is found to occur in every type of activity investigated." It has been pointed out, however, that higher rates of ethnic minority group community involvement tend to be directed toward voluntary associations related to the "ethnic community" (Olsen, 1970, pp. 695–696). This appears to be particularly the case with Mexican-American families who have historically experienced "blockages" in their interaction with the external or majority social system (Sotomayor, 1971, p. 319). Wright and Hyman (1966, p. 32) have also reported that minorities are somewhat less involved than Whites in the traditional "majority-oriented" civic and voluntary associations.

Having considered variables already in the model which are affected by ethnicity, we can now turn to an examination of variables not in the model which (1) are affected by ethnicity, and (2) are antecedent to other variables in the warning response model. This has the effect of adding depth to the model or expanding it to accommodate factors related to ethnicity which also effect warning response. Three such variables will be considered: socio-economic status, perceptions of the credibility of authorities, and locus of control.

Although recent years have seen increases in per capita income for minorities, ethnic minority groups remain less affluent than Whites (Bianchi & Farley, 1979; Pettigrew, 1971; Vander Zanden, 1966). With regard to coping with natural disasters, it has been argued that minorities experience greater relative difficulties than whites because they have lower incomes and money reserves, are more likely to be unemployed, less likely to have disaster insurance, and more likely to have problems in communicating with institutional providers of both information about disaster risks and post-impact relief (Bauman & Sims, 1978; Dacy & Kunreuther, 1969; Jones, 1972, p. 133; Moore, 1958; Nelson & Winter, 1975; Perry et al., 1981a; Terrell, 1971). Furthermore, socio-economic well-being has been shown to be related to two variables in the warning response model: development of a warning belief and community involvement. As mentioned previously, Moore (1958) reported that income differences (which in his data correlated with race differences) existed in the extent to which respondents believed that warning messages of impending disaster constituted an issue to take seriously. In a study of citizen response to warnings, Mack and Baker (1962, p. 49) found that low education-low income people and high education-high income people were less likely to interpret a warning signal as valid than individuals of moderate education and income. Socio-economic status is also related to community involvement, in that the low income-low education groups tend to be less involved in community organizations. On the basis of a massive review of empirical studies, Tomeh (1973, p. 97) concludes "that persons of higher SES (socioeconomic status) are more likely to participate in voluntary formal organizations than are their counterparts in low SES groups." Cohen and Kapsis (1978, p. 1065) found that the hypothesis that lower income is positively correlated with lower rates of participation holds even when ethnicity is controlled.

It should also be acknowledged that there are likely to be interactive effects of ethnicity with socioeconomic status. Indeed, in the absence of empirical research on the question, one might speculate that with regard to differences in interpreting warning messages, assessments of risk, and compliance with an evacuation warning, social class variables may explain at least as much variance as ethnicity. Sorting out such interactive effects and evaluating the relative importance of these two variables is, however, an empirical task. Both are included in the proposed comprehensive warning response model on the strength of theoretical reasoning. It is here acknowledged that all factors included in the model are probably not of equal weight in explaining warning response behavior. Our primary purpose here is conceptual synthesis rather than empirical specification. Of course, with respect to this latter activity, one would expect that subsequent research will produce evidence upon which the theoretical framework presented here can be revised and refined.

In general, it is known that ethnic minorities are less likely to perceive White authorities as credible information sources (Davis, 1974, pp. 136–140; Staples, 1976, p. 42). In the context of disaster warning systems, McLuckie indicates that ". . . different classes and ethnic groups have varying conceptions of . . . the credibility of community organizations which might be involved in issuing warning messages" (1970, p. 38). Theorists have argued that ethnic minority group members' suspicion of authorities stems from their general history of contacts with official representatives of the majority group; particularly among low income minorities, contacts with police, social caseworkers, and other social control agencies are less often reinforcing or positive. The history of discrimination against minority groups in the United States tends to continue to be reflected in the distrust such groups tend to place in the majority social system.

Studies have shown that perceptions of the credibility of authorities who issue a warning are correlated with individual's assessments of personal risk and the development of a warning belief (Mileti, 1974; Perry, 1979b; Perry et al., 1980b). It is known that the source from which the individual receives disaster warnings is positively related to his beliefs about the level of risk associated with impact. In general, the higher the credibility of the source the more likely the person is to believe he is in danger and the more likely he is to undertake some protective action (Carter, Clark, Leck, & Fine, 1977; Perry et al., 1980b, p. 73; Stallings, 1967, p. 7; Windham et al., 1977, p. 39). Studies have also shown that the greater the credibility of the warning source, the more likely the individual is to develop a warning belief (Mileti, 1975, p. 75; Mileti & Harvy, 1977, p. 5; Williams, 1957, p. 16). In a study of flood evacuation in Denver, Colorado, Drabek (1969) found that citizens warned by what they perceived to be a credible source were more likely to believe the warning. Similarly, Perry et al. (1980b) report that citizens whose first warning came from a credible source were less likely to attempt to confirm the warning with alternate sources and more likely to perceive the threat described in the warning message as real.

In addition, recent studies of disaster behavior suggest that a person's belief about his/her level of control over natural events is correlated both with ethnicity and warning response behavior. Sims and Bauman (1972, p. 1389) report that the extent to which an individual believes that he controls his own life or what happens to him is positively related to his willingness to undertake positive protective actions in response to tornado warnings. On the other hand, people with an external locus of control ". . . place less trust in man's communal knowledge and control systems; they await the fated onslaught, watchful but passive" (Sims & Bauman, 1972, p. 1391). This phenomenon has been referred to by clincial psychologists as self-efficacy (Bandura, 1977). The idea is that if an individual believes that in spite of any action he may undertake, it is not possible to achieve protection, then he is less likely to heed a warning. Burton (1972) has also pointed out that when citizens believe that a hazard is beyond the control of man's technology, they seem to ignore the threat and are reticent to adopt planning measures to protect themselves in the event of disaster impact. Two studies report that ethnicity appears to be correlated with locus of control. In a study of flood response in Charlotte, North Carolina, Ives and Furseth (1980, p. 14) report that "a significant subgroup of Blacks, however, view flooding as an uncontrollable natural event and are less confident in their ability to deal with the hazard." Likewise, Turner, Nigg, Paz, and Young (1979, p. 3) found that Blacks and Mexican-Americans "were more *fatalistic* about earthquake danger, skeptical about science and the predictability of earthquakes," than Whites. In terms of the warning response model, these studies suggest that there are links between ethnicity and locus of control, and between locus of control and both the likelihood of having an adaptive plan and the probability of undertaking a protective response. It should also be noted that variations may exist not only between majority and minority groups, but also among different minority groups. It is clear that considerable research on minority group behavior in disaster needs to be done (Perry et al., 1981a).

Locus of Control

Finally, studies of human behavior in disaster suggest that a person's beliefs about his level of control over natural events is correlated with warning response behavior. Sims and Bauman (1972, p. 1389) report that the extent to which an individual believes that he controls his own life or what happens to him is positively related to his willingness to undertake protective actions in response to tornado warnings. On the other hand, when faced with a threatened tornado, people with an external locus of control ". . . place less trust in man's communal knowledge and control systems; they await the fated onslights, watchful but passive" (Sims & Bauman, 1972, p. 1391). This phenomenon has been referred to by clinical psychologists as self-efficacy (Bandura, 1977). The idea is that if an individual believes that in spite of any action he may undertake, it is not possible to achieve protection, then he is less likely to heed a warning. Burton (1972) has pointed out that when citizens believe that a hazard is beyond the control of man's technology, they seem to ignore the threat and are reticent to adopt planning measures to protect themselves.

A Theoretical Model of Evacuation Response

Up to this point, a framework has been developed which describes citizen decision-making in emergencies by synthesizing elements of an emergent norm approach to collective action with a bounded rationality conception of decision-making. Based upon this picture of the way decisions are made, and a review of research on human behavior in disasters, we have isolated a number of variables which together circumscribe the important factors related to citizen response to disaster warning. In an effort to summarize this information in a form that is more easily understood and referenced, this section outlines a mode of warning response behavior. Although the term model has a highly specific meaning for philosophers of science and methodologists (Blalock, 1969, pp. 27–43; Brodbeck, 1968; Kaplan, 1964, pp. 258–267; Turner, 1967, p. 236), it is here used to mean a representation of social processes in a broad sense. Using Zetterberg's (1966, pp. 63–79) approach, this model is composed of a series of inter-dependent propositions or hypotheses which describe the inter-relationships among a network of variables. Each proposition may be seen as a summary statement, describing the apparent relationship among at least two variables. The claims made by each proposition rest upon the results of the studies reviewed earlier and upon the strength of the theoretical rationale developed by combining emergent norm and bounded rationality hypotheses. Thus the model itself, like all models, is time bounded—each proposition should be seen as subject to modification (and even elimination altogether) based upon the results of further research which may be conducted in the future. In social science we proceed to amass knowledge by eliminating false claims based upon research findings. That is, we begin with a claim such as ''citizens' first reaction to a flood warning is disbelief'' and design studies to test that supposition. As long as research confirms the supposition, social scientists treat it as an accurate representation of social behavior. When a negative case—one in which disbelief was not the first reaction—is found, we must either reject the hypothesis as entirely false or add a qualifying statement that makes the claim consistent with the new research findings. For example, one might amend the proposition to read ''disbelief is the first reaction to disaster warning, except in communities with high levels of emergency preparedness where emergency managers have educated the population regarding the hazard itself and the nature of the warning system.'' Thus, in a western Washington State town subject to seasonal riverine flooding with an active emergency services department, during flood season one would not expect disbelief to be the first reaction after hearing a flood warning.

Social science, then, advances by disproving hypotheses; we can never say, based upon any amount of research, that a given claim is always true or ''proven.'' We do have more faith in hypotheses that have been repeatedly tested and not demonstrated to be false, but we rely upon continued and progressively more refined research to specify the precise conditions under which we may expect any given proposition to be correct. The research process must be seen as a long-term endeavor, which over time provides the information necessary to reject or modify the claims of propositions and hypotheses. For this reason, all models are fragile in the sense that new knowledge may demand that they be changed. Understood in this light, as tools which may change over time rather than rules which are forever stable, models can be highly useful devices for understanding human behavior.

With these qualifiers in mind, we can now turn to the elaboration of a warning response model. Since the research reviewed in this chapter focuses upon a particular type of warning response—evacuation—each of the model's constituent propositions describes the relationship between one of the primary variables and the probability of evacuation. Subpropositions listed under each primary proposition seek to further specify the relationship between a primary variable and other variables which are antecedent to it. The warning response model is listed below in the form of twelve primary propositions and seventeen subpropositions.

> **PROPOSITION 1.** The more precise an individual's adaptive plan, the higher the probability of evacuation.
>
> > **1a.** Prior experience with similar disasters increases the chance that an individual will develop an adaptive plan.
> >
> > **1b.** The more detailed the warning message content, the more likely it is to provide the elements of an adaptive plan.
> >
> > **1c.** Individuals characterized by an external locus of control are less likely to develop adaptive plans.
>
> **PROPOSITION 2.** The greater the individual's believe in the warning (perception of threat as real), the greater the probability of evacuation.
>
> > **2a.** Prior experience with similar disasters increases the likelihood of developing a warning belief.
> >
> > **2b.** As the number of warning messages received increases, so does the degree to which the threat is perceived as real.
> >
> > **2c.** Receipt of a warning from a credible source increases the degree to which the threat is perceived as real.
> >
> > **2d.** The presence of environmental cues associated with a disaster increases the extent to which the threat is perceived as real.

      2e. Successful confirmation of a warning message increases the extent to which the threat is perceived as real.

PROPOSITION 3. The higher the level of perceived personal risk, the greater the probability of evacuation.

      3a. Prior experience with similar disasters is positively related to level of perceived personal risk.

      3b. Ethnicity is inversely related to the level of perceived personal risk.

      3c. Socio-economic status is inversely related to the level of perceived personal risk.

      3d. Receipt of a warning from a credible source increases levels of perceived personal risk.

      3e. To the extent that the warning message specifies the location and severity of impact, levels of perceived risk among persons within the impact area will increase.

PROPOSITION 4. To the extent that family members are together at the time of warning or otherwise accounted for, the probability of evacuation is increased.

      4a. The nature and frequency of kin relationships is related to the definition of family members who need to be accounted for in emergencies.

PROPOSITION 5. Individuals characterized by an external locus of control are less likely to evacuate or engage in any type of protective action.

      5a. Membership in an ethnic minority group increases the chance that an individual will have an external locus of control.

PROPOSITION 6. The greater the frequency of contacts with kin, the greater the number of warnings an individual will receive.

PROPOSITION 7. The greater the frequency of contacts with kin, the more likely one is to receive additional warning information (content) through these contacts.

PROPOSITION 8. Membership in an ethnic minority group is related to the nature and frequency of contacts with kin.

PROPOSITION 9. The greater the level of community involvement, the greater the number of warnings an individual is likely to receive.

    9a. Membership in an ethnic minority group is positively related to level of community involvement.

    9b. The lower the individuals' socio-economic status, the lower the level of community involvement.

PROPOSITION 10. The greater the level of community involvement the more likely one is to receive additional warning information from these contacts.

PROPOSITION 11. Membership in an ethnic minority group is positively correlated with lower perceived credibility of authorities.

PROPOSITION 12. Membership in an ethnic minority group is inversely correlated with socio-economic status.

The preceding propositions or statements summarize empirical findings on citizen warning response, interpreted within an emergent norm–bounded rationality theoretical framework. Figure IV.2 shows the postulated network of relationships specified in the model in the familiar graph or diagram form. Among the many relationships specified in the model, it should not be forgotten that there are four primary variables or conditions which insure citizen compliance with a decision to evacuate on request: (1) the individual must have some adaptive plan; (2) he must believe that the consequences of not evacuating place him in a position of high personal risk; (3) he must believe that the warning message accurately describes a pending environmental threat; and (4) he must either have his family (household) assembled to evacuate as a unit *or* know that missing family members are not in danger. The other variables described in the model serve to specify conditions which affect, either directly or indirectly, the four critical variables of personal risk, warning believe, adaptive plan and family context.

Finally, the most important question posed in connection with any model is

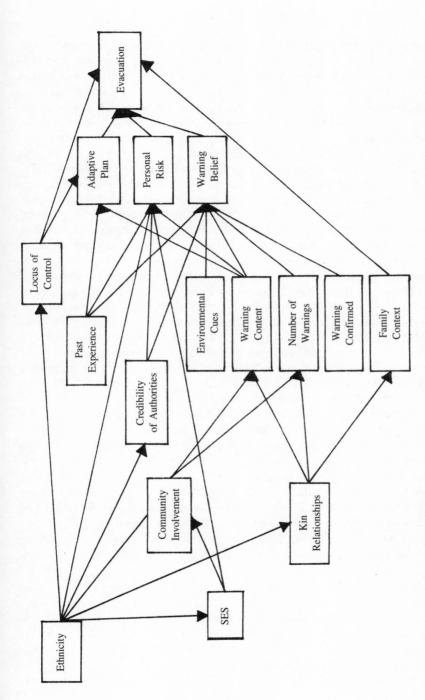

Figure IV.2. Model of factors important in individuals' decision to evacuate (arrows represent relationships, either direct or inverse).

"now that it has been developed, of what use is it?" The model developed in this chapter describes citizen performance in disaster warning situations, and provides information on human behavior which can be used by emergency managers (1) to anticipate how individuals are likely to act when given a warning and (2) to use this information to develop emergency response plans which maximize the chance of citizen compliance. That is, knowledge of how people respond to emergencies can be used both to structure the *process* of planning for emergencies and to organize the *elements* of any given plan. In Chapter VI, we will examine what this model suggests for the planning process, while Chapter VII is devoted to the implications for plans themselves. Thus, the remaining chapters are oriented toward emergency management strategy and tactics, devising techniques to accomplish the job. Before turning to the questions of the planning process and plan elements, we will consider an important and persistent issue in the management of emergencies, the question of the social psychological response of citizens to warnings and to disaster impact.

Interestingly, much attention has recently been focused upon the question of the psychological consequences of environmental threats for citizens exposed to them. Recently, court orders forced the U.S. Nuclear Regulatory Commission to assess the likely psychological impact of restarting one of the two nuclear reactors located at Three Mile Island, Pennsylvania. The issue involved questioned whether restarting a reactor, and thereby restoring a technological threat in the environment, have a negative psychological effect upon citizens living nearby, particularly those involved in the evacuations described in Chapter III. The problem of negative psychological responses to environmental threats and disasters is to a certain extent independent of, but as important implications for, the emergency decision-making processes described in this chapter. That is, if disasters create negative long-term psychological reactions in victims, how will such reactions affect the process of making a decision to comply with or ignore a disaster warning message. Or, even if no long-term effects accrue, are there short-term psychological effects—producing panic for instance—that might interfere with a citizen's capacity to reason or act in an emergency. In Chapter V we will address the question of psychological impacts, based upon descriptive studies of human behavior in disaster, and assess the relevance of such impacts for managing the consequences of natural and man-made disasters.

Social Psychology in Emergency Management

For decades, social scientists have been unable to agree on the extent to which experiencing a natural or man-made disaster is related to the development of psychopathological symptoms. While there is some consensus regarding the existence of a "disaster syndrome"—a dazed state found in the immediate post-impact period—the extent to which more persistent negative psychological consequences may be attributed to disaster impact remains controversial. Indeed, scientists appear to be polarized; some argue that disasters cause severe negative psychological reactions in victims, with the opposite camp claiming that any psychological effects, if they exist at all, are transient and minor.

The purpose of this chapter is to examine the question of psychological reactions to disasters as it impinges upon the problem of managing emergencies. From a conceptual standpoint, emergency managers need to be concerned about two aspects of the social psychology of disaster response. First, and most pressing from the standpoint of managing any given emergency, is the problem of short-term citizen response to the disaster warning and impact. In addressing this problem, attention will be given to describing the disaster syndrome and its implications for warning response, the problem of panic flight and the concept of the therapeutic community response. Concern here is with documenting the types of short-term psychological reactions observed in field studies of disaster behavior and specifying the options open to emergency managers for coping with the consequences of such reactions.

The second aspect of the psychological consequences of disasters examined in this chapter focuses upon the problem of understanding longer-term effects of disasters upon citizens. In this case, attention centers upon the later post-impact and recovery phases, where the emergency manager may have to anticipate the possible effects of negative psychological consequences upon the ability of citizens to understand and comply with both recovery measures and plans for managing subsequent impacts of the same disaster agent. In this connection, two tasks are addressed. First, the controversy regarding the extent to which natural disasters are correlated with negative psychological outcomes will be critically examined, giving special attention to understanding conceptual and methodological difficulties. Second, the empirical literature on field studies of disaster response will be reviewed and an attempt will be made to assemble the rudiments of a conceptual framework for understanding the longer-term psychological consequences of disasters. The conceptual framework will focus not upon whether disasters cause psychopathology, but will concentrate upon the problem of identifying the various avenues through which natural disasters may impinge upon individuals' psychological stability.

SHORT-TERM PSYCHOLOGICAL EFFECTS

It is often assumed by some citizens, and unfortunately by some emergency managers, that people respond to the immediate threat of disaster and immediately after impact in a disorganized or perhaps disoriented fashion. Particularly in what might be called the journalistic or popular press, and more recently in "disaster" movies, the general theme is put across that disasters tend to be managed by the very few brave and clear-thinking souls who lead or protect the masses of frightened and passive victims. Thus, conventional wisdom seems to tell us "that typical patterns of response take the form of (a) panic, (b) shock, or (c) passivity" (Dynes & Quarantelli, 1976, p. 234). It is therefore sometimes thought that short-term victim responses fall into one of two categories: undirected, disorganized activity (such as panic flight) or stunned, passive nonaction.

Interestingly, as Enrico L. Quarantelli has repeatedly demonstrated, neither of these responses represents the reaction of the majority of disaster victims (Quarantelli, 1954, 1957, 1960a, 1978, 1980b; Quarantelli & Dynes, 1972). Indeed, most citizens do not develop shock reactions, panic flight occurs only rarely and people tend to act in what they believe is their best interest in the situation. The discussion in Chapter IV was meant to indicate that most citizens respond constructively to environmental threats by bringing as much information and as many resources as they can to bear on the problem of how to cope with the anticipated disaster. In general, emergency managers should devote more attention to determining how citizens will interpret and act upon either environmental cues or emergency instructions than to worrying about quelling panic or spurring docile victims to action. In this section we will review the above cited *uncommon* responses to disasters: shock and inactivity ("the disaster syndrome"), and panic flight. To keep the issue in perspective, in terms of emergency management, both of these reactions occur so infrequently that in most cases, they can be considered insignificant problems from a practical or operational standpoint.

There have been some documented reports of what has come to be called the disaster syndrome. This condition is characterized by a state of shock associated with docility, disoriented thinking and sometimes a general insensitivity to cues in the immediate environment. Perhaps the earliest discussion of the disaster syndrome in social science literature is the anthropologist A. F. C. Wallace's (1957) research on mazeway disintegration. In his work Wallace described the shock behavior which characterized surviving victims whose friends and family members died. There are three important things to remember about the disaster syndrome or shock reaction. First, research indicates that it appears most frequently in sudden-onset, low forewarning kind of disasters; the syndrome appears to be associated with disaster events involving much physical destruction and/or death (cf. Fritz & Marks, 1954). Second, the disaster syndrome is transient in that it persists for a maximum of a few hours, rarely being detected outside the immediate post-impact period. Finally, when it does occur it affects a relatively small proportion of the disaster stricken population. In one of the few methodologically sound studies of the phenomenon, Fritz and Marks (1954, p. 33) found that only 14% of their random sample showed any evidence of the early symptoms associated with the disaster syndrome.

In general, the impact of natural and man-made disasters is not associated with significant increases in mental health problems in the afflicted population. This does not necessarily mean that disasters produce no psychological consequences in the long-run or pass for the most part unnoticed. It is certainly true that citizens who experience disaster impacts do experience stress which can be manifest in various symptoms. Stress reactions sometimes documented after natural or man-made disasters include sleep disruptions, anxiety, nausea, vomiting, bed-wetting, and irritability. Some of these, however, are somewhat longer-term onset problems than the disaster syndrome, although they tend to be equally transient. For the most part, citizens seem to be able to develop functional coping mechanisms for these disorders with a minimum of (if any) intervention by outsiders. What remains important here from the standpoint of emergency management is that such short-term stress reactions do not seem to interfere with disaster victims' ability to act responsibly on their own or to follow instructions from emergency response officials. Isolated cases of shock are reported among some citizens in some disasters, but such reactions are relatively rare and certainly could not be described as normative.

Perhaps the most stubborn myth regarding human behavior in disasters is the idea that a major problem in hazard management is panic flight among citizens (Perry, 1983). In general, "panic can be defined as an acute fear reaction marked by a loss of self-control which is followed by nonsocial and nonrational flight behavior" (Quarantelli, 1954, p. 272). While such panic flight is a staple of the science fiction and horror books and movies, and periodically is mentioned in connection with crowd behavior (for example, in riots after soccer games), it is a rare response to natural or man-made disasters.

It is possible that the myth of frequent panic flight in response to disasters owes some of its origin to misperceptions on the part of observers. Sometimes an observer will misinterpret the behavior of disaster victims simply as a function of not being aware of the contingencies to which they are responding (cf. Killian, 1954, p. 68). It is not exactly irrational to want to put distance between oneself and a fire, or to move quickly to leave the vicinity of crumbling buildings following an earthquake. In these examples, and other cases, citizens are assessing a threat in the environment and coping with it by achieving distance from the threat.

Not all examples of panic flight can be explained away as observer errors. While it is indeed very rare, panic flight does occur under certain circumstances. In his classic paper on the problem, Quarantelli (1954) outlines two specific conditions for the development of panic. It should be remembered that Quarantelli's conditions are based upon an intensive review of panic events in the archives of the National Opinion Research Corporation as well as the documentable research literature. Also, both of the conditions are defined in terms of the individual's perceptions or beliefs; thus the conditions are based on what individuals *believe* to be true, not upon so-called objective definition. The first specific condition for panic is that the individual must experience a feeling of helplessness, or an inability to bring the threat under control by his own actions. This establishes, at least from the viewpoint of the individual, that an approach to reducing danger to himself by manipulating the apparent source of the danger is not a feasible option. The second specific condition for panic is that the individual must believe that he *may* be unable to escape from an impending threat. Researchers have documented that panic occurs only when participants are aware of the *possibility* of being trapped *and* there is no *possible* avenue of escape. Quarantelli (1954, p. 274) notes that:

> Coal miners entombed by a collapsed tunnel who recognize they will have sufficient air til rescuers can dig through to them do not panic . . . [panic occurs in reaction] . . . to the immediate dangerous consequences of possible entrapment rather than to being trapped as such.

The conditions for the development of panic flight behavior, therefore, involve a series of perceptions on the part of an individual. One must believe that the threat cannot be controlled by personal action and that there is a possibility of escape. Usually, there is some element of perceived time pressure as well: it is believed that a few avenues of escape exist and that they may be closed off. This latter point is sometimes cited by psychologists to account for the hurried flight aspect of panic.

In summary, panic is not entirely unheard-of in response to natural or man-made disasters, although the particular conditions for panic flight appear to be more likely in connection with man-made events. Panic is not, however, a common or frequently observed reaction to any type of disaster. When panic flight is observed, it seems to involve a relatively small proportion of the people exposed to the threat and does not usually persist for any period of time. From the standpoint of managing emergencies, particularly in connection with public information and issuing warnings, a persistent problem with panic is that authorities will permit their concern with creating "public panic" stop them from keeping the public informed about environmental threats (Iklé & Kincaid, 1956; Iklé, Quarantelli, Rayner, & Withey, 1958; Quarantelli, 1960a). In cases where information has been withheld, officials have justified their actions by arguing that the problem of controlling a community in panic flight posed just as many dangers as whatever environmental threat may be involved. In this section I have documented that there is no justification for such moves by emergency managers. In the first place, the specific conditions for panic flight are rarely something that officials can create or retard and second, large scale panic flight is virtually unheard of. In keeping with our discussion, in Chapter IV, of the way citizens make decisions in emergencies, officials are always better off to share the best available threat information with citizens-at-risk. In so doing, authorities are more likely to be regarded by citizens as having access to special threat information (which is being shared) and are therefore more likely to develop shared expectations about the threat with authorities. Furthermore, when citizens and authorities share similar expectations given an environmental threat, citizens are more likely to positively receive and act upon protective action recommendations from officials.

Finally, we will close discussion of short-term psychological responses to threat by examining what Barton (1969) has called the altruistic community and what others have referred to as the therapeutic community response (Fritz, 1961a, 1961b, 1968; Midlarsky, 1968; Wilmer, 1958). In the context of at least the immediate post-impact period, it has been observed that disasters may be seen as having integrative effects upon the "community of sufferers" and in the short-run promote cohesion both among victims and between victims and other citizens in the larger community (cf. Fritz, 1961b, pp. 9–17). It was mentioned above that disaster victims tend to be pro-active rather than docile, and often initiate such activities as emergency first aid and search and rescue on their own before authorities arrive on the scene. It is also known that nonvictim members of the afflicted community tend to engage in positive helping behaviors directed at victims. This rendering of aid may be described as part of a therapeutic community response to disaster impact.

Part of the therapeutic community response arrives as a function of convergence behavior in disasters (Fritz & Mathewson, 1957). When disaster strikes a community, that community often becomes the focus of an aid-giving effort on the part of surrounding communities and individuals, larger political entities (counties, states and the federal government) and private organizations. The result is a continuous in-pouring of offers of help, volunteers themselves, and equipment and material. On the one hand, such convergence can provide local emergency managers with much needed personnel and resources necessary to effectively respond to the disaster. On the other hand, unless local emergency managers have or can generate quickly a plan to utilize and deploy these resources, the convergence can produce unprecedented communication and response difficulties. In general, then, emergency managers need to be aware of the likelihood of such convergence and maintain at least some plan for utilization and deployment. The point here is that convergence processes tend to pour people into a disaster area who can be organized or who will organize themselves to assume supportive roles relative to disaster victims. Zurcher (1968) has, for example, described the formation and performance of volunteer work crews in connection with a 1966 tornado which struck Topeka, Kansas. Zurcher's research, and that of later researchers, indicates that the presence of such volunteers—arriving as part of "normal" disaster convergence—has not only a positive impact upon the local authorities' resource base for emergency management, but also upon the morale of victims. That is, victims can perceive the presence of such help as evidence that the consequences of the disaster are not totally overwhelming and that indeed the catastrophe may be something that can be overcome. Thus, feelings that victims must suffer alone are mitigated against, and the more positive view that help is not only on the way, but has arrived, is promoted. This latter orientation may be seen as one which increases positive short-run morale of victims and decreases the chance that victims will go into shock or otherwise develop short-run negative psychological consequences.

A second aspect of the concept of a therapeutic community can be seen as dealing with more general sympathetic behavior on the part of nonvictims which is not appropriately characterized as part of the convergence response. Reference is here made to the volunteering of direct help to victims in the form of needed clothing, food and lodging. Perhaps the earliest documenting of this type of therapeutic response is found in Prince's (1920, p. 137) study of an explosion in Halifax, Nova Scotia, where he points out that:

> . . . The idea spread of taking the refugees into such private homes as had fared less badly . . . . It became the thing to do. The thing to do is social pressure. It may be unwilled and unintended but it is inexorable. It worked effectively upon all who had an unused room.

Since the time Prince conducted his study, a considerable literature has developed on the extent to which disaster victims can be seen as drawing upon the helping behavior of other community members (Midlarsky, 1968; Watson and

Collins, 1982; Vallance and D'Augelli, 1982; Young et al., 1982). Particularly in disasters which occur in Western societies, such helping behavior directed at (and among) victims may be seen as a normative response. What is important from the standpoint of emergency management, however, are the consequences of the climate created by such altruism.

> The result of these psychological and social processes is a therapeutic social system that helps to compensate for the sorrow and stress under which many members are living with an unexpected abundance of personal warmth and direct help. (Barton, 1969, p. 207)

Thus, once again we see that following disasters there are community social processes which operate that tend to promote some positive outcomes for victims and thereby mitigate or at least reduce the likelihood of short-term negative psychological consequences. It is not argued, of course, that such helping behavior ameliorates all negative reactions in victims—both natural and man-made disasters are by definition negative, harrowing experiences for victims. For example, later in this chapter we will discuss the very real negative psychological consequences associated with grief reactions. An attempt is being made here to stress balance mechanisms. Certainly the disaster impact is negative, but studies have shown that there are also positive forces operating in the post-impact period which are subsumed under the rubric of a therapeutic community response.

It is in this broader context that one should understand all three aspects of short-term psychological response to disaster—the disaster syndrome, panic flight and the therapeutic community—discussed in this section. Before moving on to a discussion of longer term psychological consequences, it is important to mention one qualifier regarding the *persistence* of the therapeutic community response over time. It has been discussed here as a phenomenon of the post-impact period in connection with other *short-term* phenomena; at most the present discussion focuses upon activities which extend a few days beyond impact. Barton, however, sees the therapeutic community as ''an outpouring of altruistic feelings and behavior beginning with mass rescue work and carrying on for days, weeks, possibly even months after the impact'' (1969, p. 206). There has not been, since Barton's work, sufficient research on the persistence of the therapeutic community response to allow one to confidently accept or reject the hypothesis that such behavior can last for months or at least long periods after impact. In fact, Quarantelli and Dynes (1976, 1977) have pointed out that the decline of community conflict following disasters and the apparent increase in community consensus are short-lived phenomena. Although it does not assess the question of the longevity of the therapeutic community directly, the work of Quarantelli and Dynes does suggest that it may not be a long lasting condition. This conclusion is supported somewhat by the experience of billeting evacuees during the heavy bombing of London during World War II; in that case short-term response to billeting evacuees was positive, but between-family tensions began to rise as the months passed (Titmuss, 1950). In any case, there is agreement regarding the development of a therapeutic in the short-term aftermath, and that it should be seen as promoting some level of positive outcomes for disaster victims.

THE LONGER-TERM PSYCHOLOGICAL EFFECTS CONTROVERSY

At the outset of this chapter, it was indicated that over the past four decades two identifiable and essentially opposing positions have evolved among researchers studying the effects of natural disasters upon victims' mental health. One position holds that natural disasters constitute catastropic life events which produce adverse psychological reactions among victims. These reactions are seen as problematic both immediately post–impact and throughout the long range; possibly encompassing a period of several years or perhaps the victims' entire remaining life span. The empirical support for this perspective came initially from psychiatric interpretations of natural disasters (Menninger, 1952; Tyhurst, 1957a, 1957b), was buttressed by a series of sociological studies of tornadoes (Moore, 1958a, 1958b; Moore & Friedsam, 1959; Moore et al., 1963) and has recently gained support from studies of flood victims (Erikson, 1976; Gleser, Green, & Winget, 1981; Lifton & Olson, 1976; Tichener & Kapp, 1976).

The competing position suggests that although some individuals experience adverse reactions to natural disaster, the extent of negative psychological impact is not substantial. These researchers acknowledge that psychological reactions frequently occur in the short-run (to a maximum of a few hours post-impact), but it is argued that apparent longer-run reactions are infrequent and probably a function of a variety of factors, among which disaster impact is only one. This point of view can be traced to Charles Fritz' early analyses of the National Opinion Research Corporation (NORC) disaster studies (Fritz, 1961a; Fritz & Marks, 1954; Fritz & Williams, 1957) and is supported by numerous studies which have involved a variety of disaster agents including floods, hurricanes and tornadoes (cf. Barton, 1969; Bates et al., 1963; Drabek & Key, 1976; Drayer, 1957; Erickson et al., 1976; Quarantelli & Dynes, 1972; Sterling et al., 1977; Taylor, 1976).

These competing positions, therefore, rest upon the apparently contradictory findings of empirical studies. In such cases, one usually attempts to resolve the controversy first by assessing the quality of the research designs (e.g., asking methodological questions) and second by reviewing the *theoretical* underpinnings of each competing view, comparing basic assumptions, logical adequacy, parsimony, internal consistency, and other factors (cf. Schrag, 1967, p. 220). The controversy surrounding the psychological impact of natural and man-made disasters, however, seems to have developed largely in the absence of formal theory. This is not to say that *rationales* haven't been offered; they have come from advocates of each position. For example, initially Fritz (1961b) and later Barton (1969) suggested the concept of the "therapeutic community" as an important factor in minimizing adverse psychological reactions. What is lacking on both sides though, is an explicit, theoretical framework which could guide the directions of scientific inquiry and against which empirical findings may be evaluated (cf. Gillespie & Perry, 1976, pp. 48–49).

Furthermore, without such a theoretical structure, exchanges among proponents of different views tend to become laden with rhetoric. With no conceptual standard against which to evaluate empirical studies, there is little basis for resolving apparent inconsistencies in findings and the polarization becomes more pronounced. Indeed, Lazarus (1978, pp. 35–40) and Logue and Hansen (1980, p. 28) have pointed out that the preoccupation of researchers with locating negative or positive *instances* of psychological effects has lead them to largely ignore the question of the *process* through which disasters might or might not affect citizens' emotional stability. It is only through understanding the process of how disasters impinge upon individuals, and how individuals perceive and cope with these problems, that one can begin to assess the psychological consequences of such events for citizens and, from an emergency response standpoint, to design programs which minimize any negative consequences.

The problem remains, however, of understanding how scientists can adhere to two seemingly opposite positions, with each group claiming empirical support for its respective position. To effectively examine this apparent problem, one must address two general issues; namely, what is meant by negative psychological consequences and how does one link disaster impact with psychological consequences.

A critical aspect of understanding the psychological consequences controversy is identifying the phenomena to be studied; that is, deciding what is meant by "psychological consequences." In the disaster literature, only scant attention has been given to this problem. Usually, definition is either left implicit and the phrase "mental illness" used to cover the widest range of meanings, or among empirical studies some operational definition of "psychological consequences" is equated with an observable measure such as victim self-report, interviewer diagnosis, or admission to care. This is not to suggest that one should undertake the herculean, and probably impossible, task of "rectifying" the numerous, disparate theories of psychopathology and create a single definition of mental illness. It is essential, however, when evaluating studies of the psychological consequences of disasters, to carefully attend to specific definitions and operationalizations, as well as the underlying conceptions of psychopathology.

Many conflicting claims regarding the relationship of natural and man-made disasters and mental illness may be resolved by acknowledging that researchers have used different conceptions of emotional impairment when designing studies and consequently have chosen different measurement strategies which tend to yield *uncomparable* results. Those who have found a correlation between disaster and mental illness have tended to employ a psychodynamic perspective, which directs concern with anxiety states, subjective unhappiness and other maladjustment evidenced through psychiatric diagnosis (cf. Scott, 1958, p. 29). These studies also depend largely upon victim self-report and clinical interviews as measures of psychological consequences. On the other hand, studies which have not found a strong relationship between disaster and mental illness tend to use a behavioral model of psychopathology sensitive to individuals' maladaptive behaviors, usually measured by rating scales, observers reports or admissions to psychiatric care (Ullman & Krasner, 1970, pp. 327).

One should be aware that the above mentioned "measures" are sensitive to different aspects of human behavior and constitute different criteria for establishing the presence of psychological consequences. Thus, it is *not* appropriate to assume that they are acceptable *equivalent* indicators of mental disorder. Instead of interpreting the empirical findings as conflicting, then, one should conclude that the different measures employed offer evidence that some types of psychological reaction are common in the aftermath of disasters and other types are not. Hence, we have much evidence that people usually answer in the affirmative when psychological consequences are "defined by the victims themselves in response to the question, 'Have you noticed any emotional stress among family members as a result of the disaster'?" (Moore & Friedsam, 1959, p. 136). When the psychological consequence of interest is admission to psychiatric care, however, it is evident that this reaction is rare and that relatively few disaster victims seek such institutional help (cf. Bates et al., 1963; Bennett, 1970, p. 456). Thus, careful review of the measurement strategies of existing empirical studies directs attention away from the problem of apparently conflicting findings and toward the more productive task of cataloging the nature and frequency of different types of psychological consequences associated with natural disaster.

Up to this point, attention has been devoted to the problem of understanding the concept of psychological consequences as it relates to the study of human response to disasters. Now attention may be turned to examining a methodological pitfall encountered by existing studies. As Taylor (1976, p. 7) has pointed out, most of the study designs used to date involve a rather straightforward attempt to determine "whether any cases of mental illness can be found after a major disaster either in the short or long run." The difficulties with this approach are both conceptual and methodological. As stated, the research task appears to be one of examining individuals post-disaster and either finding or not finding mental disorder. In fact, the issue of interest should center upon finding disorders which can be linked with disaster impact. A pair of concepts from the epidemiology literature are helpful in understanding this problem: prevalence versus incidence of mental disorder.

Prevalence refers to the amount of mental disorder (treated and untreated) existing in a specified population over some defined time period—sometimes called period prevalence (Susser, 1968, pp. 205–215). Epidemiological studies have documented prevalence of psychological disorder in communities ranging from low figures of 1.7 percent in some rural areas (Eaton and Weil, 1955) to 23.4 percent in the Midtown Manhattan Study (Srole, 1962) and more than 50 percent in the Sterling County Study (Leighton, 1963). Incidence describes the number of new cases of mental disorder which arise in a specified population over a specified time period (Dohrenwend & Dohrenwend, 1972, p. 283). Figure V.1 shows the relationship of incidence to prevalence; the ordinate represents the level of mental disorder and the abscissa represents time with three points indicated. If disaster impact occurs at T_2 then it is clear that simply locating cases of mental disorder during the post-impact period does not answer questions about

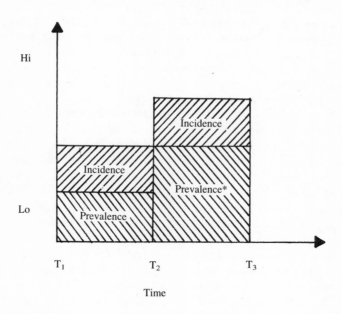

Figure V.1.   Graph of the relationship between period incidence and period prevalence of mental disorder.

*Prevalence for the time period T_2–T_3 equals prevalence plus incidence for the previous time period, minus remissions.

the psychological consequences of disaster. Some cases of disorder would be *expected* due to prevalence and incidence even in the absence of disaster. There-fore, the appropriate research task is to determine what fraction (if any) of the incidence for period T_2-T_3 can be traced or directly attributed to the findings of studies purportedly supporting both sides of the controversy. Hudgens (1974, p. 120) summarizes this argument succinctly:

> . . . as I interpret the results of recent studies . . . investigators demonstrated a causal con-nection between stressful life events and subsequent worsening of conditions already under-way . . . it does not seem to me that investigators have yet convincingly demonstrated that life stress can cause madness in a person previously of sound mind.

The preceding discussion begins to account for the possibility of contradictory findings in terms of the ''after measure only'' type research design which is commonly used in disaster pathology. It has been argued that theoretically, at any given time, there exists some level of mental illness in any given population. Thus, an after only design which does not account for the base rate of mental illness is generally inappropriate for answering questions about the relationship between disasters and victim's psychopathology. Furthermore, it has been ar-gued that this is essentially post-hoc methodology has contributed to the per-petuation of an over-simplified view of the problem; namely that disaster is a direct and unconditional cause of mental illness.

Accurate assessment of the proportion of incidence attributable to disaster impact requires an understanding of the process through which disasters impinge upon victims *and* an understanding of the ways in which individuals perceive and cope with such intrusions (Perry, 1979c). Given the preceding discussion of the nature of psychological disorder as well as methodological pitfalls, it is apparent that simple uni-causal models are not particularly useful for understanding the psychological consequences of natural disaster. It has been argued that an inade-quate emphasis upon theory and conceptualization has contributed to the per-petuation of an oversimplified view of the problem; namely, that disaster is a direct and unconditional cause of mental illness (cf. Lifton & Olson, 1976). The perspective which appears to appropriately address the problem sees disaster as a contributory cause—as one of a number of factors which together determine psychological consequences. In the following section, the empirical literature on human response to natural disasters is carefully reviewed. Special concern is given to the problem of developing a tentative framework to serve as an ordering device within which research findings may be integrated.

Recent research conducted by Thomas Drabek and his colleagues (Drabek et al., 1975; Drabek & Key, 1976; Erickson et al., 1976; Sterling et al., 1977) has outlined a general framework to explain the effects of disaster impact upon the physical health self-perceptions of victims. By building upon this research tradition, an attempt will be made here to expand upon and formalize this approach by identifying channels through which natural disasters impinge upon individuals and by introducing additional detail when specifying relevant theoretical dimensions. Thus, the review of literature will be organized in terms of three general dimensions which Drabek has argued are critical in understanding how natural disasters impinge upon individuals. These dimensions are: (1) characteristics of the disaster impact; (2) characteristics of the social system; and (3) characteristics of the individual. In the sections which follow each dimension is addressed in turn and literature indicating the importance of specific variables associated with the relevant dimension is reviewed.

Characteristics of Disaster Impact

One of the most integrated and detailed typologies of collective stress situations (disasters) was devised by Barton (1969), who argues for the primary importance of two aspects of disasters which mediate the subsequent social and physical consequences: duration and scope of impact. The idea of ''duration'' references the time involved as well as the character of disaster impact. Time, however, is the critical dimension. Whether duration is long because of multiple or many secondary impacts (such as continuing volcanic eruptions) or because of a long steady impact (e.g., a severe drought), the result is the same: a long duration ''may gradually drain resources and lower aspirations so that the whole system moves toward a less satisfactory equilibrium, or toward collapse as a system . . . a brief duration disaster still may leave long-lasting injury and destruction, but relief and recovery can be carried on *unhampered by further impacts*'' (Barton, 1969, p. 40, emphasis added). Again, the longer the duration of impact, the greater is the chance that kinship and friend-networks will be disrupted and the greater the likelihood of property damage.

Scope of disaster impact refers to a primarily geographical dimension: the size of the impact area. The obvious correlates of increasing scope are increases in the sheer number of people who can be affected and increases in the absolute amount of property exposed. Among natural disaster agents, hurricanes tend to have a large scope of impact while tornadoes tend toward a limited scope. It should be pointed out that all the factors reviewed here correlate with *type* of disaster agent. Therefore, these factors are treated as characteristics of disasters which have implications for other classes of variables more directly related to psychological consequences.

Characteristics of the Social System

While characteristics of the disaster tend to affect psychological consequences indirectly, variables which measure characteristics of the social system more often involve direct effects. From the research literature, six factors have been identified which are characteristic of social systems and which have been found to mediate the psychological impact of natural disasters: level of community preparedness, the presence of kin networks and friendship networks, the extent of property damage, community participation, and presence of institutional rehabilitation. These factors are interrelated and will be discussed in terms of the *patterns* of their interrelationships.

Level of community preparedness describes the state of emergency preparations undertaken by communities, including any planning for the management of disaster impact, as well as plans for post-impact reconstruction. The level of community preparedness affects (either directly or indirectly) all of the other factors discussed as social system characteristics. It may be thought of as the "stockpile" of pre-existing resources (including plans) to deliver emergency services of all types—especially for the maintenance of physical and mental health—to a given community. Drayer (1957, p. 154) has pointed out that, over time, high levels of community preparedness in response to "recurrent natural disasters tend to [promote] adequate psychological preparation of the population, particularly if the disasters have a tendency toward seasonal periodicity with enough frequency to give each succeeding generation some degree of personal experience with them." Furthermore, high levels of preparedness tend to correlate with the existence of a capability on the part of local emergency managers to effectively use the personnel and equipment which arrive on the scene as part of the convergence response discussed above. Also, high preparedness communities are better able to productively exploit the therapeutic community response which: "supports action by the public [formal] authorities and large scale organizations devoted to relief and reconstruction" (Barton, 1969, p. 283). Therefore, the development of a therapeutic community reaction enhances the opportunity for formal and informal psychological support for victims in both the short and long run (cf. Perry et al., 1974; Quarantelli & Dynes, 1970; Roen et al., 1966).

It was mentioned above that the level of community preparedness was inversely related to the destruction of kin networks and friendship networks. Kin networks are here conceived in terms of people's interaction and exchange patterns with their kinsmen. Numerous studies of community disaster report that intense kin relationships are highly supportive and promote post–disaster recovery success among victims (Bolin, 1976, p. 90; Cobb, 1976; Drabek et al., 1975; Eaton, 1978; McCubbin, 1979; Tolsdorf, 1976). Thus, to the extent that kinship networks are destroyed, one should expect negative psychological consequences for victims. On the other hand, to the extent that affected individuals are supported by intact kin networks, one should expect lower levels of negative consequences.

The effects of friendship networks are very similar to those described in relationship to kin networks. In both cases, we are describing the stress-buffering role of social support (Dean & Lin, 1977). Friendship networks refer to people's patterns of interaction with friends (and/or neighbors). Barton (1969, pp. 63–124) has pointed out that intact friendship networks insure victims access to much post-impact aid; since relatives only infrequently live adjacent to one another, immediate aid is likely to come from victims' friendship networks. It has also been argued that when both kin and friendship contacts are available, kin relationships are more important in victims' successful adaptation, especially in the long run (Drabek & Boggs, 1968). Nevertheless, in the short run, or when kin bonds are weak or absent, the role of friendship networks appears to be an important one.

Community participation refers to the individual's patterns of participation in voluntary associations and other community organizations (cf. Perry & Greene, 1982; Perry, 1982). Barton (1969, pp. 63–124) has pointed out that the extent of people's integration into the community affects hazard awareness in general, and specifically their knowledge of the nature of post-impact aid which is available and the proper contacts to make to obtain aid. Numerous studies of disaster recovery have shown that failure to promptly recover lost possessions or to begin to replace damages or lost possessions is correlated with victim self reports of depressed feelings, anxiety, and despair (Fried, 1964; Gerontology Program, 1976; Haas et al., 1977, pp. 30–37; Huerta & Horton, 1978, p. 543).

Finally, research has suggested that extent of property damage is related to both social, psychological and economic recovery from the effects of natural disaster impact. If one thinks of property in anthropological terms as our culture inventory, it must be acknowledged that material things plan an important role in people's definitions of self (Wallace, 1961, pp. 171–193). In examining reactions to disaster, Wallace suggests that "the sudden perception of physical destruction of the natural environment and material culture with which one is identified seems to elicit fundamentally the same paralytic [psychological] response . . . ." (1957, p. 23). Hence, widespread destruction of property in itself is likely to produce some negative psychological effects in the short run. The extent of property damage is also related to the nature, amount and speed of institutional rehabilitation made available to stricken communities. In general, the greater the damage, the more extensive is the institutional aid (loans, donations, etc.) which flows to the community from external sources (Haas et al., 1977). Evidence also suggests that the presence of extensive institutional rehabilitation serves to reduce negative psychological consequences among victims in the long run (Fogelman and Parenton, 1959, pp. 133–135).

Characteristics of the Individual

Two factors which constitute characteristics of individuals are particularly important in understanding the psychological consequences of natural disaster: pre-impact psychological stability, and grief reactions. In discussing epidemiological concepts, it was indicated that many studies may have "found" a direct link between disaster impact and mental disorder possibly because they neither controlled for nor assessed pre-impact psychopathology. In general, an individual who is psychologically unstable *before* disaster impact, is likely to remain so *after* impact. The only qualifier needed here is that a very few investigators have reported that *some* "unstable" individuals (particularly those diagnosed as senile) have been shown to *briefly* exhibit "stable" behavior (usually task oriented helping actions) in natural disaster circumstances, followed by relapse. Since this finding has not been consistently reported and in each case the individual quickly reassumes a "mentally ill" role, it is here acknowledged as an intriguing anomaly.

Perhaps one of the most prominent sources of psychological discomfort, whether chronic or acute, is the death or severe injury of a kinsman or a close friend. In the case of natural and man-made disasters where death or injury can occur during a short time span *and* one may even witness the event, the psychological consequences for survivors may be tremendous (Fritz & Marks, 1954, p. 40). In discussions of various stress response syndromes in reaction to disasters, in general, surprisingly little attention has been paid to grief reactions (cf. Horowitz, 1974; Kastenbaum, 1974; Lifton & Olson, 1976; Titchener & Kapp, 1976; Tyhurst, 1957). Bugen (1977) has developed a theoretical model for understanding human grief reactions which is based upon the pioneering work of Lindemann (1944). Bugen contends that the *intensity* and time duration of psychological reactions associated with grief may be characterized in terms of two dimensions: the closeness of the survivor's relationship to the deceased and the survivor's perception of the preventability of the death. Thus, when the relationship is central (in the case of one's spouse) and the death was preventable (e.g., if the couple were warned but failed to evacuate prior to a hurricane), one would expect the survivor's reaction to be intense and prolonged. Other conditions yield different reactions. What this implies for disaster research is that one must assess the nature of relationship and perceptions of preventability to understand a survivor's psychological reaction. Although both concepts exist in the disaster literature (cf. Bucher, 1957; Crawshaw, 1963), they are not often juxtaposed and have not previously been used in any integrated conceptual framework. The concept of grief reactions of different intensity and duration begins to shed some light on psychiatric studies which offer conflicting claims about the longer term psychological consequences of exposure to disaster deaths (Kastenbaum, 1974). When one takes Bugen's model into account, the fact that some survivors suffer longer-duration disturbances than others is readily explainable.

An Interpretive Framework

The preceding sections examine three dimensions relevant to understanding the channels through which natural and man-made disasters impinge upon the psychological stability of individuals (victims). Eleven important factors (variables) have been identified and literature related to each has been reviewed. The emphasis however, has been upon conceptualization and organization. The review of literature was intended to be thorough but not exhaustive since such reviews are available elsewhere (cf. Barton, 1969; Dynes, 1970; Mileti et al., 1975). The objective was to sort out findings and summarize data which specify interrelationships among variables likely to be important in explaining the psychological consequences of natural disasters.

Two additional points should be made before presenting the interpretive framework. First, this work should not be confused with the presentation of a causal theory or causal model; to describe it in such terms would be misleading. Instead, this framework marks the beginning of the theory building process, not its completion. Empirical findings have been examined, inductively constructed images of time order devised, and inferences made about possible relationships among factors. As Blalock (1971, p. 8) points out, such reasoning marks the first step toward causal theory development. The prime objective in presenting this framework is to summarize in a managable form, the results of a large number of empirical studies. The task of assembling the framework of course involves making assumptions about posited inter-relationships, but the bases for these assumptions have been elaborated above.

The second point relates to the treatment of demographic variables—age, sex, socioeconomic status, race, etc. The only other recently published theoretical efforts in this area (England & Kunz, 1977; Sterling et al., 1977) explicitly include demographic variables in their models. The role of demographic variables is here acknowledged in matters such as the definition of appropriate grief reaction and perceptions of kin and friendship networks. In the interest of clarity of presentation, however, demographics have been left *implicit* in the interpretive framework, and it is here acknowledged that demographics should be included as exogenous variables in the development of more refined conceptual models.

Figure V.2 diagrams the interrelationships among the eleven factors identified and their relationships to negative psychological consequences following disaster impact. This framework may be structurally summarized as a series of fourteen propositions (that is, research questions or hypotheses).

1. The higher the level of community disaster preparedness, the less extensive will be the destruction of kin and friendship networks as a function of disaster impact.

2. The larger the scope of impact, the more extensive the destruction of kin and friendship networks.

3. The larger the scope of impact, the greater the extent of property damage.

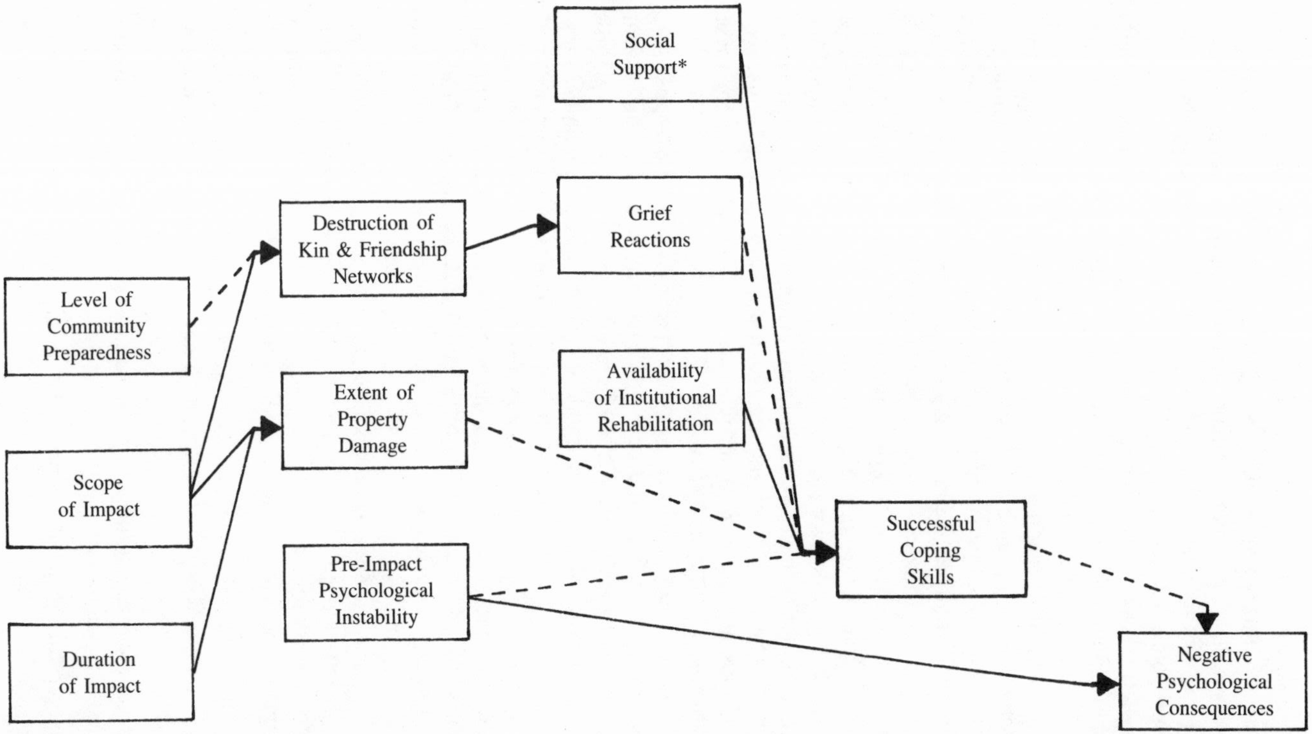

Figure V.2. Model of factors important in the psychological impact of natural disasters (solid arrows represent positive relationships, broken arrows represent inverse relationships).

*Social Support includes three distinct variables: kinship networks, friendship networks and community participation.

4. The longer the duration of impact, the more likely is the destruction of kin and friendship networks.

5. The longer the duration of impact, the greater the extent of property damage.

6. The more extensive the destruction of kin and friendship networks, the greater the probability of grief reactions.

7. The greater the extent of property damage, the greater the availability of institutional rehabilitation aid.

8. The greater the extent of property damage, the less likely is the development of successful coping skills (adaptation).

9. The presence of a history of pre-impact psychological instability decreases the likelihood of developing successful coping skills (adaptation).

10. The greater the levels of social support, the greater the likelihood of developing successful coping skills.

   10a. The greater the individual's integration into kinship networks, the greater the likelihood of developing successful coping skills.

   10b. The greater the individual's integration into friendship networks, the greater the likelihood of developing successful coping skills.

   10c. The higher the level of community participation, the greater the likelihood of developing successful coping skills.

11. The greater the availability of institutional rehabilitation aid, the greater the likelihood of developing successful coping skills.

12. The more severe the grief reaction, the less likely the individual is to develop successful coping skills.

13. The development of successful coping skills inhibits the probability of negative psychological consequences.

14. The presence of a history of pre-impact psychological instability increases the likelihood of negative psychological consequences.

SUMMARY

In summary, this chapter has focused upon the problem of assessing negative psychological consequences which may accrue from the impact of natural disasters. It has been emphasized that to date, most disaster studies have not been designed in a way that permits the detection of *disaster-related* psychopathology.

The primary purpose here is not to argue that there are either predominately positive or negative consequences of disasters. Instead, an interpretive framework was developed which isolates important variables and specifies the channels through which disaster impact impinges upon individuals and might produce some psychological consequences, either positive or negative. The value of this framework lies in the fact that it represents an explicit attempt to conceptualize and integrate existing empirical knowledge.

From the standpoint of understanding the psychological consequences of citizen exposure to disasters, a number of summary comments are also in order. The disaster literature documents the idea that people rarely—except under specific conditions—panic or exhibit severely maladaptive behavior in connection with the disaster event (Quarantelli and Dynes, 1972; Quarantelli and Dynes, 1977; Taylor, 1977). Indeed, during the immediate post-impact period a few investigators have reported that *some* "unstable" individuals (particularly those diagnosed as senile) have *briefly* exhibited "stable" behavior—usually task-oriented helping actions (cf. Perry & Lindell, 1978, p. 111).

With regard to negative psychological consequences, there is a general consensus among investigators that there does appear to be an identifiable "disaster syndrome"—a dazed state common in the immediate post-impact period of disasters characterized by high levels of physical destruction. This is usually an immediate reaction which passes quickly. A variety of other symptoms have been documented which also appear to be transient: bed wetting, general ("free floating") anxiety, depression, difficulty in sleeping (Logue et al., 1979; Moore, 1958a, 1958b; Moore & Friedsam, 1959; Tyhurst, 1957a). Goldstein (1960) and Wilson (1962) underscore the idea that "normal" disaster reactions clear up quickly; Quarantelli and Dynes (1970:68) indicate that "only in a minority of cases do victims exhibit a shock reaction," and the full course of the "disaster syndrome," when it does occur, may run only a couple of hours (Killian, 1954, p. 68; Wallace, 1956; Wallace, 1957, p. 24).

The literature also shows that longer term negative psychological reactions are equally infrequent in occurance. Studies indicate that in the post–emergency period, disasters show little or no effect upon citizens' patterns of interacting with family members (Drabek et al., 1975; Erickson et al., 1976) or on other primary group linkages (Drabek and Key, 1976). Furthermore, disasters are not correlated any appreciable incidence of severe psychiatric disorder particularly if such disorder is manifest in severely maladaptive behaviors (Bates et al., 1963; Gilbert, 1958; Mileti et al., 1975; Quarantelli, 1980). Indeed, a recent controlled study covering a period of three years found no significant long-term effects of experiencing a natural disaster on the health self-perceptions of victims (Sterling et al., 1977).

There are three general exceptions to the rule that disasters are not associated with observed negative psychological consequences among those exposed to the event. First, when disaster impact causes high levels of physical destruction and thereby affects the majority of people in a given social system, there appears to be greater psychological disruption among some victims (Fritz, 1957; Wallace, 1956b). In such cases shock reactions appear to occur in some citizens, but the total proportion of people affected seems to remain small. Second, some people exhibit grief reactions in the post-impact period which may persist over time (cf. Bugen, 1977; Lindemann, 1944). Such reactions are typically observed where victims are exposed to dead or severely injured individuals, and particularly when relatives of victims are involved (Fritz & Marks, 1954). A third class of people who seem to exhibit negative psychological consequences after a disaster are people who were exhibiting symptoms before the disaster, or those with a history of coping difficulties. In summary, the disaster literature indicates that following disaster impact most people in a community exposed to the disaster do not experience negative psychological consequences. In a very small proportion of people persistent symptoms may appear, but usually under the special circumstances noted above.

Both social scientists and emergency managers need to consider at least two broad categories of psychological stress: (1) that which produces visible symptoms of a maladaptive nature in citizens and interferes with their ability to function in daily living, and (2) that which produces either no symptoms or symptoms which do not seem to affect the individual's ability to function. Research indicates that only a very small proportion of the people exposed to disasters report any stress which they attribute to the disaster that persists very long. Also, epidemiological studies of communities following disasters fail to report the high levels of institutional admissions or out-patient mental health care that one would expect to find if there did exist a clear causal link between disasters and mental disorder. It should be clear, however, that there are conditions under which one would *expect* negative psychological consequences. In connection with such disaster events, there are strategies and treatments available for managing emergency mental health care service delivery (Cohen & Ahearn, 1980; Golan, 1978) and emergency managers should be sufficiently conversant with local community mental health care resources to be able to incorporate such services into disaster recovery plans.

The second class of consequences apparently stemming from psychological stress is somewhat less straightforward to deal with. Indeed, there is some question about how to conceptually deal with apparent stress which generates no symptoms; behavioral sociologists and psychologists have argued that without the presence of some troublesome symptom, there is no stress. Stress which generates symptoms which do not interfere with the individual's functioning is also difficult to classify. Here we are dealing with "symptoms" which are not functionally debilitating, but that would probably be reported on an epidemiological survey. Studies of natural disasters suggest that the extent to which an individual perceives that the hazard constitute some level of risk to her/his health and safety is probably correlated with this "type" of psychological stress. From the standpoint of disaster management in the immediate post-impact period, stress which produces no maladaptive behaviors is simply not of concern—and probably undetectable by any practical means anyway. It is likely that such individuals would be proportionately few, and would either undergo remission on their own or seek out some form of mental health service if the anxiety became sufficiently bothersome.

Therefore, these studies reviewed here suggest that the process of making decisions in emergencies which was described in Chapter IV is not likely to be substantially affected by psychopathology related to prior involvement in disasters. Furthermore, short-term negative psychological responses which would impair a citizens ability to engage in decision-making during emergencies seem to occur infrequently enough to minimally interfere with emergency management activities. Assuming that negative psychological consequences are not a major problem in emergency response, we can now consider the environment in which emergency managers must accomplish their mission. In discussing observed citizen responses to volcano, flood and nuclear reactor threats in Chapter III, and in our model of emergency decision-making presented in Chapter IV, considerable emphasis was given to the issues of educating the public regarding environmental threats and involving citizens in the emergency management process. In Chapter VI we will more carefully look at the *process* of developing public policy for environmental hazards, the structure of emergency evacuation plans, techniques to promote citizen participation and the role of emergency managers.

Chapter VI

The Context and Practice of Evacuation Planning

Local community evacuation planning and management is a dynamic process which may be seen as generally involving three collectivities of actors: emergency managers, the public, and political-governmental decision-makers. Chapters I, II, and III addressed the interactions of all these local community actors with the larger emergency management system, both in theory and when responding to a flood, a volcanic eruption and the reactor accident at Three Mile Island. Chapter IV assessed the process by which members of the public made decisions in emergencies, while Chapter V explored the questions of short-term and long-term psychological consequences of disasters for the citizenry and whether such effects might adversely impact their ability to comply with disaster warnings. For the most part then, the emphasis has been upon human performance during time of acute threat—both the performance of officials who implement emergency plans and the performance of citizens who may or may not comply with it. The purpose of this chapter is to examine the sociopolitical context in which evacuation planning, and emergency planning in general, takes place. This involves looking at the roles played by political-governmental decision-makers and emergency managers in planning for and responding to both natural and man-made hazards.

It should be remembered that population evacuation is one of several generic functions which are associated with *many different types* of community emergencies. That is, as we pointed out in Chapter II, it may be necessary to move citizens from an endangered place to a safer location in connection with floods, hazardous materials emergencies, volcanic eruptions, nuclear power plant accidents, hurricanes, or other environmental threats. However, while evacuations are not hazard-specific, community hazard management typically—particularly when political decision-making bodies are involved—takes a phenotypic approach and tends to address hazards one at a time. Because this is the case, this chapter begins by addressing some general issues—those related to community hazard planning—and progressively becomes more specific, focusing upon the problem of designing and implementing evacuation plans. The sections of this chapter address three major issues related to evacuation planning. First, attention will be given to examining public policy and hazards planning, focusing upon describing the major actors and important properties in local community hazard management. This analysis of the local community is more specific than our initial description, in Chapter I, of the role of localities in emergency management. The second part of the chapter addresses the problem of deciding what elements need to be included in any given evacuation plan and identifies the basic principles which underlie effective evacuation planning. Finally, the closing section focuses upon the role of the local emergency manager in generating both citizen compliance with emergency plans and citizen participation in the planning process.

PUBLIC POLICY AND HAZARDS PLANNING

The management of any given natural or technological hazard is a public decision that involves a variety of community actors. Anderson (1969, p. 5) describes the public policy process as a sequence consisting of five stages:

1. Agenda setting: the first step in the process is to get an issue on the public or political agenda.
2. Policy formulation: once an issue is on the agenda, a set of alternatives are identified and evaluated.
3. Policy adoption: after the alternatives are identified, one or more public bodies act to adopt the prefered alternative.
4. Policy implementation: the preferred alternative is then implemented by the appropriate public or private actors.
5. Policy evaluation: the actions of the implementing agencies are evaluated to determine if policy goals have been met.

From the standpoint of managing natural and technological hazards, two of these stages or the processes which they represent are of particular interest. In practice, of course, the two stages are interrelated, but they may be analytically separated for illustrative purposes. The first component involves the choice to manage (or not manage) a hazard, usually made by government officials, by recognizing the threat and setting community goals and standards regarding that threat. One may group Anderson's first stages of agenda setting, policy formulation, and policy adoption under the general category of policy formulation (cf. Levine, 1972). Second, one may group the last two stages of implementation and evaluation under the general rubric of policy implementation, where this is defined as the process of charting a course to achieve specified goals—that is, developing a plan and putting it into practice—and reviewing the actions undertaken to assess the extent to which they are consistent with original policy goals.

This dichotomizing of Anderson's five stages reflects the idea that in community hazard management, different actors tend to be involved in policy formulation versus policy implementation. Natural hazards issues often may be catapulted onto the agenda and through the ensuing policy stages as a result of a crisis or an emergency. In other cases, natural hazards policies—which may be thought of as preventive—may advance through the first two stages of the policy process, but not be adopted and thereby not need to be implemented. In other cases, one sees the development of community interest and/or pressure groups which engage in hazards specific lobbying and become involved in hazard manage issues to the extent that they affect or are affected by other issues. Corbett and Svenson (1981, p. 1) describe three traditional positions from which critics might oppose hazard management: (1) hazard management may be seen as a means of extending bureaucratic control over land use or promoting organizational survival; (2) hazards management involves extending community resources which should be devoted to other more pressing community needs; and (3) hazard management means "over-management" in that there is the risk that public officials will needlessly expend community resources attempting to manage low probability threats. As a result, even though the threat of a natural or technological hazard may be serious, a governing body may not adopt policies which would mitigate the impact of such crises. The structured public policy environment is composed of the various components of local government which interact with private groups and the state and federal governments as described in Chapter I. The following discussion focuses upon the environment in which local community hazard management takes place.

Local governments are a crucial element in natural hazards policy. For example, local governments make land-use decisions, enact construction codes and manage emergency response efforts. Policy formulation, including agenda setting and adoption decisions, can be made by elected officials (for example, city or county councilmen) or appointed officials (for example, city or county managers). Policy implementation (including evaluation) is carried out by administrative or public safety departments in the local government. To formulate or adopt a hazards management policy, local government must: (1) be aware that the threat exists and consider it important relative to other issues; (2) believe that the threat is susceptible to management; and (3) develop or be presented with a politically feasible policy for management. It is possible to understand the role of local government in hazard management, and its seemingly spotty record of performance, by examining each of the three above aspects to the hazards management process.

In practice, most community governments assign a low priority to comprehensive hazard management, although some local governments may take an interest in one particular hazard. In a recent survey of state and local political influentials, Wright and Rossi (1981) found that problems associated with five natural hazards (flooding, fire, hurricane, tornadoes and earthquakes) were ranked near the bottom of the list of 18 problems facing local governments. This suggests that in general natural hazards particularly tend to be defined as less serious or pressing problems compared to the other issues.

Studies of specific hazards have produced similar findings. For example, Wyner's (1981, p. 24) study of California communities facing the threat of earthquakes report that local officials do not devote much attention to defining an acceptable level of earthquake risk in their community. In failing to develop a policy for hazard management, these officials made no explicit decision and have in effect opted for a policy of no (or minimal) management. Also, some communities have expressed resistance to the national flood and insurance program, which is designed to encourage local governments to manage the flood hazards (Keeling, 1980). In order to develop a natural hazards management program both citizens and officials of a community must be aware that hazards exist and believe that a risk of significant negative consequences is posed. Numerous studies have reported that hazards or risk perception is a necessary first step in obtaining risk management action (Burton et al., 1978; Davenport & Waterstone, 1979; Hewitt & Burton, 1971). There are differences in how community officials and citizens perceive risk, of course, and these differences have implications for the nature of the hazard management policy which may be undertaken. Also, the level of uncertainty associated with the potential disaster often plays a major role in the definition of these different perceptions. Officials who have responsibility for public safety must take very seriously a potential threat that could injure numerous citizens in the community. Individual members of the public, on the other hand, might take such a threat much less seriously unless they perceive themselves to be among the handful at direct risk (Hultaker, 1977, p. 14).

One may also find situations where community members or interest groups believe a hazard to represent a great danger and strive to place the issue on the political agenda. Often in such cases, members of the public who attempt to generate a political response to the hazard are experts in a given hazards area. Grass-roots pressure for community adoption of a given hazards management policy may also come from "aware" lay citizens who understand the nature of the hazard.

A second important requisite in hazards management policy formulation is that local government officials must believe that the hazard which is the object of public policy is susceptible to management. Specifically, officials must believe that a hazard can be managed. Management here may refer to any of a variety of activities, including preventing the hazard altogether—such as developing me-chanical standards for vehicles which transport hazardous materials—or adjust-ing human use patterns with respect to some hazards—for example, keeping homes and businesses out of flood plains. It remains important, however that there be some identifiable human action which can be undertaken to minimize negative consequences associated with the threat. It is interesting to note that when there is significant disagreement among technical experts regarding the extent of an environmental threat, its manageability, or survivability, political bodies often hesitate to adopt positive hazards management postures. When technical experts provide no consistent guidance, the management of the hazard moves more firmly into a political realm and may be subject to the same kinds of forces as other more political or social value questions. In the United States, the question of civil defense measures has taken on a political dimension in part due to disagreement among experts regarding the threat (cf. Perry, 1982).

Finally, for a local government to act it must have presented to it a policy for hazard management that it politically feasible. That is, the policy must appear to be effective in managing the hazard, it must not run counter to established community values, and it must be economically feasible. It is interesting to note the importance of having an acceptable proposal upon which government may act. As Davies (1974, p. 2) points out:

> Legislatures must work almost exclusively as boards of review . . . [to be successful, a bill should be] accompanied by supporting advocacy which convinces legislatures that the bill is sound and that they will not incur serious political vulnerability if they support it.

This point of view is consistent with Atkisson and Petak (1981, p. 4) who argue that

> . . . contrary to the folklore of American government, the typical legislator and public policymaker is neither a molder of public opinion, a pioneer in public problem identification and problem-solving activities, a designer of legislation, or the creator of a legislative politi-cal environment within which it becomes possible to enact or to successfully oppose the enactment of any specific policy proposal.

The idea then, is that for a hazard policy to be politically feasible it must be presented to the local government in a form on which action can be taken, as well in a form that minimizes political vulnerability. Alternatively, the local officials can, and tend to, mold proposals so that they are acceptable.

In summary, there appear to be two primary avenues through which hazard management policies come before local government, with the latter being most common. First, local officials can, because of their broad public safety respon-sibilities or interests, incorporate some aspects of hazards management in their political agendas. Second, citizens or interest groups can lobby to have public officials address the issue of hazards management. In practice, a combination of both local official and citizen interest will be important to creating or sustaining community hazards management policy.

With respect to hazard management in the local community, both administrative departments and public safety departments tend to be involved in policy implementation and secondarily involved in agenda setting or policy formulation. Such departments may participate in policy formulation as identifiers of new threats or of gaps in existing hazards management policy, as technical experts who may be called upon by the local government to judge outside proposals, or as lobbyists in favor of or opposed to some specific policy. In the final analysis however, the fact that administrative and public safety departments have responsibility for interpreting and implementing public policy relative to hazards management overshadows the role in terms of policy formulation. Thus, the activity of administrative and public safety mission departments focuses upon action: mitigating against, preparing for, responding to and recoverying from acute environmental threats. Recognizing a potential danger is one motivating factor for each of these activities, since if no problem or potential risk is perceived, no action is likely to be undertaken. Administrators of departments in a community tend to be most concerned with planning and coordination in connection with disasters, rather than immediate response, search and rescue, or other operational aspects of emergency management. This of course excludes those administrators such as police chiefs, fire chiefs or emergency services officials, who have public safety and emergency response as their primary responsibility. City managers and county administrators may have general oversight responsibilities for the functioning of their city or county, or for a particular area such as transportation, housing, or public works. It must be remembered however, that the responsibilities of such officials are much broader than hazards management, and numerous political priorities intervene to reduce the time they can devote to such concerns.

Officials whose duties include land use planning, building regulation, public works and utilities are more likely to be concerned with mitigation and recovery matters. This role seems to be broadening, however, to include disaster preparedness. For example, in connection with earthquakes and related hazards, it has been pointed out that "effective hazard reduction measures are critical for emergency preparedness . . . city planning directors, attorneys, and others will make as many of these decisions, likely more, than disaster directors" (Council of State Governments, 1979, p. 45). Thus, through an emphasis on mitigation and post-impact recovery, local administrators can have an indirect responsibility for emergency preparedness. An important point to remember when identifying recovery responsibilities of administrative officers is that it is preferable to link recovery planning and comprehensive community planning.

In addition to mitigation and long term recovery responsibilities, most public administrators will also play some role in the immediate response phase of a community emergency. Hence, although most administrators may prefer to leave the implementation of preparedness and response plans to their public safety offices, during the impact phase they tend to play major coordination roles. As Kartez and Kelley (1980, p. 30) point out, individual emergency plans prepared by separate offices "are most likely to stem from some overall policy or emergency response philosophy encouraged by the jurisdictions' elected officials or chief executive officers." Certainly there are jurisdictions where, because of strong personalities in some positions, independent planning efforts do take place. However, in most cases the administrative officer in a jurisdiction will have overall preparedness and response responsibilities in addition to those associated with mitigation and recovery.

In a hazards management scheme, both administrators and staff of public safety departments have more direct responsibility for response than do other administrative departments. These public safety departments include fire departments, police departments, emergency medical services and disaster preparedness offices. Depending upon the kind of disaster involved, their duties can range from immediate preparedness (warning, setting up road blocks, sand bagging, evacuation) to immediate response (search and rescue, rubble clearing) and long term recovery. Officials in disaster preparedness offices may also have responsibility for the development of parts of a community's mitigation program. Also, public safety departments may have responsibility to develop preparedness plans prior to any disaster, even though the overall direction may be set by the jurisdiction's elected officials.

Each agency responsible for public safety usually develops its own preparedness plan or that of procedures (Hildebrand, 1980). Such plans or procedures may reflect an overall community philosophy, but it is also possible that the plans will be poorly referenced to each other, resulting in minimal coordination and much dependence on initiative-taking in emergencies (Wenger et al., 1980, p. 154). It is important that when separate plans or procedures are maintained in the same community by different agencies, that there is careful coordination among them to minimize unnecessary overlap and insure the interdepartmental communication necessary to accommodate effective implementation.

EVACUATION PLANS AND PLANNING

Up to this point, interest has centered upon the context in which public policy for community hazard management is made. The primary concern in this section is to describe the nature of one particular component of this management process—the development of evacuation plans and a process of evacuation planning at the city or county level.

The process of generating a plan to evacuate citizens from places threatened by disasters varies considerably among communities, just as the nature of the plan itself varies. It is possible, however, to characterize evacuation plans in terms of select disaster agent-generated and response-generated demands with which they must deal. It is also important to mention two aspects of evacuation planning that place it in the larger context of hazard management. First, an evacuation plan is simply a strategy for moving people from a place of relative danger to a place of relative safety. Thus, an evacuation plan may be an element of, but it is not in itself a hazard management plan. Managing any hazard involves a far wider range of activities than moving threatened citizens. Second, evacuation plans may be formal or informal, mostly written or mostly unwritten. To a certain extent, the elaborateness of the plan will correlate with the size of the community for which it is developed; larger communities characterized by many departments, many personnel and perhaps higher relative turnover, tend to evolve more formalized plans. In smaller communities, an evacuation plan may be almost completely unwritten, familiar only to the public safety personnel who would actually implement it, and passed on to new employees verbally.

It should not be inferred from the above remarks that the most effective evacuation plan is one that is written down and addresses the potential problem in great detail. No plan can be expected to address every issue or cover every contingency, one which attempted to do so would probably be so complex and lengthy as to virtually preclude implementation. Indeed, one universal guideline for constructing evacuation plans is that they should be simple and flexible. There are several additional guidelines for effective hazard management which may be modified slightly to apply to the problem of generating an evacuation plan. These may be seen either as characteristics of a plan which is likely to be effective, or as an approach to planning. In any event, the following six suggestions have been gleaned from the research literature on natural and technological disasters and the practical experience of numerous emergency managers.

One of the most important aspects of evacuation planning is that it should be a continuing process; the plan is never complete. Wenger et al. (1980, p. 134) point out that ". . . there is a tendency on the part of officials to see disaster planning as a product, not a process." An evacuation plan makes assumption regarding, among many things, the conditions under which movement takes place, the responsiveness of the public, the characteristics of the threat, and the operational smoothness of interagency or interdepartmental linkages. These conditions naturally change over time and with experience, and thereby necessitate periodic changes in plans. To assume that because it has been once written down an evacuation plan is complete, is simply inaccurate. An effective evacuation plan, whether written or unwritten, must be continually updated and revised to reflect changing conditions and new knowledge. By treating a written plan as a final product, one risks creating the illusion of being prepared for an emergency when such is not the case (Quarantelli, 1977).

A second characteristic of evacuation planning is that it should encourage appropriate adaptive actions. Particularly with regard to evacuation, much stress has been given the idea that careful planning promotes quicker response. While this is true in many respects, there remains some question regarding whether response speed should be the primary objective of planning or simply a by-product. Quarantelli (1977, p. 106) has argued that appropriateness of response is far more crucial than speed: "it is far more important in a disaster to obtain valid information as to what is happening than it is to take immediate action . . . planning in fact should help to delay impulsive reactions in preference to appropriate actions necessary in the situation." Two points are important here. First, every evacuation plan should contain provisions for continuing threat assessment. Second, quick reactions based upon incorrect or misleading information can lead to inadequate protective measures. For example, in 1979, flooding along the Platte River threatened a small Nebraska town (Perry et al., 1981b, p. 16–19). Traditionally, floods had approached the town from the north, causing most damage in the north and east sections of the community. As the height of the river steadily rose, there was pressure on the primary emergency manager to "get a jump on the situation" by setting up his emergency operation center (EOC) and evacuee shelter center in the usually dry west end of town. The emergency manager resisted, opting to follow the flood emergency plan which provided for radio-equipped patrols along the river levees to determine the direction of approach of the water and on this basis to select routes of egress and location of EOC and evacuee reception facilities. When the levees finally failed, the downstream levees went first, causing flood waters to approach town from the west, inundating the south and west sections of the community first. In this case the emergency manager acted appropriately by following the plan, which included provisions for intelligence gathering, and making response decisions based upon the best available data. It is noteworthy that to have done otherwise would have risked undertaking a response that would have generated far more danger than doing nothing.

The preceding example also serves to suggest a third rule for effective evacuation plans. The changing direction of approach of water from the Platte reminds us that it is impossible to plan in great detail for very atypical events, and that one should be flexible enough to adjust response contingencies accordingly. Thus, in developing evacuation plans one should focus upon principles rather than attempting to elaborate the plan to include many specific details. Very detailed plans are problematic in four ways: (1) the anticipation of all contingencies is simply impossible (Lindell & Perry, 1980, p. 337); (2) very specific details tend to get out of date relatively quickly, demanding virtually constant updating of mechanistic aspects of the plan (Dynes et al., 1972); (3) very specific plans often include so many details that the wide range of emergency functions appear to be of equal importance, causing response priorities to be unclear or confused (Tierney, 1980, p. 100–101); and (4) the more detailed incorporated into a plan, the larger and more complex it is, the more difficult it is to communicate to personnel, and the harder it is to implement. From this perspective an evacuation plan should focus upon principles of response, minimize discussion of operational details which would tend to restrict flexibility, and clearly specify priorities. It should be remembered that the purpose of having a plan is to promote effective response; heavily elaborated plans have a tendency to become "sacred documents" which in effect hinder response capability. Fourth, evacuation planning is hardly an educational activity. Without the active compliance of citizens, an evacuation plan simply cannot be implemented (Perry et al., 1981a). In the case of evacuation plans, public knowledge need not be substantial, but at a minimum people need to know actions are expected of them, how to recognize a warning, how to identify emergency personnel, and what constitutes an "all clear" signal. This kind of information must be meaningfully communicated not only to the public, but also to operational personnel who would implement the plan, and personnel of any support organizations who might be involved in the evacuation. Thus, once the plan is devised the next, at lesat equally important, phase begins: educating planning support and operational officials, as well as the public, about the provisions of the plan. This educational activity is an integral part of the evacuation planning process and yields high dividends in terms of the effectiveness of evacuation response. Indeed, it can be an important source of feedback regarding potential problems with the plan (Glass, 1979, p. 180).

The fifth principle of good evacuation planning is that it must be based upon accurate knowledge, both of the hazard and of likely human response. There is usually adequate attention given to whether or not evacuation is an effective protective measure. That is, to determining if moving people will in fact reduce their vulnerability. Much less attention has been given to examining how people are likely to perform in an emergency and building evacuation planning around people's known reaction patterns—too often emergency plans which are administratively devised turn out to be based on misconceptions of how people react and, therefore, potentially create more problems than they solve (Perry, 1979b, p. 446). Quarantelli and Dynes (1972) have described a number of myths regarding citizen response to disaster which seem to persist in spite of much research which shows otherwise. Those charged with developing evacuation plans should consider examining the research literature on citizen behavior during evacuations in order to make plans which reflect such knowledge. As we argue in Chapter VII, knowledge of people's response patterns can also help planners identify "incentives" which may be used to enhance citizen compliance with evacuation warnings. For example, it is well known that families sometimes delay evacuating until all members have returned home, and then they leave as a unit. Studies have shown that this behavior reflects a concern for having accurate information regarding the whereabouts and safety of separated family members. A mechanism to provide such information could be included in evacuation shelter planning and may be seen as an incentive for compliance with an evacuation warning (Perry et al., 1981a). It is possible to develop numerous such incentives based upon knowledge of citizen's likely response patterns in disasters.

The sixth suggestion regarding the conduct of evacuation planning is that it must address organizational issues as well as focus upon the public to be served. The success of any evacuation effort is related to the achievement of effective interorganizational coordination among the responding groups and organizations (Perry, 1981a, p. 79). Ideally, they must work in concert toward the goal of moving citizens by accomplishing many interrelated tasks; e.g., warning message construction and dissemination, warning confirmation, traffic direction, temporary sheltering, temporary feeding, etc. To complete these tasks requires, among other things, that organizations be aware of one another's mission and styles of operation, that a communication system exists, and that there are some mutually agreed upon priorities in response, as well as rules for determining which organizations are responsible for which operations. One of the best places to resolve these and related issues is, in advance of a disaster event, in the basic provisions of an evacuation plan. Over time, as the plan is tested and the relevant organizations develop styles of routinely interacting with one another, the quality of interorganizational coordination will likely improve. It remains, however, both necessary and very useful that the evacuation plan itself provide for minimal rules for coordination and task allocation.

The Content of Evacuation Plans

To this point we have presented six guidelines for structuring the evacuation planning process. We will now briefly discuss selected aspects of the content of evacuation plans, specifically the problems of command and control. It should be pointed out that the actual movement of people is usually considered perfunctory and rarely written; specific techniques depend upon standard operating procedures (SOP) and the experience of the public safety personnel on site. Command and control issues are more likely to appear in a written form than other matters. The following discussion focuses upon four issues which usually are covered in written evacuation plans: authority to order an evacuation, executing evacuation orders, security and property protection, and personal welfare and shelter (Perry et al., 1981a).

Government, whether local, state, or federal, has both the authority and the responsibility to protect its citizens. During states of emergency, the power to act may be derived from a variety of sources, including laws, general ''police powers'' and special statutes. With regard to evacuations, it is generally true that during times of emergency citizens may be compelled, in the interests of personal or public safety, to leave an area of potential danger once it has been so designated by relevant authorities. In most cases, however, the problem of forcibly evacuating citizens need not arise. Forcible evacuations are usually avoided via reasonable presentation: research shows that in virtually all cases, when public safety officials contact citizens, explain the nature of the threat and request that they evacuate for their own protection, few refuse on legal grounds for further discussion (see Perry et al., 1981a, p. 6–9).

Acknowledging that governments have the authority to order evacuations, the question then becomes *who* makes such a decision. In almost all cases the chief executive of the relevant government has the authority and the responsibility for making the decision to evacuate. In practice an evacuation decision involves numerous actors and a data gathering process. The information gathered routinely includes the nature of the threat, its speed of onset and likely magnitude, location of impact, duration of impact, characteristics of citizens likely to be at risk, and other agent-specific data deemed to be relevant. In the process of assembling the information numerous actors from within and outside the community become involved. The chief executive may, and usually does, delegate the threat assessment and decision to evacuate citizens to one or morepublic safety officials. From the standpoint of the evacuation plan, however, decision authority (with a clear succession of alternates) should be explicitly assigned.

The second, and somewhat more involved, aspect of a written plan relates to executing the evacuation order once a decision has been made. The first concern here is with the designation of a department with primary responsibility for coordinating and overseeing the conduct of the evacuation effort. In larger communities evacuations may come under the control of an emergency preparedness director (or coordinator) who may or may not be assigned to a public safety department. In smaller communities, responsibility may rest with the fire chief or police chief, who in addition to normal responsibilities may also be the designated emergency preparedness director (Hildebrand, 1980, p. 7). Once designated, the lead department would establish the emergency operations center (EOC) or command post, and concentrate on executing the evacuation and maintaining a coordinated effort to monitor activities and respond to problems that arise while the evacuation is in progress. It is important also that the written plan offer guidelines regarding how the lead department will interface with other departments who participate in the evacuation. This usually takes the form of specifying lines of communication, specifying the location of resources which might be used, and lying out responsibility for the conduct of specific evacuation-related tasks.

The type and number of tasks assigned in a written plan is quite variable and may depend upon the size of the community involved and the resources available. However, almost all written plans address two functions: warning dissemination and traffic management. The warning dissemination function usually includes responsibility for constructing the warning message which will be delivered to the public, deciding the mode for delivering the message, and assigning personnel to the task. The warning message is intended to be a persuasive communication, and must explain (briefly) the nature of the threat, the likely times and places of impact, and some information about how leaving the area will reduce the danger. Evacuation warning messages also should contain information on suggested routes for departure and safe destinations. Different warning modes include door-to-door contacts, announcements over mobile public address systems, pre-arranged signals such as sirens, and pre-planned contact systems such as telephone "ring-down" networks (Perry et al., 1980a). Which mode is selected depends upon numerous factors including the amount of forewarning, availability of equipment and personnel, time of day, and the size and characteristics of the population to be warned. Mass media, particularly radio, may be used to relay warning information but is rarely depended upon as a primary warning mode. Usually evacuation warnings are issued by public safety personnel—police, fire fighters or national guard—because they are readily identified as responsible officials by the citizenry and because of their task-relevant expertise and training.

The traffic management function must ensure that evacuees depart the danger area via appropriate routes and move in the direction of relative safety. In some natural disasters, for example hurricanes, some departure routes may be closed off as the storm becomes more intense. Thus, there is a need to monitor evacuee movement. Traffic management also includes the problem of providing transportation to citizens who cannot otherwise evacuate, and the responsibility for assisting in evacuating special facilities such as nursing homes, hospitals, and incarceration facilities. Since warning dissemination and traffic management functions are conducted simultaneoulsy, different personnel must be involved, but a public safety department—for example, police or fire fighters—is usually assigned the task.

The third issue usually addressed in a written evacuation plan is the question of security and property protection in the evacuated area. In most communities the police or sheriff's department will be assigned responsibility for the two major tasks here: isolating the danger area and providing security for evacuated areas. These areas of intense danger tend to be given to change (particularly expansion), and sometimes characterized by a rapid dissipation of threat. The problem of providing security in evacuated areas includes preventing the return of successfully evacuated residents, and preventing nonresidents from entering the area. This task is normally handled by a law enforcement department. In most cases access restrictions are primarily aimed at protecting the safety of the public—both residents and nonresidents—by precluding their access to an area of potential danger. Such access controls also serve the purpose of keeping virtually all unauthorized persons away from evacuated homes and businesses, thereby reducing the potential for looting and vandalism. Although research indicates that in practice looting is very rare, it is also known that citizens sometimes cite fear of looting as a prominent concern (Perry et al., 1981b, pp. 148–149). Thus, in the process of preserving public safety with access controls, one also addresses the issue of public beliefs about the risks from looting and illegal behavior.

The fourth aspect of written evacuation plans deals with the problem of the personal welfare and sheltering of evacuees. The primary concern here is with designating the department and/or individuals who will participate in locating and administering public shelters. Virtually all aspects of shelter site choice and management are decided in conjunction with the American National Red Cross and, often, with the participation of the Salvation Army. In most cases, community officials are justified in relying on these organizations' experiences and knowledge of the local area in decisions regarding locating and organizing the shelter, developing specific shelter management procedures, family locator systems, and accounting and service utilization systems. The role usually assumed by community officials is that of a cooperating participant who takes part in all decisions and has the responsibility of providing current threat-relevant information which may have a bearing on the conduct of the shelter operation. In addition to these responsibilities, official community representatives may assume responsibility for any special programs designed as part of the evacuation plan which require oversight at the public shelter. Such programs are often intended as evacuation incentives and may include provision for keeping evacuee pets near the shelter facility, services for uniting or compiling information on the whereabouts of separated evacuee families, or check-in services for evacuee families not staying at the public shelter.

CITIZEN PARTICIPATION IN EVACUATION PLANNING

In the preceding section we reviewed several important aspects of the practice of evacuation planning. Six general guidelines for the conduct of evacuation planning were elaborated and the issues most frequently addressed in written plans were described. This accomplished, it is important to examine the idea of synchronizing the evacuation plan with the needs and characteristics of the local community. Specifically citizens must be involved in the planning process. As we argued above, the evacuation planning process should be on-going. It is also important that this process incorporate the community, since numerous aspects of conducting an evacuation—issuing warnings, obtaining citizen compliance, operating shelters—are related to the particular social and demographic characteristics of a community.

The purpose of this section is to review general strategies that might be used to obtain citizen input in the evacuation planning process; it is written from the perspective of a county or municipality director of emergency services. It is important to emphasize at the outset that a premise underlying this work is that an evacuation plan must have a built-in capacity to respond to and incorporate feedback. Most planning guides stress the need for periodic review and updating of plans to accommodate changes in the emergency response system. An evacuation plan should be flexible enough to incorporate comments and suggestions which come from other officials or departments within the community or related outside emergency services agencies. It is argued here that evacuation plans also need to be designed such that comments and feedback from the citizenry can be accommodated and incorporated. In particular, citizen participation helps to insure that a warning message effectively communicates with the population-at-risk, that citizens understand what is expected of them under the plan, and that citizens believe that they have shared interest with authorities to make the provisions of the plan work.

These benefits may be realized only to the extent that inputs from citizens can be obtained and integrated into the planning process. It should be remembered that from a social psychological standpoint, asking citizens to participate in the planning process commits them to being part of the response process, which in itself encourages compliance with the evacuation effort. In virtually every case, however, the best way to obtain citizen participation is to seek it. This requires that emergency managers assume a proactive posture *vis-à-vis* the community. It is true, of course, that budget and staff limitations prescribe definite parameters on the extent to which a proactive role may be assumed. With these realities in mind, we will sketch a number of techniques for citizen involvement, with the awareness that some can be used with a minimum resource expenditure while others are substantially more elaborate.

There are basically three objectives to citizen involvement in evacuation planning (cf. Glass, 1979). The first is *information exchange,* where one seeks citizen feedback regarding specific procedures and policies, and provides information to citizens regarding the rationale which underlies official actions. *Educational contacts* encompass official efforts to familiarize citizens with the basic provisions of the evacuation plan itself, or the need for it in general. Finally, *support-building exchanges* are those in which one seeks to enhance the credibility of the plan (and of the planners and response personnel) in the eyes of the public. The following paragraphs enumerate several options which may be used to exchange information about local evacuation planning.

One of the first obstacles to overcome when attempting to inform the community about emergency evacuation plans is to let citizens know that community officials are engaged in planning for emergencies. Sometimes this involves informing the public that some department of emergency services exists. Unfortunately, most citizens rarely think about emergency services until a disaster strikes, and soon after they rapidly forget (Wolensky & Miller, 1981). Hence there is a need for periodic educational contacts with the community on a fairly large scale. Two techniques are well suited to this purpose: mailed brochures and mass media interviews. For a relatively low cost one can develop brochures—for example on the need for hazards management in general, or specifically describing an evacuation plan—which can be mailed in bulk to the community. Such brochures have the advantage that they serve as written information which citizens can retain for future use, as well as reminders that the emergency services department is active. In Valley, Nebraska, the volunteer fire department developed a bright colored brochure on a 5 × 7 inch cardboard with space for emergency telephone numbers on top and the meaning of different warning messages on the bottom. It was designed to be kept near a telephone, where it could also be referenced in the event of a disaster (Perry et al., 1981, pp. 18–24). Brochures can be printed relatively inexpensively in large quantities and after one mailed wave, they may also be distributed by hand in response to inquiries made by citizens. In San Bernadino County, California, short brochures are developed in conjunction with recurrent seasonal threats—general survival, desert survival, winter survival, earthquakes and floods—for direct distribution to citizens (Bethell, 1981). Furthermore, several federal agencies—the National Weather Service, Forest Service, U.S. Geological Survey, and the Federal Emergency Management Agency—routinely produce brochures on a variety of emergency topics; these can be obtained by local officials (usually at low cost) and distributed to citizens by mail or by hand as informational bulletins. Such mailings can be made on a periodic basis, perhaps quarterly, and may be designed to bring current information on emergency services activities and season hazards. In cases where limited budgets either limit the number of mailings or simply altogether preclude such activities, it has been suggested that emergency managers might speak with state authorities about sending relevant pamphlets with hunting and fishing licenses and boat and recreational vehicle registration renewals (Bethell, 1981). Also, arrangements can be made to have brochure material printed in documents which are routinely available to the public. For example, the Skagit County (Washington) Department of Emergency Services has arranged with the local phone company to have a set of "blue pages" inserted in phone books (Sheahan, 1982). Although the precise content is yet to be determined, present plans include listing emergency phone numbers, brief instructions for reporting and responding to recurrent local threats, and perhaps location of potential evacuation reception centers. This very innovative strategy achieves wide distribution at low cost. Furthermore, since the instructions are printed in a commonly used and retained public document, the likelihood of loss or misplacement is substantially reduced.

Another method of communicating information to a large segment of the public at a low cost is through interviews of emergency services personnel in the local mass media or informational "spots" as public service programming. One means of insuring that such interviews occur in a timely fashion is to periodically contact local newspapers or weekly magazine feature editors with a seasonally appropriate suggestion for a story as well as some information on a given hazard: winter storms, summer/fall tornadoes, or spring floods, (Sheahan, 1982). A similar approach can be used with local radio and television "talk shows" and news programs (Bethell, 1981). By approaching different radio stations and using different time-slots, a creative emergency services official can reach many different segments of the community in a short period of time.

Both of the techniques described above have the advantage of reaching large audiences at moderate cost, and the disadvantage of using essentially one-way communication. The emergency services official gets his or her message out, but except in rare circumstances the audience cannot respond. The following techniques involve the opportunity for two-way communication, and rely principally upon existing personnel and equipment. The first technique is simply to encourage emergency services staff to serve as listening posts and information disseminators in their own neighborhoods. This involves picking up and distributing (largely verbal) information at the grassroots level. The value of such exchanges, particularly over the long run, should not be underestimated.

A second technique for interacting with the public involves setting up a "hazard information" telephone number. This need not be any more elaborate than advertising an office phone number and training existing staff to handle inquiries, or using a recorded message. Citizens could be informed of the information line—perhaps via a mailed brochure—and staff could develop a procedure for promptly responding to questions. This type of phone-in arrangement is quite useful in that it serves to gather and disseminate information on a routine basis, and has the potential to be expanded into a rumor control and/or warning confirmation line during times of disaster (Perry, 1981, p. 75). There are cautions which one should bear in mind when using telephones to disseminate hazard relevant information or as a mechanism for rumor control during a time of emergency. In general, particularly over the course of a year, one would not anticipate large volumes of calls in connection with citizen inquiries. Such non-emergency-time calls probably would not tax either the ability of staff to respond or the capability of telephone equipment to handle calls. If a telephone number is to be used during emergencies to disseminate information, however, officials in even small communities should anticipate the possibility of very large volumes of calls which potentially overload telephone exchanges. Two strategies might be used to prevent or minimize difficulties associated with high volumes of calls. First, one could use several phone numbers—in addition to an emergency services office, perhaps a fire department, police department, city manager's office, public works office, and/or social services office—in an effort to distribute calls across numerous exchanges. This option demands, of course, that coordination between offices be maintained so that all citizens receive the same information from each office. Second, one can—at some cost—arrange for special telephone equipment to handle large numbers of calls, either with appropriate personnel to answer inquiries or recorded messages. In any case, it must be remembered that if telephones are to be used either to disseminate information in general or during emergencies, adequate measures must be taken to insure that the system can be responsive to the needs or demands of the community to be served. A system which quickly overloads or results in the simultaneous dissemination of conflicting messages in an emergency produces greater negative consequences than would likely be the case if no system existed in the first place.

A third technique for communicating with the public is to establish direct contact with citizens in the community. This is traditionally done through speaking at neighborhood meetings and meetings of community organizations and schools. Neighborhood meetings can deal with very specific and timely topics; they can reach otherwise difficult to contact groups; and they provide both face-to-face contact and an opportunity for dialogue. For example, a community or neighborhood club might welcome a speaker on how to prepare for a hurricane at the start of hurricane season. Detailed information could be provided on what to expect in their specific neighborhood, and evacuation routes and procedures could be discussed. A discussion of this specificity is not as feasible on a community-wide basis, although meetings at community organizations and schools are still very important in disseminating hazards information and emergency procedures. An important issue here is remembering that neighborhood groups and community organizations tend to have fairly homogeneous memberships, so in order to communicate with a significant portion of the community one must make contacts with a number of different types of groups.

Finally, a more direct level of citizen involvement can be achieved by creating citizen advisory committees and citizen cadre opportunities. Advisory committees are usually small in size and attached to departments, but can be used for specific topics as well, including the problem of evacuation planning. When an advisory committee is created, a considerable commitment is being made. At a minimum, regular meetings should be held and officials must devise an acceptable mechanism for soliciting information, evaluating it, and then either using it or explaining why it was not used. The citizen advisory committee, if administered appropriately, can provide valuable, timely information on specific points of planning interest, and also serve a strong support-building function in the community. While citizen advisory committees tend to involve people in the administrative aspects of evacuation planning, citizen cadre opportunities tend to involve volunteers in selected operational duties. Citizen cadres require some degree of training and usually function as auxiliary personnel acting in support of regular emergency personnel. Citizen cadres have been used as sandbagging personnel in floods, as traffic direction officers, in search and rescue operations, to provide security in evacuated areas, and to help administer family locator services and other shelter services. The idea behind the use of citizen cadres is to incorporate people into the evacuation response process in a constructive way. At best, such auxiliary personnel can be used to ease the tremendous demands placed on regular manpower during the operational phase of an evacuation. Furthermore, an appropriately trained volunteer represents a community member with a reasonable working knowledge of the evacuation procedures and the logic behind them. Such persons serve as convincing support-builders *vis-à-vis* the larger community in that they can explain and justify emergency procedures to others.

In summary, the general purpose of all the techniques discussed above is the same: to allow emergency authorities to better know their community and to familiarize citizens with emergency response planning and operations. It is probably not feasible to attempt to use all of these techniques in the same community. They are elaborated here as possible programs which can be selected, relative to existing budgetary and other constraints, and adapted to the specific needs of a community.

THE ROLE OF EMERGENCY MANAGERS

In Chapter I and particularly in this chapter, we have reviewed the role of local communities in emergency management. Earlier in this chapter the structure of the locality—primarily local government—was explored relative to the question of community hazard management and specifically in terms of evacuation planning. Throughout those discussions we alternately focused upon a variety of "roles"—mayor, county council member, police chief, fire chief, public works administrator, etc.—and described the different demands placed upon them in the process of responding to natural and man-made emergencies. In concluding this chapter, we will briefly examine a role or job position that appears in many city and county structures, and toward which this book is oriented: the emergency manager.

In the past, even as recently as the late 1950s and through the 1960s, emergency services were fragmented; to determine what department or official was responsible for planning and/or response, one had to specify which type of emergency was being referenced. The public could identify the position—if not the incumbent—of civil defense director. However, the vision was one of a largely invisible person or persons, presumably attached in some fashion to defense authorities (whoever they were), charged for the most part with "civil defense duties." From the citizens point of view, other emergency services were embodied somehow in the police or fire departments. The routine activities of these organizations focused upon responding to what citizens defined as personal emergencies, and police and firefighters were (and sometimes are still) the most visible actors during natural and technological disasters.

In the past decade or so, the world has changed substantially with respect to natural and man-made hazards. It has become increasingly difficult to see emergency management as something that can be done by police and firefighters as an adjunct to their regular duties. Due to many factors, including human settlement patterns and failure to develop zoning regulations which are enforceable, natural disasters are affecting greater numbers of people than ever before. As we pointed out in Chapter I, the culprit is not an increase in the occurrence of natural disasters. Instead, more people are living in flood plains, on slopes subject to mud and land slides and in unreinforced dwellings near faults, too close to the spillways of man-made dams, and in other places which make them subject to the negative consequences of natural forces. It is also becoming apparent that potential risks from technological sources, including nuclear war, are increasing with the growth and change of existing technologies and with the development of new technologies. The public, as well as officials at all levels of government, are becoming sensitive to the idea that the number and varieties of hazardous materials transported by land, sea, and air are increasing. For example, large quantities of hazardous materials—including gasoline, nuclear wastes, and liquid natural gas—are moved by truck and by rail through even large urban areas. A related aspect of the risk of technological disasters can be seen in the practice of citing hazardous facilities such as oil refineries and nuclear power plants near large population centers. This changing hazard environment has been at least in part responsible for the development of the idea that most jurisdictions should have something called an "emergency manager." Thus was born, in the middle 1970s, a position for an administrator who devotes most of his time to the emergency management.

A substantial problem which has arisen in connection with the creation of emergency managers is the question of defining the role itself. In light of the above discussion of the changing hazard environment, one can specify several desirable characteirstics for emergency managers. First, since disasters are affecting more citizens now than ever before, their management, or more specifically how to minimize negative consequences, is at the forefront politically. Thus, to be more effective, an emergency manager must have some political acumen. Also, with increasing politicalization of the role, an emergency manager cannot be "invisible" any longer.

Second, it was acknowledge above that more, and different, natural and technological hazards now affect more citizens. Thus the technical knowledge that an emergency manager must have is increasing. No longer can one get by with a general familiarity with civil defense and a little knowledge of a few natural hazards. Although the technical knowledge need not be deep or profound, an emergency manager needs to know enough about a variety of hazards to be able to determine when outside help is needed and where to obtain that help.

Also, as the need for increased technical knowledge implies, emergency managers must cultivate their skills at communicating and coordinating among different people and organizations. As we have seen, comprehensive emergency management refers to the problem of developing the capability for handling all phases of activity—mitigation, preparedness, response and recovery—in all types of disasters by coordinating the efforts and resources of many different agencies. Hence the role of emergency manager must reflect the concept that hazard management simply requires interdependence. All of the resources required for effective hazard management cannot be assembled into a single department. Instead, the emergency manager keeps track of resources and their location and plans how such resources may be employed at appropriate times to manage natural and technological hazards. This means that an emergency manager must, for example, keep alive communications with such diverse organizations as departments of public works, police and fire fighters, elected public officials at various levels of government, and representatives of the private sector such as the Red Cross, the Salvation Army, local search and rescue groups, and industrial concerns.

Based upon the above discussion, it is apparent that an emergency manager needs to be an administrator, a politician, and a technical expert who can share his expertise both with the public and with elected decision-makers. Executing this role can be very difficult, particularly since the dualism concept has not entirely disappeared from the minds of the public and political decision-makers. There still remains strong pressures to keep emergency managers invisible for the most part, but to hold them accountable during and after natural and technological disasters. To effectively perform as an emergency manager, the role encumbent must incorporate the need for political acumen, technical knowledge and coordination into a long-range strategy for administering hazard management.

Finally, in the last section of this chapter, it was pointed out that evacuation planning is an ongoing process which should incorporate the community, since numerous aspects of conducting an evacuation—issuing warnings, obtaining citizen compliance, and operating shelters—are related to the particular social and demographic characteristics of the community. A still more important aspect of involving the community or citizens in the evacuation planning process relates to the role of the emergency manager. Recall that the emergency manager's job is to a certain extent political. That is, an emergency manager gets involved in the politics of hazard management in at least two ways. First, he serves as an expert witness and gives technical guidance to political decision-making bodies regarding policy formulation—namely deciding which hazards should be managed. Second, the emergency manager implements hazard policy decisions and in so doing decides how any given hazard is to be managed thus affecting in a personal way the lives of the public.

Under these conditions, one should remember that the public is a constituency and that elected decision-makers understand constituencies and their importance in politics. If an emergency manager cultivates the public as one of his constituencies, it can enhance his ability to perform the task of emergency management. That is, the emergency manager must survey the hazard environment and determine which hazards require managing and assess, based upon technical expertise, the volume of resources that should be devoted to the problem. Since elected officials tend to make decisions for citizens regarding which hazards are to be managed and what proportion of public resources will be devoted to that management, to effectively execute his charge, the emergency manager must influence these decision-makers. His ability to exert such influence is greatly enhanced if the public acknowledges and respects the Department of Emergency Services as the center of technical expertise regarding emergencies.

This means that emergency managers must address the issue of: "How does one cultivate the public and make them a part of the planning process in a constructive way?" Put slightly differently, without letting public relations become a fulltime job and without letting public involvement become an obstacle to carrying out emergency management, how does one involve the public? The techniques for citizen participation developed in this chapter are specifically designed for long-term use and provide several alternative strategies for involving or "cultivating" the public. Furthermore, use of the citizen participation techniques discussed above simultaneously achieve two objectives: constituency building and increasing the chance that citizens will understand and consequently comply with community emergency procedures.

In summary, the purpose of elaborating principles of evacuation planning and techniques for public involvement for the planning process is to allow emergency managers to better know their community and to familiarize citizens with the process and practice of emergency management. It is probably not feasible to attempt to use all of the principles and techniques developed in this chapter in the same community. They are elaborated here as possible programs which can be selected, relative to existing budgetary and other constraints, and adapted to the specific needs of a community. The consistent theme has been that the role of emergency manager is changing, and role encumbents must adjust to a new set of demands. These demands include the politicalization of emergency management, increasing needs for technical expertise, and the ability to coordinate a number of agencies in accomplishing hazard management. The principles for evacuation planning involve acknowledging the need for technical expertise and communication and incorporating these needs into a strategy for long run emergency management. The discussion of public involvement in evacuation planning takes into account both the politicalization of the role of the emergency manager and underscores the idea that no emergency planning can be effective without the cooperation of the public.

Having addressed most of the mechanics of evacuation plans and the planning process, the next logical concern is with the question of what can emergency managers and planners do to increase the likelihood that threatened citizens will comply with disaster response measures devised by authorities. Chapter VII grapples with this problem by drawing upon the propositions describing citizen behavior during the emergency period developed in Chapter IV.

Chapter VII

Enhancing Citizen Compliance with Disaster Warnings

The purpose of this chapter is to examine the issues of design and evaluation in connection with community emergency warning systems. First, we will review the structure and operation of warning systems to establish the context in which evacuation warnings are issued. The second part of the chapter is devoted to applying the information derived from the warning response model developed in Chapter IV to the problem of enhancing evacuation warning compliance. That is, data on citizen warning response are brought to bear on the problem of evacuation planning by considering measures which might be taken by planners to enhance the likelihood that citizens will comply with an official warning. Thus, attention is focused upon the relationship between planning authorities and citizens through the development of incentives to evacuate. In this context, an incentive is any procedure or provision devised by authorities and incorporated into evacuation plans which *increases* the subjective probability that threatened citizens will comply with a warning to evacuate (Perry et al., 1980b, p. 433). Incentives may be seen as one approach to hazard reduction; they are measures undertaken before any specific disaster incident which promote successful adaptation to an environmental threat. The final section of this chapter addresses the problem of developing a set of criteria for evaluating a communities' emergency response plan. The objective in so doing is to develop a series of general guidelines which can be used to identify gaps in existing planning.

For the sake of clarity, it should be pointed out at the outset that discussion of "incentives" to evacuate here implies that such procedures will be instituted on a voluntary rather than enforced basis. As we pointed out in Chapter II, enforced evacuation—characterized by an order to evacuate and the forcible removal of those who do not comply with the order—while not frequently used, would ensure that an endangered area would be emptied of people, making incentives unnecessary. Many states in the United States have provisions in their legal codes for forcing people to leave an endangered area, and enforced evacuation is often used outside the United States. Perhaps the most important reason that enforced evacuation can be problematic centers upon the relative inefficiency of the technique. Coordinating the exodus from a threatened area and providing some form of reception for evacuees is a sufficiently difficult task without authorities being forced to engage in social control activities related to the forcible removal of those who refuse to comply with the warning. Indeed, if people don't voluntarily comply, the only alternative for enforced evacuation is to arrest and forcibly remove residents. Such mass arrests produce the undesirable *convergence* of additional personnel and material to a threatened area when the objective is to remove all people (cf. Fritz & Mathewson, 1957). Given these difficulties, it becomes apparent that ensuring evacuation of a threatened area via enforced compliance is in general less suitable than other approaches based upon voluntary compliance. Furthermore, it is in the context of voluntary compliance that the concept of *incentives to evacuate* assumes critical importance.

WARNING SYSTEMS IN EMERGENCY PREPAREDNESS

The problem of warning threatened populations about impending disaster is multifaceted and the present discussion requires that at least two elements be addressed. One element is the warning system itself. Warning systems consist of procedures and processes which are general in the sense that a single warning *system* may be used for a variety of hazards, both natural and man-made. The other element refers to the nature of the warning message or specifically to the "adaptive" response suggested to the threatened population. Appropriate adaptive responses vary with the nature of the threat involved—for example, evacuation in the case of hurricanes and riverine floods, basement shelter against torandoes. This book has focused upon warnings which convey the necessity for a particular adaptive strategy: pre-impact evacuation to a "safe" location for a short-term stay. The following paragraphs outline the warning process with specific attention to how the warning system operates within the context of emergency preparedness and response.

Historically, social scientists tend to view warning from a social systems perspective as a process which is the product of social organization. Such models typically emphasize processes operating on an aggregate level; concern is with the full warning process, beginning with detection of impending disaster and concluding with consideration of human response. Thus, a system's view of the warning process highlights disaster detection, communication of warning messages, and human response to warning. To fully appreciate the warning process, however, requires its explicit introduction within the larger framework of community preparedness and response planning.

Especially in recent years, social scientists as well as emergency managers have devoted increasing attention to the importance of disaster preparedness plans. Indeed, in describing the National Weather Service Warning programs, Mogil and Groper (1977, p. 320) point out that:

> Improved forecasts and warnings of severe local storms and other hazardous weather events may prove useless unless community preparedness plans are developed and people learn how to react promptly and positively to weather watches and warnings.

The point here is that warning systems are designed to provide a message or "cue" that danger is imminent. There has been much research on the optimum content of warning messages (McLuckie, 1970; Mileti, 1975; Williams, 1964), and it is known that the place and time to communicate a detailed adaptive plan is *not* the warning message issued just prior to disaster impact. Ideally, warnings describe the threat, its probable time of impact and *suggest* appropriate adaptive behaviors. It is considered optimal (in terms of efficiency and protection of individuals) if the "suggested" actions may serve as brief cues to the individual which bring to mind more elaborate adaptive strategies which have been previously communicated. For example, a warning to evacuate some threatened area is considerably more effective if residents are aware of various evacuation routes, checkpoints, and safe locations *at the time they receive the warning* (cf. Mileti, 1974; Mileti & Beck, 1975; Perry, 1979a). Preparedness programs, then, may be conceptualized in part as "calling up" (via a warning message) an individual's "stored" information regarding adaptive behavior.

Figure VII.1 draws upon Williams' (1964, p. 83) model of warning systems and includes consideration of the role of community preparedness. This chart is meant to emphasize that traditional views of warning systems as mechanisms that only deliver a warning message are neither particularly adequate nor accurate; the level of community preparedness and a community's response capabilities will be reflected in the results delivered by nearly every warning system. It is also important to mention that in Figure VII.1, and throughout this chapter, "warning message" refers to a warning communicated by *local authorities* to a threatened population. This warning is distinct from warnings delivered from one government agency to another, such as "meteorological warnings" of the type issued by the National Weather Service. Meteorological warnings describe technical aspects of impending disasters and may be seen as cues for local officials to make decisions about instituting emergency measures. In discussing incentives however, we are only concerned with the structure and design of warning messages issued to citizens by the local officials.

An indicator of the increasing acceptance of the importance of preparedness is the attention being given the subject by such organizations as the National Governors' Association and the U.S. Conference of Mayors. The National Gov-

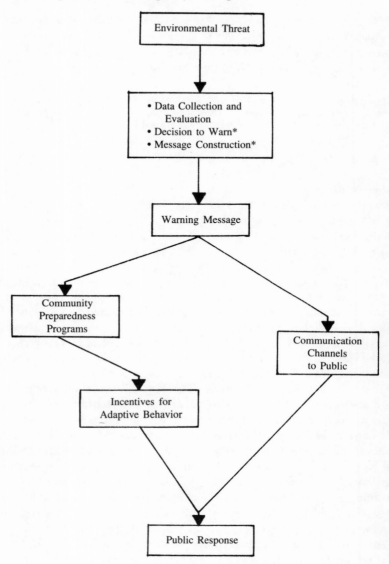

Figure VII.1. A model of a community disaster warning system (arrows designate the direction of information flow and the order of sub-system activation).

*Refers to activities of local authorities

ernors' Association has recently completed a comprehensive study of overall emergency management, focused at the state level but identifying many important preparedness issues that arise at the local level (National Governors' Association, 1979a, 1979b, 1979c). The U.S. Conference of Mayors is currently conducting an assessment of the needs and priorities of Mayors in emergency preparedness and response. The Council of State Governments has also recently completed a study of states and natural hazards to identify important factors in the development of effective preparedness programs and to acquaint state officials with new federal emergency management policies (Council of State Governments, 1979).

Also, several agencies with disaster responsibilities have developed programs designed to make them more responsive to local needs in the development of emergency preparedness programs. An example of this is the National Weather Service program to assign disaster preparedness meteorologists to Weather Service Forecast Offices (Mogil & Groper, 1977, p. 321). These disaster preparedness meteorologists meet with and serve an educational function for state, county, and local officials as well as civil defense and other community organizations. Such planning efforts to supplement warning programs have been credited with significantly reducing loss of life, injuries, and property damage, particularly in tornado disasters (cf. Galway, 1966; Ostby & Pearson, 1976).

In connection with citizen warning response, disaster preparedness programs usually involve determining appropriate adaptive behaviors and planning strategies for implementing such protective actions, and educating the relevant population with regard to the particular plans (Lewis et al., 1977, p. 99). In the case of pre-impact evacuation relative to riverine floods, for example, the relevant tasks would include identification of possible safe areas for shelters, mapping optimal departure routes, provisions for any necessary official transportation, provisions for security in areas which may be evacuated, and communicating the results of this planning effort to the community. It is well known, however, that even the most carefully devised and disseminated plans are useful only to the extent that citizens comply or participate. Viewed in this way, evacuation incentives assume a role of considerable importance: they represent measures which can be integrated into disaster preparedness programs that enhance the probability that citizens will cooperate in a time of emergency.

INCENTIVES TO EVACUATE

The concern here is with evacuations which are instituted prior to disaster impact, involve a short-term absence of individuals from the threatened area, and are characterized by voluntary compliance. From this perspective, incentives to evacuate must be devised in advance—they represent the results of careful planning and *not* simply a response to some immediate threat to the community. This discussion identifies possible incentives from the literature and discusses the empirical findings of this study regarding the efficacy of such incentives. These incentives are by no means new ideas; as the citations indicate, some were suggested years ago. They have not previously, however, been brought together, scrutinized from a social scientific standpoint and discussed in terms of an overall approach to emergency preparedness and response.

A final qualifier should be mentioned in connection with the discussion of evacuation in general. In discussing the use of incentives in preparedness plans, we must presume—for analytical purposes—that detection of the impending disaster occurs such that sufficient *time* is available to issue a warning and to actually evacuate the relevant population prior to disaster impact. As we pointed out in Chapter II, the amount of lead time available to authorities depends upon a variety of factors, including the existence of a detection technology for an environmental threat, as well as the efficiency of interorganizational relations between agencies charged with managing emergencies. It is acknowledged that in the study of disaster warning systems, time is a very crucial factor. No matter how well a system might be designed or how many incentives to evacuate might be used, if the lead time is short, possible success can be severely hampered. In other words, a well-designed emergency preparedness plan may not be effectively implemented if there is no warning period. It should be emphasized, however, that even in the absence of forewarning elements of a preparedness plan should be helpful in the response phase, particularly during post–impact removal of the population and in general search and rescue activities.

Given the above qualifications, attention may be focused upon incentives to evacuate and their incorporation into emergency preparedness planning. In approaching the problem of isolating evacuation incentives, four issue areas have been chosen from the warning response literature which represent problems in evacuation implementation: sheltering, transportation, the role of the family, and security and property protection. Each of these issue areas will be examined in turn, reviewing the empirical basis for concern, citing examples, and enumerating possible incentives that could be employed to encourage participation from potential evacuees.

Sheltering

The nature of shelter facilities provided to evacuees has been the source of considerable controversy among disaster researchers. It has been frequently reported that evacuees tend not to use public or planned shelters. In connection with the Yuba City flood, Stiles (1957) reports that only about 20 percent of the people who evacuated actually reported to Red Cross shelters. Likewise, Moore et al. (1963, p. 92) found that 58% of the people who were evacuated in response to Hurricane Carla went to the homes of friends and relatives rather than to official shelters. While some investigators have interpreted these findings to indicate that public shelters are less necessary, it should be emphasized that the research literature is by no means entirely consistent with regard to evacuee utilization of public shelters. Even if many evacuees seek help from friends and relatives, there still remain at least some people who depend upon public shelters.

As a point of depature, research on evacuations suggests that one can draw at least three general conclusions about evacuees' sheltering behavior (Perry et al., 1981b, p. 109). First, when kin are within a reasonable distance of the disaster site and some forewarning is possible, evacuees clearly prefer the homes of relatives as shelter. As the amount of forewarning decreases, people tend to seek shelter in the homes of friends. When forewarning is short *and* community disaster preparedness is low, evacuees often seek only high ground as a means of escaping an environmental threat. This is a situation in which communications to the threatened population about the impending disaster are low; apparently people first seek known protection to gain enough time in which to evaluate the situation further for themselves. Second, the use of public shelter increases when community preparedness is high, when the entire community (geographically speaking) must be evacuated, and when the evacuees anticipate that the necessary period of absence will be long. Generally though, public shelters seem to attract, even under the conditions described above, approximately one-fourth of the evacuees at a given site. Third, in communities which experience recurrent impacts of some particular disaster and a disaster subculture (Anderson, 1965) exists, use of public shelter tends to be low, with people primarily seeking shelter in the homes of friends or relatives.

Another issue periodically raised in the research literature is the question of how people who go to a particular place for shelter know of its availability. Often, it is argued that the warning message is the "proper" place to communicate information about shelter availability and researchers often assume this is the principal source of such information. Studies report, however, that comparatively small proportions of evacuees claim that they heard about the shelter to which they went as part of a warning message.

The way in which most evacuees "discover" the shelter facilities to which they eventually go is through the evacuee making the first contact. Especially in the case of those who find shelter with friends or relatives, most evacuees tend to initiate the contact which usually takes the form of a phone call. There are, however, two frequently observed departures from this pattern. Evacuees sometimes report that they knew of the availability of the shelter they chose because it was part of their family emergency plan. One would expect thispattern to appear with greater relative frequency in communities characterized by recurrent disasters which afford citizens an opportunity—over time—to develop such family plans. A second pattern involves what Drabek (1969, p. 345) has described as "evacuation by invitation," whereby people residing in a flood-threatened part of Denver, Colorado, were contacted by relatives and friends who "invited" them to come to their homes. At the time, Drabek (1969, p. 346) suggested that "in localized disasters [i.e., floods with forewarning] of this type, the process is highly important." Two additional qualifiers are that this effect is intensified in communities with a history of recurrent disasters and that the longer the period of forewarning, the greater is the proportion of evacuations by invitation (Perry et al., 1981a).

From the standpoint of developing evacuation incentives, two interesting points may be derived from the previous discussion. First, when given an opportunity to choose, people tend to prefer to evacuate to the homes of friends and relatives rather than to public shelters. Second, the warning message is not necessarily the place where most people hear about the availability of shelter.

These points argue strongly for the development and use of reasonably flexible shelter plans for evacuees, particularly in small communities which are part of or close to large metropolitan areas. It may, for example, be both cost effective and efficient to use temporary "shelter checkpoints" where evacuees could report to gain additional information about the evacuation effort and then *either* depart to stay with friends or relatives or be assigned to stay in a public facility (cf. Fritz & Mathewson, 1957). Such a plan would minimize the need for elaborate and extensive shelter facilities, permit evacuees their choice of arrangements, and allow for a more careful accounting of those who do evacuate. Shelter checkpoints would also offer an ideal place for recording evacuees' names and their shelter destinations to facilitate the operation of "family message centers," where concerned relatives or friends from outside the disaster area could quickly find data on evacuees. This kind of shelter "accounting" also allows officials to keep a temporary record of who evacuated, how many evacuated, and where they went. This amounts of extending the system currently used, for example, by the Red Cross to register shelters users, to the larger population of evacuees. Note that a "shelter checkpoint" should be a specified destination in a "safe" area which could probably also be a public shelter. It should therefore *not* be confused with "roadside checkpoints" which tend to snarl traffic and generally impede the flow of evacuees from the threatened area.

Another variation on the traditional approach to public sheltering might involve distributing information to residents of frequently threatened areas that would describe in advance safe areas as well as routes to these areas for potential evacuees. Residents could then be instructed to make contact with friends or relatives in the safe area and arrange in advance for shelter in that home in the event of disaster impact. In this way as soon as an evacuation warning was issued, evacuees could depart, arrive at their host home (whether the home of a friend or relative) and simply call some official checkpoint to indicate that they were safely out of the area. Residents of threatened areas who could not locate family or friends in designated safe areas could either stay at a public shelter or perhaps through local civic organizations arrange to meet with residents of the safe area and discuss the possibility of potential shelter. It is acknowledged that this strategy is more useful in the case of riverine floods or civil defense type evacuations which are characterized by relatively predictable impact areas; its utility with hurricanes or other disasters where scope of impact is great and direction and place of impact varies widely is probably limited.

Finally, research indicates that citizens infrequently report that the warning message was the source of information about the availability of the place to which they evacuated. In general the modal pattern seems to involve a citizen receiving a warning message and then making phone calls to (1) confirm the message and (2) find a place to go. Another possible incentive, then, would involve developing warning and evacuation information centers. Citizens could be instructed to contact these centers for warning confirmation and/or more detailed instructions regarding shelter. Such a system could be based on telephone or radio contact and could also serve a rumor control function. Furthermore, since confirming instructions could be somewhat standardized, such centers would minimize problems which traditionally arise when citizens receive contradictory or conflicting warning messages and instructions while seeking confirmation or specific evacuation information.

It should be noted here that a difficulty frequently cited with strategies such as the above which involve the use of telephones is the problem of snarled communications. Fritz and Mathewson (1957) discussed telephone convergence on a disaster area as a significant problem. In fact, many disaster planning handbooks emphasize that one should never advise citizens to use their telephone (Healy, 1969; Leonard, 1973). It is also well known that such rules are systematically violated; people call into an area to check on relatives and residents call out to issue reassurance to friends and relatives as well as to call for official confirmation warnings. Since the late 50s and early 60s when many of the studies suggested avoiding telephones were conducted, technical advances have been made in the telephone industry. Quarantelli and Taylor (1977) argue that technical innovation, coupled with the idea that people disobey the request not to use telephones anyway, is sufficient to suggest that evacuation incentives (such as those described above) which utilize some telephone contacts are not at all infeasible.

An additional option which does not depend exclusively upon telephones involves broadcasting, on a continual basis, relevant information about the hazard and about evacuation procedures and destinations. The broadcast medium could be either radio or television (assuming the local availability of both), but it is important that the station be officially designated as the community's source for disaster information *and* that the public be aware of this designation. Establishing *credibility* of the warning source can be nearly as important as the information disseminated. It should be mentioned that, in recent years, the Emergency Broadcast System (EBS) "has been expanded so that it can also be used during day-to-day emergencies at the state and local levels" (Defense Civil Preparedness Agency, 1978, p. 2). Thus, it may be possible to simplify such a warning and evacuation information dissemination strategy by working within EBS.

Transportation

The coordination and use of evacuation plans involve issues which do *not* arise in connection with emergency response plans where the protective actions necessary do not involve the *movement* of people. When a warning message calls for evacuation, local officials are asking people to undertake a specific adaptive action where timing is often critically important and effective adaptation of the community as a whole depends upon a coordinated exodus. There are two possible lines along which one might approach the problem of developing incentives related to transportation: one can attempt to more effectively regulate the cars on the road or attempt to develop a system of regulated "official" transportation.

Most people who evacuate leave in their family car and consequently, especially when one thinks of people who use relatives' and friends' vehicles also, there are a large number of cars on the road at about the same time which must somehow be channeled out of the area to be evacuated. Numerous studies have indicated that evacuations can be more effectively accomplished if the people involved have a plan—a route of egress and safe destination. This also helps to minimize traffic coordination difficulties as well as the problem of families *not* evacuating or evacuating to an even more dangerous location (cf. Drabek, 1969; Hamilton et al., 1955; Lachman et al., 1961; Sillar, 1975).

Since available research findings do suggest that people who are not given an evacuation plan are slow to take action, one transportation-related incentive to evacuate could center upon the establishment of safe destination and plausible route information which could be distributed to citizens in advance as part of general community emergency preparation. Such a plan need not be particularly elaborate and could be made available to the public in the form of a labeled map. The Federal Emergency Management Agency has plans to disseminate such maps via newspapers in connection with its Crisis Relocation Planning (Defense Civil Preparedness Agency, 1978), but the same kind of maps could be printed on index cards for public distribution. Particularly in the case of riverine floods, where flood plains and patterns might be known, such a plan would put important information on how to leave into the hands of the population to be evacuated. More importantly, however, specific instructions on routes and destinations could help to minimize traffic coordination problems by taking into account road capacities and other traffic flow variables.

Another approach to transportation incentives that would minimize the material citizens must maintain until an evacuation is necessary involves making detailed route and destination information available at the time of warning. This could be accomplished using either of two strategies. As we suggested in the preceding section, citizens could be given a telephone number, either in advance or as part of the warning message, to call for detailed evacuation instructions. Upon calling the number, citizens could report their location and be given appropriate evacuation instructions for that position. Note that especially when warnings are delivered via mass media, this telephonein strategy serves numerous functions simultaneously: (1) the call confirms the warning message, (2) helps the individual to determine whether he/she is in the area to be evacuated (i.e., personal risk assessment), and (3) helps the individual obtain information on safe destinations and exit routes. This type of plan has the disadvantage that it would probably involve special—and expensive—modifications to telephone equipment to handle high volumes of calls.

In some communities, particularly very small ones, evacuation warnings are routinely issued on a face-to-face basis; designated emergency officials—often fire fighters or police officers—issue the warning to each household in the threatened area. In such cases, officials could explain the warning and hand residents a single sheet of paper with map and other appropriate instructions. In itself, this procedure would speed and simplify the evacuation process, since details (to which the citizen could refer later) would be supplied in written form and only a minimum verbal explanation would be needed. The amount of lead time and the number of personnel available for delivering warnings serve as limiting factors when this strategy is used. This strategy, and any other approach which involves predetermining evacuation routes or destinations, is of use only when emergency managers can accurately forecast likely impact areas so that the plans in fact send citizens to safe locations.

Finally another approach to evacuation incentives related to transportation which does not involve the strategy of regulating the direction and flow of private vehicles through an emphasis upon routes and plans can be derived from addressing the problem of transporting evacuees to shelter in vehicles controlled by emergency managers. Most evacuation plans assume that the majority of evacuees will supply their own transportation, but limited official transportation is routinely made available to account for citizens who have no vehicle and cannot otherwise arrange transportation or for moving institutionalized or handicapped citizens. An incentive to evacuate can be found in systematizing and publicizing the availability of this transportation. This can be accomplished by specifying departure times and locations for official transportation either as part of a community emergency plan or within the warning message itself. While it is known that most families tend to transport themselves, those unable to do so would be given an opportunity to evacuate in an orderly fashion, even on short notice

(Drabek & Stephenson, 1971, p. 200). Furthermore, if evacuees can be transported in designated emergency vehicles, the number of cars on the road is reduced, increasing the ease with which an area can be evacuated.

Role of the Family

Since Lewis Killian's (1952) classic study of role performance in disasters, investigators have been sensitive to the influence of the family on behavior under stressful circumstances. With respect to evacuation, it is known that families tend to evacuate as units (cf. Drabek & Boggs, 1968; Perry et al., 1981a) and that the separation of family members often involves anxiety and attempts by evacuees to reunite families, sometimes by returning to previously evacuated areas (cf. Fritz & Mathewson, 1957; Quarantelli & Dynes, 1972; Titmuss, 1950). Other investigators have pointed out, however, that keeping families united is not necessarily as important as simply having information available regarding the whereabouts of family members (cf. Haas et al., 1976; Hans & Sell, 1974, p. 49). This reasoning suggests that evacuation would be facilitated if some means were available through which families could communicate if separated. The establishment of "family message centers," where *evacuees* could obtain information on the whereabouts and condition of family members, could be included in evacuation shelter planning and may be seen as an incentive for compliance with an evacuation warning. Similar systems have been used in Darwin, Australia, after the Christmas 1974 cyclone and proved to be relatively effective.

Such a family message center—which would of course only maintain minimal, short-term records—could be structured around a shelter check-in system like those described in earlier sections of this chapter. It must be remembered that check-in systems, message centers and virtually any evacuation "incentive" also involves a cost in terms of time and effort both on the part of emergency personnel *and* evacuees.

Both the American Red Cross (Simes, 1978) and the Salvation Army (Cline, 1976) have programs which center upon locating disaster victims and "registration" procedures at shelters. With additional support, these existing programs may be expandable into "family message centers" which would process and disseminate information on families which had evacuated some threatened area. Thus, a message center could be structured along the lines of a "check-in" service for evacuees. It is possible that the center itself could be centralized and accessed by telephone: different shelters could call with name lists as available and people who wished to use the service but not use public shelters could report directly to the central location.

Security and Property Protection

There is a large volume of field research which indicates that the problem of looting is rare in natural disaster (cf. Quarantelli & Dynes, 1970, p. 168).

Indeed, looting apparently occurs so infrequently that it is unnecessary and perhaps even a poor use of personnel to deploy police or national guard troops in large number to guard evacuated areas. Dynes et al. (1972, p. 33) argue that only *symbolic* security measures are necessary to "create the illusion" of property protection. It is probable that the idea of symbolic security is a reasonable approach to real problems of property protection. We must consider, however, not necessarily the real problems, but the evacuees' *perceptions* of the problem, when designing evacuation incentives.

It is widely assumed by disaster researchers that if evacuees feel that their property will be safe from potential looters, they will be more likely to comply with an evacuation program. Although it should beindicated that short term evacuation probably objectively minimizes the need for protective forces, the literature on evacuee perceptions as well as our data suggest that security remains an important concern (Dynes et al., 1972, p. 34). Hence, as part of an incentive program, local communities could communicate the general nature of whatever official security measures will be undertaken to the public. As Dynes indicates, such measures need not be elaborate; the purpose of communicating them is to inform potential evacuees that some measures *are* being taken. This contributes to the citizens' view of official efforts as "having the situation well in hand," and would tend to relieve the potential evacuee of any concern that "I have to guard myself."

If efficiency is an important concern, it may be worthwhile to incorporate community members into the protection process. This would involve assigning a few selected individuals security duties within their own neighborhoods. These people would coordinate with local police departments and act much like auxiliary police personnel. Such a program would appear to be particularly useful since it would free some police personnel for other work, reduce slightly the number of residents who would have to be evacuated simultaneously, and provide the "peace of mind" security described by Dynes. This would also help to convince the citizens that they are part of their own community protection plan—a circumstance which enhances citizen participation in community preparedness plans.

This review of incentives to evacuate is meaningful largely in the context of planning to manage the *consequences* of natural and man-made disasters. Of course, incentives do not constitute an evacuation plan. At best, they should be seen as suggestions for structuring some elements of a plan. Furthermore, the enumeration of incentives presented here is meant to be suggestive rather than exhaustive. One important objective of this section has been to underscore the idea that research can be productively used in the planning process.

The incentives described here are based upon or drawn from empirical research on people's performance under disaster conditions. This reflects the view, expressed in Chapter VI, that it is important to build emergency planning around people's known reaction patterns. Too often emergency plans which are administratively devised turn out to be based upon misconceptions of how people react (cf. Drabek & Stephenson, 1971, p. 202; Dynes et al., 1972, p. 31) and, therefore, potentially create more difficulties than they solve. In the final analysis, it would appear to be wise to develop emergency plans which guide and channel citizen actions into complementary and productive protection behavior patterns.

EVALUATING EMERGENCY RESPONSE PLANS

This book has been devoted to examining the problem of citizen decision-making in emergencies, the process of hazard management, and techniques for the design and implementation of community evacuation plans. Throughout, an attempt has been made to communicate both general principles of emergency management and specific strategies for the use of evacuations as a tool for protecting endangered citizens in a variety of natural and man-made threats. Furthermore, in the process of examining evacuation-related problems, considerable attention has been given to the more general issue of emergency response planning. In this case, emergency response planning refers to the broader environment of which evacuation plans are only one part. In terms of comprehensive emergency management, reference is made to the plans for activities which are anticipated to occur in the response phase; namely the authorities' strategy for responding to any given emergency, whether it be the derailment of a tank car carrying liquid natural gas or the impact of a riverine flood.

It is possible to characterize the extent to which any particular community is "prepared" for an emergency along a variety of dimensions. There are numerous theoretical approaches to defining preparedness, as well as some very specific "checklist oriented" strategies for assessing the likely capability of local authorities or specific organizations to respond to emergencies (Commonwealth of Virginia, 1980; Defense Civil Preparedness Agency, 1978; Federal Emergency Management Agency, 1980; Hanson, 1981; Hildebrand, 1980). The purpose of this closing section is to sketch out six general criteria along which a local emergency manager or interested official or citizen may characterize the emergency response plans of his community or organization.

In effect, the emphasis here is not upon evaluation in the traditional sense, but upon a broad schema for constructive self-criticism. Indeed, it seems that in recent years there has been an incredible proliferation of written "emergency response" plans, some mandated by law, some due to public pressure, others simply traditionally done, and far too few created strictly in the hope of better emergency management. Faced with a maze of plans—many of which are "filed" with local government emergency services offices—both emergency managers and citizens need a simple way of thinking about, and ultimately understanding, emergency response plans. Emergency managers may have a dozen plans on file from different governmental or private organizations and need to understand how such plans, which by necessity will probably involve overlapping use of community resources, can be coordinated. Also, emergency managers are frequently asked to review plans and classify them into the broad categories of "being adequate" or "in need of improvement." The objective of this section is to sketch out six criteria along which emergency response plans can be assessed.

Six aspects of the process of responding to emergencies have been selected as evaluative criteria: the problem of notification, damage assessment, public information, protective strategy, responsibility for planning and operations, and personnel training. These criteria reflect issues already discussed in this chapter and Chapter VI regarding the management of emergencies in general and specifically the problem of evacuation. It should be mentioned that these criteria are not chosen because they are exhaustive, representing all important features of emergency response strategies. Instead, they should be seen as minimum requirements; six issues which must be addressed in the process of responding to an emergency. Furthermore, the elaboration of the criteria is not done with any specific type of emergency in mind. They are meant to be general enough to apply to both man-made and natural threats.

Finally, criteria for the evaluation of emergency response plans can be considered to fall into two classes: substantive criteria and supporting criteria. Substantive criteria deal with the adequacy of the content of the plan. This includes the areas of notification, damage assessment, public information, and protective strategy. Supporting criteria refer to those aspects of the plan that address non-operational or noncrisis needs. These criteria, responsibility for planning and operations, and personnel training, deal more with the initiation and maintenance of the plan than with the operation or implementation of the plan.

Notification

A discussion of substantive evaluative criteria logically starts with the onset of the threat. That is, the point at which local emergency managers either detect or are otherwise notified of an environmental threat can be seen as the beginning of the emergency response process. If we use town or county emergency managers as our point of reference, the origin of the alert that they receive depends to a certain extent upon the nature of the threat agent. For example, notice of riverine floods and tornadoes usually comes from the National Weather Service, notice that a hazardous materials transportation accident has occurred may come from either the shipper of the material or its carrier, or in the event of a nuclear power plant accident notice might come from the plant operator, the Nuclear Regulatory Commission or a state department of emergency services. Citizens, of course, have also been important sources of reporting apparent environmental threats to local authorities. The point here is that authorities may be informed of a potential threat from one, or more likely some combination of sources. This suggests that an emergency response plan should contain provisions for two kinds of activity relative to the problem of notification. First, a procedure should exist that allows local authorities to *receive* notification of environmental threats on a round-the-clock basis. Usually this is achieved by establishing a "duty officer" concept in some form. In some larger emergency services department, a rotating duty system which keeps one or more persons at the office to actually monitor incoming communications may be developed. In other cases, arrangements may be made with routine sources of threat information—National Weather Service, U.S. Geological Survey, etc.—to call in reports after hours to designated emergency services personnel. To be fully effective, such an approach should also include arrangements with local fire department, police, and county and state police to notify emergency services personnel when citizen (or private organization) reports of environmental threats are received. Without regard to what procedure is ultimately employed, this aspect of notification should receive explicit attention in an emergency response plan.

The second aspect of notification of interest here is that emergency managers, once alerted themselves, should have a plan to notify other offices or organizations which might play a role in responding to the environmental threat. This notification process should end only when all of the parties that have a duty or capacity to respond to the emergency have been informed. The need for such a process arises as a function of the role of local emergency managers as coordinators of the response to a community emergency. Again, the particular people and offices notified will vary among different threat-agents. In all cases, though, the essential functions of notification is to identify the organizations which will be responding, alert these organizations that they should begin to coordinate their own communications, and initiate the emergency response process itself. Thus, it is necessary for emergency managers to establish explicit criteria for determining who is likely to initiate the notification process, which parties they should notify, which communications channels are available and should be used, and what information should be transmitted.

This process of notification should be expected to differ among jurisdictions (i.e., whether a city, county or state is involved), among different types of hazard (natural or man-made), and in some cases with respect to different threat agents (e.g., if nuclear waste is involved in a transportation accident, the Nuclear Regulatory Commission must appear among those notified). As an example, let us consider the problem—and likely flow of events—associated with a transportation incident which involves a radiological threat. In most cases, it is to be expected that the driver of the truck or crew of a train will, as employees of the carrier, make an attempt to notify their dispatcher and a state or local police office. In any event, it is quite likely that local or state police will be the "first agency on the scene." The first on the scene will, in turn, notify other local and state agencies including the lead state agency which will inform still other agencies at the state and local level and make the link to the federal response system. In view of the preeminent responsibility of the states for the health and safety of their citizens and the role of the carrier as an agent of the shipper, it is common for these parties to play leading roles in responding to the incident. The length of time that it takes to notify these lead parties could, under certain circumstances, take an appreciable period of time. A serious truck accident involving the death of a driver, might, for example, produce such a delay. To date however, notification times have been reassuringly small. Hornsby, Ortloff, and Smith for example, reported on a yellow cake spill in southeast Colorado in which the shipper was notified within approximately one hour of the truck wreck by the local county sheriff's office. This was in spite of the fact that the accident took place in a rural area in the middle of the night and the driver of the truck was pinned inside the truck cab (Hornsby et al., 1978). Taylor (1978) reports notification times of 10 and 20 minutes for a train derailment and a truck accident, respective, and notes a one and a half hour lag in receiving notification of a different train derailment. In all three cases these times refer to the length of time it took to notify the *shipper*. He does not report the length of time that it took to notify the local authorities. Finally, there should be a recognition that the information to be transmitted to the state's lead agency for radiation control will be coming from personnel who may have little familiarity with radioactive materials. Consequently, it is desirable to have standardized forms available to agencies likely to be first on the scene so that the appropriate information can be obtained in a timely manner.

Damage Assessment

Damage assessment is probably most often thought of in terms of post-disaster impact activities. That is, it is something done in connection with determining eligibility for different types of "disaster declarations" which are in turn related to the nature of extra-community aid for which a jurisdiction may apply. In fact, damage assessment should be a *continuing process* that begins during disaster impact and is completed well into the post-impact phase. Conceptualized this way, damage assessment becomes part of a feedback process to emergency managers that provides information regarding community status *vis-à-vis* the relevant disaster threat. Emergency managers use such information in deciding how resources should be initially deployed, as well as for deciding how to shift or redeploy resources to take into account changes in the impact pattern of the environmental threat. For example, in managing emergency response to a riverine flood, after an initial dike or levee failure, a damage assessment party may report other weak spots in the levee which might be sand-bagged (or otherwise reinforced) to prevent damage from a second breach.

It should be noted that, particularly in the case of certain types of man-made threats such as those associated with hazardous materials, damage assessment may not always be a simple or straightforward process. For example, specialized instruments are required to accurately assess the magnitude and location of a release of radioactive material or to confirm that no release has occurred. This can pose a more substantial problem for emergency workers than does the need for speedy notification of an accident in the first place. Although information can be transmitted instantaneously, the transport of specialized equipment takes time. In some situations this means that uncertainty persists for some time as to the location and magnitude of release of hazardous materials. In some incidents, knowledge of the nature of the material being transported, together with the visual inspection of the integrity of the container can reliably confirm that no threat exists. In other situations, only the use of the appropriate sensing instruments can be expected to clearly identify the location and magnitude of the hazard. Speedy deployment of these instruments to the incident site can be greatly facilitated if there is a centralized inventory of resources available for radioalogical assessment. This may include the location of instruments and the identity and location of personnel trained in their use.

Public Information

One of the most significant problems in dealing with the public in an emergency is the tremendous confusion that can be generated when each involved party supplies information directly to the public. The ambiguous or conflicting statements that can result shake the public's confidence in the ability of those in authority to effectively safeguard lives and property. The data presented in Chapters II and III show how this operated at Three Mile Island. Previous research on natural disasters indicates that the public is disposed to comply with the legitimate requests of those in authority, even if the requests result in some level of discomfort or extra effort and expense. Thus, every emergency response plan should contain provisions for transmitting information both to the public-at-risk (those immediately subject to the environmental threat) *and* to the public-at-large. Communications to the public-at-risk should be identified as emergency warning or advisory messages and subject to the rules of message construction presented earlier in this chapter. Emergency managers also need to develop plans to communicate with the general public who are *not* believed to be at risk. At a minimum, authorities need to have a capacity to disseminate information which allows citizens to determine whether or not they are at risk. This procedure was not well handled, for example, during the reactor accident at Three Mile Island and seems to have resulted in many citizens defining themselves as in danger when from a technical standpoint they probably were not. From the standpoint of managing an emergency, inappropriate definition of risk by citizens can be very problematic. Having too many people incorrectly define themselves as in danger could, if evacuations were involved, result in unnecessary clogging of exit routes. Having too few people define themselves as in danger introduces the problem of slow warning response times and general hesitance to comply with suggested protective measures.

Protective Strategy

Every emergency response plan should contain provisions for choosing a means of protecting threatened citizens from harm. Obviously, the appropriate protective strategy varies with both the nature and with the magnitude of the environmental threat. Although there are cases where a single protective option is appropriate—for example evacuation in response to a severe riverine flood—it is often possible to specify different protective options for a single threat. In the case of volcanic eruptions, one might consider advising the public to stay indoors and wear protective masks in the event of light ashfall, or if the ash fall is heavy or mudflows threaten, evacuation may be appropriate. The importance of carefully considering protective strategies is perhaps most pronounced in connection with man-made threats. For example, in some transportation-related incidents involving hazardous materials, it may not be possible for the employees of the carrier, personnel from the first agency on the scene, or other responsible parties to immediately isolate the area affected by the accident and to control access to this area. It is, in addition, desirable that those not experienced in the handling of incidents involving radioactive materials be made aware of the necessity of accounting for persons who might have been exposed to radiation so that they may be examined for evidence of contamination or, subsequently, for adverse effects of exposure. Inventories of equipment suitable for establishing an exclusionary area should be available on a ready basis to local emergency services personnel, if not, they should be carried on the transport vehicle. The location of medical facilities available for the treatment of contaminated emergency response personnel and victims should be accessible on short enough notice that this consideration would not be an obstacle to rapid treatment of victims. Even more desirable than detaining persons possibly exposed, is the rapid achievement of an onsite capability for radiological monitoring and decontamination of emergency personnel and others. Protective action guides should be made available in order to regulate the exposure of emergency personnel to radiation.

Responsibility for Planning and Operations

An emergency response plan should clearly indicate the authority under which the plan has been written, and the standards by which assignment of responsibility for various functions under the plan are made. There should be documentation that potential inter-organizational ambiguities have been resolved to the satisfaction of all parties likely to be involved. These inter-organizational problems include relationships among agencies at a given level of government, inter-level relationships as well as relationships between public agencies and private sector parties.

Personnel Training

Perhaps the most frequently slighted of all the desired characteristics of an emergency response system deals with the level of effort put into testing the system to determine its effectiveness and efficiency under fairly realistic conditions. Exercising the system requires that all parties have copies of the plan, are aware of their responsibilities, and follow through the steps necessary to perform their functions. This requires regular—at least once a year—exercises of the plan which need to be observed and critiqued by qualified observers. In some jurisdictions, certain *portions* of the plan will be tested many times a year as a function of responding to real environmental threats. This may give grounds for confidence in the ability of the agencies involved to respond effectively, but should not lead to overconfidence in the ability of the plan as a whole to produce effective response in situations which have not been tested.

Among other valuable contributions, exercises can identify hidden problems that might delay or even prevent successful accomplishment of an agency's prescribed response function. For example, in one exercise for a fixed nuclear facility, the agency responsible for identifying evacuation areas did not discover until the plant personnel notified them of the affected zones and sectors, that their map of the county did not indicate true north. As a consequence, they could not orient their overlays so as to accurately identify the areas requiring evacuation. The result was a significant delay in the initiation of the evacuation.

Chapter VIII

Prospect: Evacuation and Comprehensive Emergency Management

The preceding seven chapters of this book have covered, in varying degrees of specificity, a large number of issues related to community emergency management. Initially an attempt was made to describe comprehensive emergency management as a philosophy and approach to dealing with environmental threats. This included discussions of the tasks associated with managing emergencies, the actors involved in the United States emergency management system and the tools at their disposal for accomplishing their missions. Specific interest was then shifted to the use of pre-impact evacuation as a generic function for managing some types of emergencies. After a discussion of evacuation as a social process, data were analyzed on citizen evacuations in connection with a flood, a volcanic eruption, and a nuclear reactor emergency. We then began an *inductive* exercise drawing upon our data and the results of other research efforts and constructed, in Chapter IV, a conceptual model wherein the relationships among important factors in evacuation warning compliance were described. In Chapter V a second model was *induced* from the research literature to explain the likely short-run and long-run psychological consequences of natural and man-made disasters. In connection with both models, care was taken to describe implications for emergency management. Subsequently, in Chapters VI and VII, a *deductive* process, using the model built in Chapter IV as a base, was employed to identify emergency management practices compatible with our knowledge of citizen behavior in disasters. Thus the task undertaken in preparing this volume was ambitious; perhaps beyond the skills of any social scientist. At best it is intended to provide some conceptual clarification of comprehensive emergency management and an integrated review of evacuation as a generic function. At worst, it could be seen

161

as an encyclopedia of evacuation research and practice. In this chapter, we will briefly review the problems of comprehensive emergency management and the role of evacuation as a generic function, with an eye toward future developments.

COMPREHENSIVE EMERGENCY MANAGEMENT

The general aim of this book has been to examine evacuation planning and implementation within the context of comprehensive emergency management. To say the least, this has not been a simple or straight-forward task because conceptually, comprehensive emergency management is not particularly well elaborated. Formally speaking, it is a realtively new idea, introduced in 1978. The genesis of CEM is probably best understood in terms of the *convergence* of changes in the way governments approached the administrative organization of dealing with disasters and the way in which disaster management itself was viewed.

At the federal level, there have been agencies charged with managing domestic and defense emergencies since Franklin D. Roosevelt's first administration. Initially these agencies were housed in the White House or the War Department, and focused either on civil defense or any of a variety of domestic emergencies, beginning with the Great Depression. In 1950, President Harry S. Truman established separate agencies for dealing with war-related emergencies and natural disasters, thereby creating a distinction between technological and natural disaster threats that persisted for decades.

Beginning with the Kennedy administration in 1961, the Office of Emergency Planning, which became the Office of Emergency Preparedness (OEP) in 1968, was given the responsibility of planning for and responding to domestic disasters, primarily those perpetrated by natural agents. OEP was first located in the White House and subsequently house in the executive office of the president. During most of this time, protecting citizens from war-related and some other technological threats was the task of the Office of Civil Defense which became the Defense Civil Preparedness Agency (DCPA) in 1972. Both these agencies were part of the Department of Defense.

In1973, while the civil defense function remained in a single agency, President Nixon dissolved the Office of Emergency Preparedness by executive order and transferred its primary functions to other federal agencies. Thus, first the Office of Preparedness (1973–1975) and then the Federal Preparedness Agency (FPA), both part of the General Services Administration, were charged with supervising and coordinating federal readiness for natural disasters (Perry, 1982, p. 7). The Federal Disaster Assistance Administration (FDAA), established in the Department of Housing and Urban Development, was assigned primary responsibility for assisting victims of natural disasters.

This configuration of federal disaster planning and response agencies persisted into the late 1970s. Also through the 1970s, both the Congress and the executive branch expressed concern that federal programs for disaster management were too fragmented. It was argued that this fragmentation hampered effective disaster planning and response, masked duplicate efforts, and made national emergency preparedness a very expensive enterprize. The director of FPA (General Leslie W. Bray) acknowledged that when the emergency preparedness function was removed from the executive office of the president and assignedsubagency status, many people believed that the function had been down-graded, or given lower priority, and his job of coordination became more difficult. The states argued simultaneously that their task of planning for and responding to disasters was complicated and hampered because they were forced to deal with and coordinate among so many federal agencies. In 1975, a study of these problems sponsored by the Federal Preparedness Agency concluded that:

> The civil preparedness system as it exists today is fraught with problems that seriously hamper its effectiveness even in peacetime disasters . . . It is a system where literally dozens of agencies, often with duplicate, overlapping, and even conflicting responsibilities, interact. (Joint Committee on Defense Production, 1976, p. 27)

In addition to these administrative and structural difficulties, there was also concern that the scope of the tasks performed as emergency management was too narrow. Furthermore, the issue was raised that too many resources were devoted to disaster response and recovery and too few to the problems of prevention and control.

It was in response to these concerns that the Carter administration began the process of reorganizing federal agencies charged with emergency management in 1978. As we pointed out in Chapter I, this reorganization resulted in the creation of the Federal Emergency Management Agency. The three major federal disaster agencies—FPA, FDAA and DCPA—were consolidated within the new agency along with several other smaller programs, including the National Weather Service Community Preparedness Program, dam safety coordination, the Earthquake Hazard Reduction Office, Federal Insurance Administration, National Fire Prevention and Control Administration, the warning and emergency broadcast system, and a terrorism management program. As a federal agency, FEMA is still in the process of evolving; there have been and probably will continue to be changes in organizational structure and in the way FEMA relates to other organizations in its environment. From the perspective of the structure of the emergency management system in America, the important issue here is that FEMA was created and exists as a single federal focal point for emergency management. To a certain extent, the FEMA structure was also recreated (or in some cases already existed) in states where state emergency services departments became more important focal points in emergency management. These structural changes in the way emergency management was administered set the stage for a fuller acceptance and implementation of an "all hazards" approach to emergency preparedness and response.

The second component of the growth of the philosophy of comprehensive emergency management deals with changes in the way that the task of managing emergencies themselves were viewed. This refers to a question that has also been given much attention in earlier chapter of this book; namely, what activities go into emergency management? As the previous discussion implies, the fragmented state of federal agencies charged with emergency preparedness and response for so many years encouraged both practitioners and researchers to compartmentalize research and management of different environmental threats. This tendency to separate different threats was also encouraged by the aforementioned "descriptive and journalistic" approach to disaster research that concentrated on recounting human responses to disasters grouped in terms of disaster agents (fire, hurricane, flood, etc.) rather than emphasizing a broader social scientific approach to human behavior in emergencies (Gillespie & Perry, 1976).

Beginning in the 1950s with the field studies of human response to disasters conducted by the Nation Opinion Research Corporation (University of Chicago) a transition in disaster reserach began. Under the leadership of Charles E. Fritz, this research effort began a trend toward increased concern with the development of conceptual schemes for understanding and *explaining* human response to disasters in general. Thus, the thrust of social scientific research began to turn *from* describing disaster events *to* understanding the demands and stresses resulting from disaster impact and cataloguing various strategies for coping with such demands and stresses. In 1954, Fritz joined the staff of the Committee on Disaster Studies of the National Academy of Sciences-National Research Council and continued to promote the analytic study of disaster events. Indeed, the 19 volumes of disaster studies generated by the NAS-NRC committee are still viewed as classics of disaster research and until 1963 served as primary examples of the analytic study of disasters. It is of great significance historically that these studies dealt with all types of disasters, natural, man–made and civil defense-related. Thus was laid the empirical groundwork of case studies which became so important in early work on the question of the possibility of cross-hazard comparisons of human disaster response.

In 1963, Enrico L. Quarantelli—a veteran of the NORC studies—established with Russell R. Dynes the Disaster Research Center (DRC) at Ohio State University. This was an important event in the conceptual growth of disaster research for two reasons. First, DRC continued (as it still does) the tradition of conducting studies of all types of disaster agents with a focus upon analyzing both disaster management practices and citizen behavior. Second, DRC represented a focal *place* for the social scientific study of disasters and an institution for training and credentialing disaster *researchers*. Another important aspect of the work at DRC is that under the sponsorship of the Office of Civil Defense and later the Defense Civil Preparedness Agency, studies of natural and man-made disasters were conducted which included discussions of the applicability of research findings to understanding human behavior inthe event of a nuclear attack on the United States. However humble these early comparisons may have been (cf. Kreps, 1981), they were the first systematic attempts to generalize findings about citizen response in natural disasters to what had previously been thought of as radically different kinds of disaster events. For our purposes, their importance is not to be seen so much in terms of advances in the depth of our knowledge of disaster management and response as in their contributions to the idea that at least some knowledge of behavior in natural disasters might apply to man-made disasters as well.

The Disaster Research Center was largely sociologists, and drew students not only from the United States, but other countries as well. Over time, the community of "disaster researchers" expanded as other university-based programs developed. Disaster researchers began to contact and coordinate with other scholars and researchers from other disciplines with a much longer history of studying natural hazards; particularly geographers, geologists and natural resource managers. Thus grew the idea, as well as the empirical study, of the possible applications of hazard management and human response principles across different hazard agents. The question of leadership here is certainly subject to argument depending upon one's perspective. The movement associated with DRC can be seen either as a guiding force (as it certainly was for sociologists) or as the joining of relative newcomers with the older tradition of hazards research among geographers and related environmental scientists. What remains important, however, is that during the 1960s there developed among researchers a tolerance for the idea that what is known about some types of disasters might be usefully applied to other types of disasters.

From the perspective of those who used the results of disaster and hazard studies in managing the consequences of such environmental threats, the growth of the idea of the utility of cross-hazard comparisons had important implications for issues of implementation. As we pointed out in Chapter I, disaster management at the local level has long been an enterprize forced to consider problems of preparedness, response and recovery in connection with many different types of environmental threats. This broad concern was probably less a matter of insightful emergency management than a realization that in the end, local jurisdictions had to bear the brunt of the consequences of natural and man-made disasters. At the federal level, however, the idea of multiple applications of disaster studies at least in part spawned what became known as a "dual use" philosophy. As instituted by the Defense Civil Preparedness Agency, dual use meant that sponsored research should be analyzed and elaborated in such a way that any potential applications to the problems of preparing for and responding to a nuclear attack were elucidated. Coupled with the already growing interest among researchers in exploring cross-hazard comparisons, the adoption of a dual use philosophy mandated that some comparisons be made between threats which were considered radically different. One might argue that the comparison of such apparently diverse threats as nuclear attack and natural disasters made other comparisons—among natural disasters and between natural and man-made disasters—seem less extreme and more feasible.

By the late 1970s the user audience represented by the states and smaller jurisdictions was becoming more organized and more vocal regarding the issue of emergency management. Sponsored first by the Defense Civil Preparedness Agency and later by FEMA, the National Governors' Association launched a major emergency preparedness project. This milestone project approached the problem of emergency preparedness from the perspective of the states, and paid careful attention to the emergency management problems and practices of local (city and county) jurisdictions. It was in connection with this project that the term comprehensive emergency management was coined in an attempt to describe a philosophy that integrated all aspects of managing all types of environmental threats. The National Governors' Association subsequently through written reports and verbal exhortations vigorously promoted the acceptance of comprehensive emergency management in the research community, the federal government, the states and localities.

Therefore, comprehensive emergency management came onto the scene in the late 1970s, and was a function of changes in the way researchers viewed the study of different types of disasters, changes in the administrative structure of the federal apparatus for dealing with civil emergencies, and acknowledgement of the realities of disaster management that faced the states and smaller jurisdictions. CEM, as an idea, did not happen fast, but may be seen as the culmination of the convergence of several forces. The changes described above, which took place over decades, were involved in the emergence of the approach. Especially since it took such a long chain of events to reach the threshold upon which we now stand, one must be very cautious about projecting the future of comprehensive emergency management based upon less than one-half dozen years experience. Nonetheless, it is reasonable to offer a few brief comments about CEM and to review some issues which will loom large in the short-range future.

As a philosophy and an organizing concept, comprehensive emergency management is attractive. Indeed, CEM as a concern with all phases of all types of environmental threats has three very important appealing points: (1) it is parsimonious; (2) there is a consolidation of effort; and (3) there is potentially great efficiency relative to resource deployment. In practice, CEM is a complex enterprize that demands sustained attention. To implement CEM at any jurisdictional level—from city to federal—does not simply require renaming or repackaging traditional emergency management techniques and activities. As we pointed out at the close of Chapter III, too often in the past emergency authorities have persisted in operating based on myths and sometimes ignored knowledge which was available when responding to emergencies. Indeed, to successfully implement CEM, emergency managers must not only abandon problematic old practices, but must learn new practices and vigilantly employ them. Ideally, CEM results in the integration of management efforts and resources, directing them toward the common goal of protecting the public from environmental threats. Although the stage is set and progress toward this end is being made (however uneaven), it is not accurate to say that comprehensive emergency management has been yet implemented on any significant scale. To expect so at this point would probably be unreasonable though, especially considering the relative youth of the idea.

One can examine the short-range future of comprehensive emergency management by saying that progress toward achieving the ideal discussed above and in Chapter I will depend upon the resolution of four major issues. First, for CEM to develop beyond its present state requires continued growth of an emergency management system in the United States. CEM is closely tied to the existence of a network of emergency services organizations wherein mutual obligations for support and coordination are recognized. Much of the administrative or bureaucratic structure of a national system for managing emergencies has been created since 1979. Large portions of this structure, particularly at the state and federal levels, retain the status of ''paper plans''; enabling legislation or provisions have been made, but specific units are not operational. It is true that the development of an emergency management system requires time. In this process, however, one must sustain the emergency management offices and agencies that are created just as vigorously as one works toward establishing new components of the system. While the growth of an emergency management system can be (and is) a ''phased'' operation, careful attention must be given to following through at state and federal levels. If the phasing must become extended then a plan for implementation with appropriate milestones could be publicized as short-term evidence that progress is being made.

This discussion suggests a second issue upon which the future of CEM depends. Comprehensive emergency management is public policy—or is reflected in legislation more traditionally termed public policy—and as such depends upon intergovernmental relations. Although the federal component is an influential part of the emergency management system, acting alone it cannot assure the implementation of comprehensive emergency management. CEM cannot appropriately be seen as a ''top down'' planning and response activity; to function effectively it must be a network operation. Therefore, not only must federal, state and local components follow through in developing specific structures for emergency management, but the components must continue to coordinate among themselves to avoid recreating the collection of disconnected and conflicting organizations that existed at the time of the 1976 Federal Preparedness Administration study. As we pointed out in Chapter VI, comprehensive emergency management is achieved through the interaction of federal, state and local political and emergency authorities. To the extent that intergovernmental relations are characterized by a spirit of cooperation in pursuing a common goal, achievement of CEM is enhanced. Lower levels of cooperation can be expected to result in a more uneven and fragmented implementation.

The growth of comprehensive emergency management also depends upon the professional development of emergency managers. It has already been suggested that contemporary emergency managers require a quantity of specialized knowledge to effectively execute their jobs. Through FEMA and other specialized programs, some highly motivated emergency managers have already established considerable expertise. This kind of effort must be greatly expanded. To establish emergency management as a viable profession, emergency managers must identify a body of knowledge and skills necessary to execute the job. Then, a credentialing process must be adopted such that other emergency managers, political authorities, and the public can recognize a "trained" emergency manager. There are several possible avenues for credentialling emergency managers. One might, for example, expand existing programs offered by the FEMA-operated Emergency Management Institute so that after a prescribed curriculum was mastered a diploma could be awarded. An alternative approach might involve the establishment of an "Academy of Emergency Management" which could serve as a national professional association and also certify members via a system of standardized examinations. One distinct training advantage of this latter approach is that a course of studies necessary to take various examinations could be publicized and aspirants could pursue studies at local institutions—perhaps universities—to the greatest extent possible. This would minimize the need for a single, centralized training program, which might prove both administratively and financially difficult to establish and maintain.

Finally, the growth of comprehensive emergency management depends upon continued research on management procedures and generic functions in dealing with environmental threats. For emergency managers to effectively manage all phases of all types of emergencies, the research community must provide the basic information to execute the task. This requires that considerable attention be given to the study of generic functions in disasters and that a firm philosophy of cross-hazard comparisons in research be maintained. To achieve the kind of integrated knowledge necessary for comprehensive emergency management, researchers must pose and answer the question of how are management practices and citizen response *similar* in different threats. Of course it is important to identify unique aspects of emergencies, but a catalogue of differences will be less useful in the short-run to emergency managers than a catalogue of similarities among environmental threats. Furthermore, in the future as much research attention needs to be given to management techniques as has been devoted to citizen response in the past. The research community should not only suggest new techniques but should also provide evaluative information on the efficacy of new techniques as well as existing management practices.

While the resolution of each of the aforementioned issues has some bearing on the future of comprehensive emergency management, it is difficult to say at this juncture just what that future may be. While there may be some permanence to the new emergency management bureaucracy, reorganizations are not unknown in the history of the U.S. emergency management system. Also, each of the four issues represent broad goals which can only be achieved by the sustained actions of many individuals and organizations over a long period of time. Both these points greatly complicate projections of the future. Based upon general experiences with previous, although less pervasive, emergency planning and response programs, one can argue that resolution of the issues will be uneven, and hence progress toward implementing comprehensive emergency management will be slow. However slow, it appears that CEM is at least the direction in which fugure emergency management efforts will go. Perhaps the most important consequence of CEMs appearance on the scene is that it has contributed to an enhanced awareness of common goals among emergency managers nationally, and encouraged the opening of a dialogue among them regarding common problems. In themselves these developments are revolutionary and even if CEM fails altogether—which is unlikely—the way in which environmental threats are seen by the public, emergency services personnel, political authorities and hazards researchers has been fundamentally affected.

EVACUATION AS A GENERIC FUNCTION

Particular attention has been given to the design and implementation of community evacuations in this book. Care was taken to review and bring together in this volume most of the research results and administrative information available on the topic. We have covered the process of evacuation planning, the content of evacuation plans, strategies for citizen participation, and incentives for citizen compliance with evacuation warnings. An effort has also been made to discuss evacuation planning and response in the broader context of community hazards management, and guidelines have been offered for evaluating community emergency preparedness. In light of what has been written here, one might get the impression that hazards researchers know a great deal about evacuation. It is true that evacuation, or more generally warning response behavior, is a topic that dominates much of the existing disaster research literature. Rather than feelings of comfort, however, this condition should generate feelings of great concern among hazards researchers. Those who have worked with emergency managers in attempting to design or implement evacuation programs are only too aware of how many research questions remain unanswered. In fact, there is precious little research on inter-organizational coordination, citizen participation, and warning compliance incentives, to name just three areas. This is all the more disconcerting because evacuation *is* one of the better-studied of disaster phenomena; it emphasizes how little research is available on the full range of emergency management issues.

It would be inappropriate—and probably counter-productive—to attempt to summarize here all that has been said about evacuations in the preceding chapters. Instead, the *approach* used to examine the problem should be emphasized. The importance of the approach lies in what it implies for the study, as well as the implementation, of evacuations. In the past there has been a tendency to look at the problem of evacuating threatened populations as simply the movement of the people, without recognizing its status as part of ongoing emergency preparedness and without acknowledging that successful evacuations are dependent in many cases upon effective use of community resources. The approach taken here has attempted to address these difficulties in two ways. First, we have conceived of evacuation as a process, not an outcome, and have sought to discuss it in the context of the larger problem of community emergency management. One can think of evacuation—and other generic functions—as a tool, but not one to be picked up only when it's needed and laid down until the next emergency. To function effectively, evacuation programs require continuing attention as *part of the process of community emergency management.* Second, we have paid close attention to the links between what emergency managers do and how citizens respond. Many early studies have expertly documented citizen behavior, and some recent research has dealt with authorities' management of evacuations. At this point, however, too little research is available on citizen reactions to specific management techniques. The slim literature on incentives for citizen compliance with emergency warnings represents only a modest beginning of the research needed on how officials' actions can shape citizen behavior.

Finally, in the process of reviewing the evacuation literature upon which Chapters IV and V are based, two issues arose recurrently which demand some attention here. Both are related to the management of evacuations by authorities and merit attention both as objects of future research and as points requiring special attention from designers and implementors of evacuation plans. The first of these relates to the broader question of citizen adaptive behavior after receiving an evacuation warning. We have attempted to understand and account for not only why people evacuate or refuse, but also for other kinds of protective actions or contingencies citizens may adopt when they are warned to evacuate. Quarantelli et al. (1980) have pointed out that emergency managers who view evacuation decision-making as a zero-sum game—people either leave or stay—run the risk of not recognizing that evacuation warning recipients are a heterogeneous group who may respond in many different ways to a request to evacuate. Studies of several flood threats have shown that evacuation warning recipients often engage in a variety of responses—attending to environmental cues, property protection, personal protection, even preparations that fall short of leaving—which might be best seen as *approximations* of evacuation compliance (Perry et al., 1981b). In Chapter IV, we attempted to outline factors in citizen emergency decision-making processes that contributed to citizen choices to engage in a protective response *different* than the one suggested by authorities in the warning message. Engaging in protective actions other than those targeted by authorities potentially places citizens unnecessarily in danger and could inhibit evacuation compliance on the part of other citizens. From a research standpoint it is important that future study designs allow for detection of citizen adaptive responses which differ from target responses desired by authorities, and that citizen choice factors which correlate with such outcomes be identified. Emergency managers should anticipate that citizens may adopt a range of protective measures and allow some flexibility in emergency response plans and operations to accommodate such a contingency. To a certain extent, problems of warning noncompliance can be minimized through careful construction of warning messages which provide some reasoning for the suggested protective action and through public education and citizen involvement programs.

A second issue which merits further attention is the problem of interagency and inter-organizational coordination in evacuation management. At the close of Chapter III it was pointed out that the actual movement of citizens—withdrawal from the threatened area—generally proceeds fairly smoothly. Relative to movement, the two issues of primary concern were motivating people to comply with the warning to evacuate (addressed in Chapter VII) and insuring appropriate supervision of the exodus (addressed in Chapter VI). While attention to these concerns is important for improving the effectiveness of evacuation programs, it was also pointed out in Chapter III that their absence doesn't necessarily mean that withdrawal will be completely inhibited; 144,000 people managed to evacuate the area surrounding the Three Mile Island reactor with a minimum of official guidance. The issue which overshadows these concerns is the problem of poor organizational preparedness.

In Chapters VI and VII we emphasized the importance of developing horizontal and vertical linkages among emergency response organizations and between these organizations and other political and private organizations which play some role in emergency management. It was even suggested that when community emergency preparedness was evaluated considerable weight should be given to the presence or absence of such interorganizational ties and channels of communication. In this connection, three matters which demand the attention of emergency managers are: (1) making the establishment of inter-organizational ties a part of the evacuation planning process, (2) reaching and maintaining consensus among responder organizations regarding a division of labor or responsibility in evacuation operations, and (3) establishing a protocol for dealing with community organizations—both during periods of emergency and the "long run"—so that the collective resources of the community may become part of the emergency management process.

With regard to research implications, Quarantelli (1980a, p. 158) has reviewed the literature on evacuations and argued that four aspects of organizational behavior in evacuations remain almost wholly unstudied. These are organizational problems related to mobilizing community resources for evacuation, the administrative decision-making calculus used by emergency response organizations in reaching a decision to evacuate citizens, the effects of different patterns of inter-organizational coordination on the success of evacuation efforts, and organizational problems which arise in connection with sheltering and subsequent return of evacuees to their homes. At present all four of these areas represent blind spots or gaps in the record of cumulative research on the management of evacuations.

Another question involving emergency management organizations that parallels the areas of research concern outlined by Quarantelli is the idea of drills or tests of evacuation plans. In Chapter VII it was argued that all emergency response plans, whether they involve evacuation or not, should be periodically tested. The virtues of a systematic testing program are many and have the advantage of addressing matters important in both emergency operations and research. An emergency response drill allows emergency managers to quickly identify gaps in inter- and intra-organizational communication networks. Also, rehearsals permit structured contact among personnel of different emergency management organizations, and if conducted on some regular basis, they help to reduce problems associated with organizational change and turnover which might otherwise hamper response effectiveness. Finally, drills constitute a positive setting for research on organizational performance, particularly because they are ameniable to the use of "true" experimental designs which afford greater manipulative opportunities than either quasi-experimental research designs or survey based cross-sectional studies.

In closing, this section has focused upon identifying gaps in the research on evacuation as well as directing attention to management aspects of evacuations that are commonly overlooked. Perhaps the most important purpose of this discussion has been to demonstrate that while there is considerable information available on evacuation relative to other generic functions, our knowledge is by no means complete. In dealing with evacuation both as a management problem and an area for social research, care must be taken to avoid premature closure. Vigilance and persistence are just as important for the maintenance emergency management *programs* as they are in watching for environmental threats themselves.

Bibliography

Ackerman, C. *Flood hazard mitigation*. Washington, D.C.: Engineering and Applied Science Division, National Science Foundation, 1980.

American National Red Cross. *Disaster relief program*. Washington, D.C.: Author, 1975. (a)

American National Red Cross. *Hurricane action*. Washington, D.C.: Author, 1975. (b)

American Nuclear Society. Special report: The ordeal at Three Mile Island. *Nuclear News,* April 6, 1979, pp. 1–6.

Anderson, J. Cultural adaptation to threatened disaster. *Human Organization,* 1968, *27,* 298–307.

Anderson, W. A. *Some observations on a disaster subculture*. Columbus: Ohio State University Disaster Research Center, 1965.

Anderson, W. A. *Local civil defense in natural disaster*. Columbus: Ohio State University Disaster Research Center, 1969. (a)

Anderson, W. A. Disaster warning and communication in two communities. *Journal of Communication,* 1969, *19,* 92–104. (b)

Andrews, R. Lessons from seismic safety planning in California. In W. W. Hays (Ed.), *Preparing for and responding to a damaging earthquake in the eastern United States: Proceedings of conference XIV, September 16–18, 1981. Knoxville, Tennessee* (Open File Report 82–220). Reston, Va.: U.S. Geological Survey, 1982.

Applied Technology Council. *Tentative provisions for the development of seismic regulations for buildings* (ATC Publication ATC 3–06, NBS Special Publication 510, NSF Publication 78–8). Washington, D.C.: U.S. Government Printing Office, 1978.

Atkisson, A. A., & Petak, W. J. The politics of community seismic safety. In W. W. Hays (Ed.), *Preparing for and responding to a damaging earthquake in the eastern United States: Proceedings of conference XIV, September 16–18, 1981, Knoxville, Tennessee* (Open File Report 82–220). Reston, Va.: U.S. Geological Survey, 1982.

Babchuck, N., & Ballweg, J. Primary extended kin relations of Negro couples. *Sociological Quarterly,* 1971, *12,* 69–77.

Babchuck, N. & Thompson, R. The voluntary associations of Negroes. *American Sociological Review,* 1962, *27,* 647–655.

Baker, G., & Cottrell, L. *Behavioral science and civil defense*. Washington, D.C.: National Academy of Sciences—National Research Council, 1962.

Bandura, A. *Social learning theory*. Englewood Cliffs, N.J.: Prentice-Hall, 1977.

Barberi, R., & Gasparini, P. Volcanic hazards. *Bulletin of the International Association of Engineering and Geology,* 1976, *14,* 217–232.

173

Barnes, K., Brosius, J., Cutter, S., & Mitchell, J. K. *Response of impacted populations to the Three Mile Island Nuclear Reactor accident. Unpublished manuscript, Rutgers University, 1979.*

Barrett, J. *Stress and mental disorder.* New York: Raven Press, 1979.

Barton, A. *Communities in disaster.* New York: Doubleday, 1970.

Bates, F., Fogelman, C., Parenton, V., Pittman, R., & Tracy, G. *The social and psychological consequences of natural disaster.* Washington, D.C.: National Academy of Sciences—National Research Council, 1963.

Bauman, D., & Sims, J. Flood insurance. *Economic Geography,* 1978, *54,* 189–196.

Beach, H., & Lucas, R. *Individual and group behavior in a coal mine disaster.* Washington, D.C.: National Academy of Sciences—National Research Council, 1960.

Beavers, J. E. *Earthquakes and earthquake engineering—eastern United States* (Vol. 1). Ann Arbor, Mich.: Ann Arbor Science, 1981.

Bennet, G. Bristols floods 1968. *British Medical Journal,* 1970, *3,* 454–458.

Bennett, R. Living conditions and everyday needs of the elderly with particular reference to social isolation. *International Journal of Aging and Human Development,* 1973, *4,* 179–198.

Bernert, E. H., & Iklé, F. Evacuation and cohesion of urban groups. *American Journal of Sociology,* 1952, *58,* 133–138.

Bethell, W. Personal communication, 1981.

Bianchi, S., & Farley, R. Racial differences in family living arrangements and economic well-being: An analysis of recent trends. *Journal of Marriage and the Family,* 1979, *4,* 537–551.

Blalock, H. *Theory construction.* Englewood Cliffs, N.J.: Prentice-Hall, 1969.

Blalock, H. *Causal models in the social sciences.* Chicago: Aldine, 1971.

Bolin, R. Family recovery from natural disaster. *Mass Emergencies,* 1976, *1,* 267–277.

Bolt, B. A., Horn, W., MacDonald, G., & Scott, R. *Geological hazards.* New York: Springer-Verlag, 1977.

Britz, K. I. *The integration of seismic design principles into preliminary architectural design.* Paper prepared for the National Science Foundation, Carnegie Mellon Institute, Pittsburgh, 1981.

Brodbeck, M. Models, meaning, and theories. In M. Brodbeck (Ed.), *Readings in the philosophy of the social sciences.* New York: Macmillan, 1968.

Brown, G. Meaning, measurement and stress of life events. In B. S. Dohrenwend & B. P. Dohrenwend (Eds.), *Stressful life events.* New York: Wiley.

Bucher, R. Blame and hostility in disaster. *American Journal of Sociology,* 1957, *62,* 467–475.

Bugen, L. Human grief. *American Journal of Orthopsychiatry,* 1977, *47,* 196–206.

Bullard, F. *Volcanoes of the earth.* Austin: University of Texas Press, 1976.

Burton, I. Cultural and personality variables in the perception of natural hazards. In J. Wohlwill & D. Carson (Eds.), *Environment and the social sciences.* Washington, D.C.: American Psychological Association, 1972.

Burton, I. & Kates, R. The perception of natural hazards in resource management. *Natural Resources Journal,* 1964, *3,* 412–441.

Burton, I., Kates, R., & White, G. *The environment as hazard.* London: Oxford University Press, 1978.

Carr, L. Disaster and the sequence pattern concept of social change. *American Journal of Sociology,* 1932, *38,* 209–215.

Carter, M., Clark, J., Leck, R., & Fine, G. *Social factors affecting the dissemination of and response to warnings.* Paper read at the 11th Technical Conference on Hurricanes and Tropical Meteorology, Miami Beach, Florida, 1977.

Chenault, W., Hilbert, G., & Reichlin, S. *Evacuation planning in the TMI accident.* McLean, VA: Human Sciences Research, 1979.

Christiansen, R. Eruption of Mt. St. Helens: Volcanology. *Nature,* 1980, *285,* 531–533.

Ciborowski, A. Some aspects of town reconstruction (Warsaw and Skopje). *Impact*, 1967, *17*, 31–48.

Clifford, R. *The Rio Grande flood*. Washington, D.C.: National Academy of Sciences-National Research Council, 1956.

Cline, V. *Emergency service*. Seattle, Wash.: Salvation Army Northwest Division, 1976.

Coastal Area Planning and Development Commission. *Summary of a coordination, education and mitigation model for disaster preparedness in coastal areas*. Brunswick, GA: Author, 1980.

Cobb, S. Social support as a moderator of life stress. *Psychosomatic Medicine*, 1976, *38*, 300–314.

Cochrane, H. *Natural disasters and their distributive effects*. Boulder: Institute for Behavioral Sciences, University of Colorado, 1975.

Cohen, R., & Ahearn, F. *Handbook for mental health care of disaster victims*. Baltimore: The Johns Hopkins University Press, 1980.

Cohen, R., & Kapsis, R. Participation of Blacks, Puerto Ricans, and Whites in voluntary associations. *Social Forces*, 1978, *56*, 1053–1071.

Commonwealth of Virginia. *Disaster preparedness handbook*. Richmond: Office of Emergency and Energy Services, 1980.

Comstock, G., & Helsing, K. Symptoms of depression in two communities. *Psychological Medicine*, 1976, *6*, 551–563.

Corbett, J., & Svenson, A. *Perspectives on local natural hazard management*. Paper presented at the meeting of the Western Political Science Association, Denver, March 1981.

The Columbian. *Mt. St. Helens holocaust*. Vancouver, Washington: Author, 1980.

Committee on Government Operations. *Emergency planning around U.S. nuclear power plants: Nuclear regulatory commission oversight*. Washington, D.C.: U.S. House of Representatives, 1979.

Cottrell, F. *Aging and the aged*. Dubuque, Iowa: William C. Brown, 1974.

Council of State Governments. *The states and natural hazards*. Lexington, KY: Author, 1979.

Crandell, D., & Mullineaux, D. *Potential hazards from future eruptions of Mt. St. Helens volcano, Washington* (Geological Survey Bulletin 1383–C). Washington, D.C.: U.S. Government Printing Office.

Crandell, D., Mullineaux, D., & Miller, C. D. Volcanic-hazards studies in the Cascade Range of the western United States. In P. D. Sheets & D. Grayson (Eds.), *Volcanic activity and human ecology*. New York: Academic Press, 1979.

Crawshaw, R. Reactions to a disaster. *Archives of General Psychiatry*, 1963, *9*, 157–162.

Cutter, S., Brosius, J., Barnes, K., & Mitchell, J. K. Special session on Three Mile Island: Risk evaluation and evacuation responses. *Proceedings, Middle States Division, American Association of Geographers*, 1979, *12*, 80–88.

Dacy, D., & Kunreuther, H. *The economics of natural disaster*. New York: Free Press, 1969.

Danzig, E., Thayer, P., & Galanter, L. *The effects of a threatening rumor on a disaster-stricken community* (Publication No. 517). Washington, D.C.: National Academy of Sciences, 1958.

Davenport, S., & Waterstone, P. *Hazard awareness guidebook: Planning for what comes naturally*. Austin: Texas Coastal and Marine Council, 1979.

Davis, J. Perspective on crisis relocation planning. *Foresight: Civil Preparedness Today*, 1974, (November/December), 20–24.

Dean, A., & Lin, N. The stress-buffering role of social support. *Journal of Nervous and Mental Disease*, 1977, *165*, 403–417.

Defense Civil Preparedness Agency. *Standards for local civil preparedness*. Washington, D.C.: U.S. Government Printing Office, 1978.

Diggory, J. Some consequences of proximity to a disease threat. *Sociometry*, 1956, *19*, 47–53.

Dohrenwend, B. Life events as stressors. *Journal of Health and Social Behavior,* 1973, *14,* 167–175.

Dohrenwend, B., & Dohrenwend, B. Psychiatric Epidemiology. In S. Golann & C. Eisdorfer (Eds.), *Handbank of community mental health.* New York: Appleton-Century-Crofts, 1972.

Donnelly, W., & Kramer, D. *Nuclear power: The Three Mile Island accident and its investigation.* Washington, D.C.: Library of Congress, Congressional Research Service, 1979.

Drabek, T. *Disaster in Isle 13.* Columbus: Disaster Research Center, Ohio State University, 1968.

Drabek, T. Social processes in disaster. *Social Problems,* 1969, *16,* 336–347.

Drabek, T. *Search and rescue missions in natural disasters and remote settings.* Washington, D.C.: Problem Focused Research Division, National Science Foundation.

Drabek, T., & Boggs, K. Families in disaster. *Journal of Marriage and the Family,* 1968, *30,* 443–451.

Drabek, T., & Key, W. The impact of disaster on primary group linkages. *Mass Emergencies,* 1976, *1*(2), 89–106.

Drabek, T., & Stephenson, J. When disaster strikes. *Journal of Applied Social Psychology,* 1971, *1,* 187–203.

Drabek, T., Key, W., Erickson, P., & Crowe, J. The impact of disaster on kin relationships. *Journal of Marriage and the Family,* 1975, *37,* 481–494.

Drayer, C. Psychological factors and problems, emergency and long-term. *The Annals,* 1957, *309,* 151–159.

Dynes, R. *Organized behavior in disaster.* Lexington, MA: Heath-Lexington Books, 1970.

Dynes, R., & Quarantelli, E. L. The family and community context of individual reactions to disaster. In Howard Parad, H. L. L. Resnik & Libbie Parad (Eds.), *Emergency and disaster management.* Bowie, MD: Charles Press, 1976.

Dynes, R., & Quarantelli, E. L. Group behavior under stress. *Sociology and Social Research,* 1979, *52,* 416–429.

Dynes, R., Quarantelli, E. L., & Kreps, G. *A perspective on disaster planning.* Columbus: Disaster Research Center, Ohio State University.

Earle, T. Personal Communication to Marjorie R. Greene. Battelle Human Affairs Research Centers, Seattle, Washington, 1980.

Earle, T. *Public Perception of Industrial Risks.* Seattle: Battelle Human Affairs Research Centers, 1981.

Eaton, W. Life events, social supports, and psychiatric symptoms. *Journal of Health and Social Behavior,* 1978, *19,* 230–234.

Eaton, J., & Weil, R. *Culture and mental disorder.* Glencoe, Ill.: The Free Press, 1955.

Ellemers, J. E. A study of the destruction of a community. *Studies in the Holland flood disaster* (Vol. 3). Washington, D.C.: National Academy of Sciences-National Research Council, 1955.

England, J. L., & Kunz, P. R. *Disasters and personal well-being.* Paper read at meetings of American Sociological Association, Chicago, 1977.

Erickson, P., Drabek, T., Key, W., & Crowe, J. Families in disaster. *Mass Emergencies,* 1976, *1,* 206–213.

Erikson, K. *Everything in its path.* New York: Simon & Schuster, 1976.

Erley, D., & Kockelman, W. *Reducing landslide hazards: A guide for planners* (Report Number 359). Chicago, Ill.: American Planning Association, 1981.

Fabrikant, J. *Reports of the public health and safety task force.* Washington, D.C.: U.S. Government Printing Office, 1979.

Federal Emergency Management Agency. *Criteria for preparation and evaluation of radiological emergency response plans and preparedness in support of nuclear power plants.* Washington, D.C.: U.S. Government Printing Office, 1980.

Finkel, A. *Energy, the environment and human health.* Acton, MA: Publishing Science Group, 1974.

Flynn, C. B. *Three mile island telephone survey* (NUREG/CR-1093). Washington, D.C.: Nuclear Regulatory Commission, 1979.

Fogelman, C., & Parenton, V. Disaster and aftermath. *Social Forces,* 1959, *38,* 129–135.

Form, W., & Loomis, C. The persistence and emergence of social and cultural systems in disasters. *American Sociological Review,* 1956, *21,* 180–185.

Form, W., & Nosow, S. *Community in disaster.* New York: Harper, 1958.

Foster, H. *Disaster Planning.* New York: Springer-Verlag, 1980.

Foster, H., & Wuorinen, V. British Columbia's Tsunami Warning System. *Syesis,* 1976, *9*(1), 113–122.

Fried, M. Effects of social change and mental health. *American Journal of Orthopsychiatry,* 1964, *34,* 3–28.

Friedman, S. M. Blueprint for breakdown at TMI. *Journal of Communication,* 1981, *41,* 116–128.

Friedsam, H. Reactions of older persons to disaster-caused losses. *The Gerontologist,* 1961, *1,* 34–37.

Friedsam, H. Older persons in disaster. In G. Baker & D. Chapman (Eds.), *Man and society in disaster.* New York: Basic Books, 1962.

Fritz, C. E. Disasters compared in six American communities. *Human Organization,* 1957, *16,* 6–9.

Fritz, C. E. Disasters. In R. Merton & R. Nisbet (Eds.), *Contemporary social problems.* New York: Harcourt, Brace & World, 1961. (a)

Fritz, C. E. *Disaster and community therapy.* Washington, D.C.: National Research Council—National Academy of Science, 1961. (b)

Fritz, C. E. Disasters. In *International Encyclopedia of the Social Sciences.* New York: MacMillan & The Free Press, 1968.

✓Fritz, C. E., & Marks, E. The NORC studies of human behavior in disaster. *Journal of Social Issues,* 1954, *10*(3), 26–41.

Fritz, C. E., & Mathewson, J. H. *Convergence behavior in disasters: A problem in social control.* Washington, D.C.: National Academy of Sciences—National Research Council, 1957.

Fritz, C. E., & Williams, H. The human being in disasters: A research perspective. *The Annals,* 1957, *309,* 42–51.

Galway, J. The Topeka tornado of 8 June 1966. *Weatherwise,* 1966, *19,* 144–149.

Garb, S. Thermonuclear survival. *Missouri Medicine,* 1963, *60,* 860–862.

Garb, S., & Eng, E. *Disaster handbook.* New York: Springer, 1969.

Garrett, R. Social sciences research program. In G. Baker & L. Cottrell (Eds.), *Behavioral science and civil defense.* Washington, D.C.: National Academy of Sciences—National Research Council, 1962.

Geophysics Program. Eruption of Mt. St. Helens: Seismology. *Nature,* 1980, *285,* 529–531.

Gerontology Program. *Service priorities for the elderly in natural disasters.* University of Nebraska at Omaha, April 30 report.

Gilbert, J. The multivariate analysis of qualitative data. *Journal of the American Statistical Association,* 1958, *65,* 226–256.

Gillespie, D., & Perry, R. W. An integrated systems and emergent norm approach to mass emergencies. *Mass Emergencies,* 1976, *1*(3), 303–312.

Glass, A. Psychologic considerations in atomic warfare. *United States Armed Forces Medical Journal,* 1956, *7,* 625–639.

Glass, A. The psychological aspects of emergency situations. In Abram (Ed.), *Psychological aspects of stress.* Springfield, Ill.: Charles C. Thomas, 1970.

Glass, J. Citizen participation in planning. *Journal of the American Planning Association*, 1979, *45*, 180–189.

Gleser, G., Green, B., & Winget, C. *Prolonged psychosocial effects of disaster*. New York: Academic Press, 1981.

Golan, N. *Treatment in crisis situations*. New York: The Free Press, 1978.

Goldstein, A. Reactions to disaster. *Psychiatric Communications*, 1960, *3*, 26–41.

Greene, M., & Gori, P. *Earthquake hazards information dissemination: A study of Charleston, South Carolina* (Open File Report 82–233). Reston, Va.: U.S. Geological Survey, 1982.

Greene, M., Perry, R. W., & Lindell, M. The March 1980 eruptions of Mt. St. Helens: Citizen perceptions of volcano hazard. *Disasters*, 1981, *5*(1), 49–66.

Grinspoon, L. Fallout shelters and the unacceptability of disquieting facts. In G. Grosser, H. Wechler, & M. Greenblatt (Eds.), *The threat of impending disaster*. Cambridge: MIT Press, 1964.

Grove, N. A village fights for its life. *National Geographic*, 1973, *144*, 40–67.

Gruntfest, E. *What people did during the big thompson flood*. Boulder: Department of Geography, University of Colorado, 1977.

Gruntfest, E., Downing, T. E., & White, G. Big Thompson Flood exposes need for better flood reaction system to save lives. *Civil Engineering*, 1978, *78*, 72–73.

Haas, E. *The Philippine earthquake and Tsunami disaster*. Paper read at the annual meeting of the Society for the Study of Social Problems, New York, 1977.

Haas, E., & Ayre, R. *The Western Sicily Earthquake of 1968*. Washington, D.C.: National Academy of Engineering, 1970.

Haas, E., & Mileti, D. *Socioeconomic impact of earthquake prediction on government, business and community*. Boulder: Institute of Behavioral Sciences, University of Colorado, 1976.

Haas, E., & Trainer, P. B. *The Tsunami Warning System in British Columbia*. Boulder: National Hazards Research and Information Center, University of Colorado, 1973.

Haas, E., Cochrane, H., & Eddy, D. *The consequences of large scale evacuation following disaster*. Boulder: Institute for Behavioral Science, University of Colorado, 1976.

Haas, E., Cochrane, H., & Eddy, D. Consequences of a cycle for a small city. *Ekistics*, 1977, *44*, 45–51.

Haas, E., Kates, R., & Bowden, M. *Reconstruction following disaster*. Cambridge: MIT Press, 1977.

Haglund, K. A. At Hershey: Medical system near failure during Three Mile Island. *New Physician*, 1979, *28*, 31–32.

Hamilton, R., Taylor, R. M., & Rice, G. *The social psychological interpretation of the Udall, Kansas tornado*. Wichita, Kansas: University of Wichita Press, 1955.

Hans, J., & Sell, T. Evacuation risks. Washington, D.C.: U.S. Environmental Protection Agency, Office of Radiation Programs, 1974.

Hanson, J. *Getting the disaster facts*. Washington, D.C.: National Governors' Association, 1981.

Harry, J. Family localism and social participation. *American Journal of Socilogy*, 1970, *75*, 821–827.

Healy, R. J. *Emergency and disaster planning*. New York: Wiley, 1969.

Herron, G. W. The process-reactive classification of schizophrenia. *Psychological Bulletin*, 1962, *59*(3), 329–343.

Hersey, J. *Hiroshima*. New York: Wiley, 1946.

Hershiser, M., & Quarantelli, E. L. The handling of dead in a disaster. *Omega*, 1976, *7*(3), 195–208.

Hewitt, K., & Burton, I. *The hazardousness of a place*. Toronto: University of Toronto Press, 1971.

Hildebrand, M. *Disaster planning guidelines for fire chiefs*. Washington, D.C.: Federal Emergency Management Agency, 1980.

Hill, R., & Hansen, R. Families in disaster. In G. Baker and D. Chapman (Eds.), *Man and society in disaster*. New York: Basic Books, 1962.

Hinojosa, J., & Gelman, W. After the earthquake. *Practicing Planner*, 1977, March, 35–40.

Hirose, H. Volcanic eruption and local politics in Japan. *Mass Emergencies*, 1979, *4*(1), 53–62.

Hocking, F. Extreme environmental stress and its significance for psychopathology. *American Journal of Psychotherapy*, 1970, *24*, 4–26.

Hodge, D., Sharp, V., & Marts, M. Contemporary responses to volcanism: Case studies from the Cascades and Hawaii. In P. D. Sheets & D. Grayson (Eds.), *Volcanic activity and human ecology*. New York: Academic Press, 1979.

Hohenemser, C., Kasperson, R., & Kates, R. The distrust of nuclear power. *Science*, 1977, *196*, 25–34.

Hornsby, R. I., Ortloff, G., & Smith, M. A highway accident which involved a spill of natural Uranium Oxide Concentrate. *Proceedings of the Fifth International Symposium on Packaging and Transportation of Radioactive Materials*. Las Vegas, Nevada, 1978.

Horowitz, J. After the earthquake. *Practicing Planner*, 1974, *4*, 35–40.

Houts, P., & Goldhaber, M. Psychological and social effects on the population surrounding Three Mile Island after the nuclear accident on March 28, 1979. In S. Majumdar (Ed.), *Energy, environment and the economy*. Pennsylvania Academy of Sciences, 1981.

Hudgens, R. W. Personal catastrophe and depression. In Dohrenwend & Dohrenwend (Eds.), *Stressful life events*. New York: Wiley, 1974.

Hudgens, R. W., Morrison, J. R., & Barchha, R. G. Life events and onset of primary affective disorders. *Archives of General Psychiatry*, 1967, *16*, 134–145.

Hudgens, R. W., Robbins, E., & Delong, W. B. The reporting of recent stress in the lives of psychiatric patients. *British Journal of Psychiatry*, 1970, *117*, 635–643.

Huerta, F., & Horton, R. Coping behavior of elderly flood victims. *The Gerontologist*, 1978, *18*(6), 541–546.

Hultaker, O. *Evakuera*. East Orange, N.J.: Upsala University Press, 1977.

Hunt, C. E., & MacCready, J. S. *The short-term economic consequences of the Mount St. Helens volcanic eruptions in May and June 1980*. Olympia: Washington State Department of Commerce and Economic Development, Research Division, 1980.

Iklé, F. Reconstruction and population density of war damaged cities. *Journal of The American Institute of Planners*, 1950, *16*, 131–139.1.

Iklé, F. The effect of war destruction upon the ecology of cities. *Social Forces*, 1951, *29*, 383–391.

Iklé, F. *The social impact of bomb destruction*. New York: McGraw-Hill, 1959.

Iklé, F., & Kincaid, H. *Some social aspects of wartime evacuation of american cities*. Washington, D.C.: National Academy of Sciences Committee on Disaster Studies, 1956.

Iklé, F., Quarantelli, E. L., Rayner, J., & Withey, S. *Withdrawal behavior in disasters*. Washington, D.C.: National Academy of Sciences Committee on Disaster Studies, 1958.

Ives, S., & Furuseth, O. *Immediate response to headwater flooding in neighborhoods in Charlotte, North Carolina* (Report to the National Science Foundation). Charlotte: Department of Geography, University of North Carolina, 1980.

Jackson, J. Negro aged. *The Gerontologist*, 1971, *11*, 52–57.

Jaffe, M., Butler, J., & Thurow, C. *Reducing earthquake risks: A planner's guide* (PAS Report #364). Chicago: American Planning Association, 1981.

Janis, I. *Air war and emotional stress: Psychological studies of bombing and civilian defense*. New York: McGraw-Hill, 1951.

Janis, I. Psychological effects of warnings. In G. Baker & D. Chapman (Eds.), *Man and society in disaster*. New York: Basic Books, 1962.

Janis, I., & Mann, L. Emergency decision making. *Journal of Human Stress*, 1977, *3*, 35–45.

Joint Committee on Defense Production. *Federal, state, and local emergency preparedness* (Hearings, 94th Congress, second session). Washington, D.C.: U.S. Government Printing Office.

Jones, J. *Prejudice and racism.* Reading, Mass.: Addison-Wesley, 1972.

Judkins, G. *The Big Thompson Disaster.* Loveland, Col.: Lithographic Press, 1976.

Kaplan, F. Enhanced-radiation weapons. *Scientific American,* 1978, *238,* 44–51.

Kartez, J., & Kelley, W. *Emergency planning and the adaptive local response to the Mt. St. Helens eruption.* Pullman: Washington State University Press, 1980.

Kaplan, A. *The conduct of inquiry.* San Francisco: Chandler, 1964.

Kardiner, A. Traumatic neuroses of war. In S. Arienti (Ed.), *American handbook of psychiatry.* New York: Basic Books, 1959.

Kasperson, J. X., Kasperson, R. E., Honenemeser, C., & Kates, R. W. Institutional responses to Three Mile Island. *Bulletin of the Atomic Scientists,* 1979, *35,* 20–24.

Kastenbaum, R. Disaster, death and human ecology, *Omega,* 1974, *5*(1), 65–72.

Kates, R. Natural hazard in human ecological perspective. *Economic Geography,* 1971, *47,* 438–451.

Kates, R. *Risk assessment of environmental hazard* (SCOPE Report #8, Internatonal Council of Scientific Unions). Paris: Scientific Committee on Problems of the Environment, 1976.

Kates, R., Haas, E., Amaral, D., Olson, R., Ramos, R., & Olson, R. Human impact of the managua earthquake. *Science,* 1973, *182,* 981–990.

Keeling, T. The national flood Insurance Program: A local perspective. In E. J. Baker (Ed.), *Hurricanes and coastal storms.* Papers presented at a National Conference. Gainesville: Florida Sea Grant College.

Kemeny, J. G. *Report of the President's Commission on the Accident at Three Mile Island.* Washington, D.C.: Government Printing Office, 1979.

Kennett, E. W. *Designing for earthquakes: Proceedings from the 1978 Summer Seismic Institutes for Architectural Faculty.* Washington, D.C.: American Institute of Architects Research Corporation for the National Science Foundation, 1979.

Kent, D. The Negro aged. The Gerontologist, 1971, *11,* 48–51.

Killian, L. The significance of multiple-group membership in disaster. *American Journal of Sociology,* 1952, *57,* 309–314.

Killian, L. Some accomplishments and some needs in disaster study. *Journal of Social Issues,* 1954, *10*(3), 68–79.

Killian, L. *An introduction to methodological problems of field studies in disasters.* Washington, D.C.: National Academy of Sciences—National Research Council, 1956.

Kirkby, A. Individual and community responses to rainfall variation in Oayaca, Mexico. In Gilbert White (Ed.), *Natural hazards.* London: Oxford University Press, 1974.

Kiyoshi, S. Little-known effects of the bomb. *Japan Quarterly,* 1967, *14,* 93–98.

Korosec, M., Rigby, J., & Stoffell, K. *The 1980 Eruption of Mt. St. Helens Washington, Part I: March 20–May 19, 1980* (Information Circular Number 71). Olympia: Washington State Department of Natural Resources, Division of Geology and Earth Sciences.

Kreps, G. *Decision making under conditions of uncertainty.* Columbus: Ohio: Disaster Research Center, 1973.

Kreps, G. *A framework for comparing nuclear and nonnuclear disasters in terms of key defining properties of disaster events and generic functions of disaster response.* Williamsburg: Department of Sociology, College of William and Mary, 1979.

Kreps, G. The worth of the NAS-NRC (1952–1963) and DRC (1963–Present) studies of individual and social response to disasters. In J. Wright & P. Rossi (Eds.), *Social science and natural hazards.* Cambridge: Abt Books, 1981.

Kunreuther, H. Economic analysis of natural hazards: An ordered choice approach. In G. White (Ed.), *Natural Hazards.* New York: Oxford University Press, 1974.

Kutchins, K. Plan for an emergency before it happens. *Journal of American Waterworks Association,* 1978, *70*(6), 308–310.

Lachman, R., & Bonk, W. Behavior and beliefs during the recent volcanic eruption at Kapoho, Hawaii. *Science,* 1960, *131,* 1095–1096.

Lachman, R., Tatsuoka, M., & Bonk, W. Human behavior during the Tsunami of May, 1960. *Science,* 1961, *133,* 1405–1409.

Lammers, C. Summary. *Studies in the Holland flood disaster* (Vol. 4). Washington, D.C.: National Academy of Sciences-National Research Council, 1955.

Lang, K., & Lang, G. Collective response to the threat of disaster. In Grosser et al. (Eds.), *The Threat of Impending Disaster.* Cambridge: MIT Press, 1964.

Langner, T. A twenty-two item screening score of psychiatric impairment. *Journal of Health and Social Behavior,* 1962, *3,* 297–306.

Langer, T., & Michael, S. *Life stress and mental health.* New York: Free Press, 1963.

Lansing, J., & Kish, L. Family life cycle as an independant variable. *American Sociological Review,* 1957, *22,* 512–519.

Lazarus, R. A strategy for research on psychological and social factors in hypertension. *Journal of Human Stress,* 1978, *4,* 35–40.

Leighton, D. C., Harding, J., Macklin, D., MacMillan, A., & Leighton, A. *The character of danger.* New York: Basic Books, 1963.

Leonard, V. A. *Police pre-disaster preparation.* Springfield, Ill.: Charles C. Thomas, 1973.

Leopold, R. L., & Dillon, H. Psycho-anatomy of disaster. *American Journal of Psychiatry,* 1963, *119,* 913–921.

Lessa, W. Social effects of Typhoon Ophelia (1960) on Ulithi. *Micronesia,* 1964, *1,* 1–47.

Levine, R. *Public planning.* New York: Basic Books, 1972.

Levine, S., & Scotch, N. *Social stress.* Chicago: Aldine, 1970.

Lewis, J., O'Keefe, P., & Westgate, K. A philosophy of precautionary planning. *Mass Emergencies,* 1977, *2,* 95–104.

Lewis, K. The prompt and delayed effects of nuclear war. *Scientific American,* 1979, *241,* 35–47.

Lifton, R. Psychological effects of the atomic bomb in Hiroshima. In G. Grosser, H. Wechler, & M. Greenblatt (Eds.), *The threat of impending disaster.* Cambridge: MIT Press, 1964.

Lifton, R. *Death in life.* New York: Simon & Schuster, 1967.

Lifton, R., & Olson, E. The human meaning of total disaster. *Psychiatry,* 1976, *39,* 1–18.

Lindell, M., & Perry, R. Evaluation criteria for emergency response plans in radiological transportation. *Journal of Hazardous Materials,* 1980, *33,* 335–348.

Lindell, M., Earle, T., Hebert, D., & Perry, R. W. *Radioactive wastes: Public attitudes.* Seattle: Battelle Human Affairs Research Centers, 1978.

Lindemann, E. Symptomatology and management of acute grief. *American Journal of Psychiatry,* 1944, *101,* 141–148.

Litwak, E. & Szelenski, I. Primary group structures and their functions. *American Sociological Review,* 1969, *34,* 465–481.

Logue, J., & Hansen, H. A case-control study of hypertensive women in a post-disaster community. *Journal of Human Stress,* 1980, *6,* 28–34.

Logue, J., Hansen, H., & Struening, E. Emotional and physical distress following hurricane Agnes in Wyoming Valley of Pennsylvania. *Public Health Reports,* 1979, *94,* 495–502.

Love Canal residents under stress. *Science,* 1980, *208,* 1242–1243.

Lucas, R. The influence of kinship upon perception of an ambiguous stimulus. *American Sociological Review,* 1966, *31,* 227–236.

MacDonald, G. *Volcanoes.* Englewood Cliffs, N.J.: Prentice-Hall, 1972.

Mack, R., & Baker, G. *The occasion instant.* Washington, D.C.: National Academy of Sciences—National Research Council, 1962.

Markush, R. E., & Favero, R. V. Epidemiologic assessment of stressful life events, depressed mood and psychophysiological symptoms. In B. Dohrenwend & B. S. Dohrenwend (Eds.), *Stressful life events.* New York: Wiley, 1973.

Marshall, E. New A-Bomb data shown to radiation experts. *Science,* 1981, *212,* 1364–1365.

Martin, D. *Three Mile Island.* Cambridge, Mass.: Ballinger, 1980.

Mayor's Disaster Review Task Force. *Disaster response: The 1975 Omaha Tornado.* Omaha, Nebraska: City of Omaha.

McCubbin, H. Integrating coping behavior in family stress theory. *Journal of Marriage and the Family,* 1979, *41,* 237–244.

McGrath, J. A conceptual formulation for research on stress. In McGrath (Ed.), *Social and psychological factors in stress.* New York: Holt, Rinehart & Winston, 1970.

McLuckie, B. *Warning systems in disaster.* Columbus: Ohio State University Disaster Research Center, 1970.

McLuckie, B., & Whitman, R. *A study of warning and response in ten Colorado communities during the floods of June 1965.* Columbus: Ohio State University Disaster Research Center, 1971.

McPherson, H. J., & Saarinen, T. Flood plain dwellers' perception of the flood hazard in Tucson Arizona. *Annals of Regional Science,* 1977, *12,* 25–40.

Mechanic, D. *Students under stress.* New York: The Free Press, 1962.

Mechanic, D. Sociocultural and social-psychological factors affecting personal responses to psychological disorder. *Journal of Health and Social Behavior,* 1975, *16,* 393–404.

Menninger, W. C. Psychological reactions in an emergency. *American Journal of Psychiatry,* 1952, *109,* 128–130.

Micklin, M., & Leon, C. Life change and psychiatric disturbance in a South American city. *Journal of Health and Social Behavior,* 1978, *19,* 92–107.

Midlarsky, E. Aiding responses: An analysis and review. *Merril-Palmer Quarterly,* 1968, *14,* 229–260.

Mileti, D. *A normative causal model analysis of disaster warning response.* Unpublished doctoral dissertation, University of Colorado.

Mileti, D. *Natural hazards warning systems in the United States.* Boulder: Institute for Behavioral Sciences, University of Colorado, 1975.

Mileti, D., & Beck, W. Communication in crisis. *Communication Research,* 1975, *2,* 24–49.

Mileti, D., & Harvey, P. *Correcting for the human factor in tornado warnings.* Paper presented at the 10th Annual Conference on Severe Local Storms, Omaha, Nebraska, 1977.

Mileti, D., Drabek, T., & Haas, G. *Human behavior in extreme environments.* Boulder: Institute of Behavioral Sciences, University of Colorado, 1975.

Mileti, D., Hartsough, D., & Madson, P. *Unobtrusive indicators of stress at Three Mile Island.* Fort Collins: Department of Sociology, Colorado State University, 1981.

Modlin, H. The post-accident anxiety syndrome. American *Journal of Psychiatry,* 1966, *123,* 1008–1012.

Mogil, M., & Groper, H. 'NWS's severe local storm warning and disaster preparedness programs.'' *Bulletin of the American Meteorological Society,* 1977, *58,* 318–329.

Mogil, M., Monro, J., & Groper, H. *The National Weather Service flash flood warning and disaster preparedness Programs.* Paper read at the second annual Conference on Hydro-Meterology, Toronto, 1977.

Moore, H. E. *Tornadoes over Texas.* Austin: University of Texas Press, 1958. (a)

Moore, H. E. Some emotional concommitants of disaster. *Mental Hygiene,* 1958, *42,* 45–50. (b)

Moore, H. E., & Friedsam, H. Reported emotional stress following a disaster. *Social Forces,* 1959, *38,* 135–139.

Moore, H. E., Bates, F., Lyman, M., & Parenton, V. *Before the wind: A study of response to Hurricane Carla.* Washington, D.C.: National Academy of Sciences-National Research Council, 1963.

Morland, H. The meltdown that didn't happen. *Harper's*, 1979, *259*, 16–23.

Murphy, L. *San Fernando, California Earthquake of February 9, 1971* (Vol. 2). Washington, D.C.: U.S. Government Printing Office, 1973.

Murton, B., & Shimabukuro, S. Human adjustment to volcanic hazard in Puna District, Hawaii. In Gilbert White (ed.), *Natural hazards*. New York: Oxford University Press, 1974.

National Academy of Sciences. *Earthquake Prediction and Public Policy* (Report of the Panel on Public Policy Implications of Earthquake Prediction of the Advisory Committee on Emergency Planning). Washington, D.C.: National Academy of Sciences-National Research Council, 1975.

National Governors' Association. *1978 emergency preparedness project: Final report*. Washington, D.C.: National Governors' Association, Center for Policy Research, 1979. (a)

National Governors' Association. *Comprehensive emergency management: A governor's guide*. Washington, D.C.: National Governors' Association, Center for Policy Research, 1979. (b)

National Governors' Association. *Emergency preparedness project: Final report*. Washington, D.C.: National Governors' Association, Center for Policy Research, 1979. (c)

Nelson, L., & Winter, M. Life disruption, independence, satisfaction and the consideration of moving. *The Gerontologist*, 1975, *15*, 160–164.

New England Municipal Center. *A hazard analysis for New England*. Durham, N. H.: New England Municipal Center, n.d.

Nigg, J. M. Societal response to the earthquake threat in the Eastern United States, issues, problems and suggestions. In W. W. Hays (ed.), *Preparing for and responding to a damaging earthquake in the Eastern United States: Proceedings of conference XIV, September 16–18, Knoxville, Tennessee* (Open File Report 82–220). Reston, Va.: U.S. Geological Survey, 1982.

Office of Civil Defense. *In Time of Emergency*. Washington, D.C.: U.S. Government Printing Office, 1968.

Office of Emergency Preparedness. *Report to the Congress: Disaster Preparedness*. Washington, D.C.: U.S. Government Printing Office, 1972.

Ollier, C. *Volcanoes*. Cambridge: The MIT Press, 1969.

Oliver, J. *Natural hazards response and planning in tropical Queensland*. Boulder, Col.: Natural Hazards Research and Applications Information Center, 1978.

Olsen, M. Social and political participation of blacks. *American Sociological Review*, 1970, *35*, 682–697.

Olson, R. A. Individual and organizational dimensions of the San Fernando Earthquake. In L. Murphy (ed.), *San Fernando Earthquake of February 9, 1971*. Washington, D.C.: U.S. Government Printing Office.

Oram, A. A reappraisal of the social and political participation of Negroes. *American Journal of Sociology*, 1966, *72*, 32–46.

Ostby, F., & Pearson, A. The tornado season of 1975. *Weatherwise*, 1976, *29*, 17–23.

Otway, H. Risk estimation and evaluation. In *Proceedings of the IIASA Planning Conference on Energy Systems* (IIASA–PC–3). Laxenburg, Austria: International Institute for Applied Systems Analysis.

Owen, H. J. *Guide for flood and flash flood preparedness planning*. Washington, D.C.: National Weather Service, Disaster Preparedness Staff.

Padley, R., & Cole, M. *Evacuation survey*. London: George Routle & Sons, 1940.

Park, R., & Burgess, E. *An introduction to the science of sociology*. Chicago: University of Chicago Press, 1921.

Parker, G. Cyclone Tracy and Darwin evacuees: on the restoration of the species. *British Journal of Psychiatry*, 1977, *130*(6), 548–555.

Parr, A. A brief on disaster plans. *EMO National Digest*, 1969, *9*, 13–15.

Pearlin, L., & Schooler, C. The structure of coping. *Journal of Health and Social Behavior*, 1978, *19*, 2–21.

Pennsylvania Emergency Management Agency. *Flash flood handbook.* Harrisburg: Author, n.d.

Perkins, C. Fiddling while volcano burns. *Seattle Post-Intelligencer,* May 10, 1980, p. A1.

Perry, H. S., & Perry, S. *The schoolhouse disasters: family and community as determinants of the child's response to disaster.* Washington, D.C.: National Academy of Sciences-National Research Council, 1959.

Perry, R. W. Evacuation decision-making in natural disasters. *Mass Emergencies,* 1979, *4*(1), 25–38. (a)

Perry, R. W. Incentives for evacuation in natural disaster. *Journal of the American Planning Association,* 1979, *45,* 440–447. (b)

Perry, R. W. Detecting psychopathological reactions to natural disasters. *Social Behavior and Personality,* 1979, *7*(2), 173–177. (c)

Perry, R. W. *Population evacuation in nuclear versus nonnuclear disasters.* Paper presented for the Committee on United States Emergency Preparedness. Washington, D.C.: National Academy of Sciences-National Research Council, 1980.

Perry, R. W. *Citizen adoption of mitigation measures in multiple impact disasters.* Seattle, Wash.: Battelle Human Affairs Research Centers, 1981. (a)

Perry, R. W. *Citizen evacuation behavior in response to nuclear and nonnuclear threats.* Seattle, Washington: Battelle Human Affairs Research Centers, 1981. (b)

Perry, R. W. *The social psychology of civil defense.* Lexington, Mass.: Heath-Lexington Books, 1982.

Perry, R. W. Environmental hazards and psychopathology. *Environmental Management,* in press.

Perry, R. W., & Greene, M. *Citizen response to volcanic eruptions.* New York: Irvington, 1982.

Perry, R. W., & Hirose, H. *Volcanic Eruptions and Functional Community Change.* Paper read at the World Congress of Sociology, Mexico City, 1982.

Perry, R. W., & Lindell, M. The psychological consequences of natural disasters. *Mass Emergencies,* 1978, *3,* 105–117.

Perry, R. W., & Lindell, M. Predisaster planning to promote compliance with evacuations. In Earl J. Baker (ed.), *Hurricanes and coastal storms* (Report No. 33). Tallahassee: Florida Sea Grant College, Florida State University.

Perry, R. W., Gillespie, D., & Mileti, D. System stress and the persistence of emergent organizations. *Sociological Inquiry,* 1974, *42,* 113–121.

Perry, R. W., Lindell, M., & Greene, M. *Human response to volcanic eruptions: Mt. St. Helens, May 18, 1980.* Seattle, Wash.: Battelle Human Affairs Research Centers, 1980. (a)

Perry, R. W., Lindell, M., & Greene, M. *Evacuation decision-making and emergency planning.* Seattle, Wash.: Battelle Human Affairs Research Centers, 1980. (b)

Perry, R. W., Lindell, M., & Greene, M. Enhancing evacuation warning compliance. *Disasters,* 1980, *4*(4), 433–449. (c)

Perry, R. W., Lindell, M., & Greene, M. *Disaster warnings and crisis relocation planning.* Seattle, Wash.: Battelle Human Affairs Research Centers, 1980. (d)

Perry, R. W., Lindell, M., & Greene, M. Mt. St. Helens: Washingtonians view their volcano. *Hazard Monthly,* 1980, *1*(2), 1–3. (e)

Perry, R. W., Lindell, M., & Green, M. Crisis communications: Ethnic differentials in interpreting and acting on disaster warnings. *Social Behavior and Personality,* 1981, *10,* 97–104. (a)

Perry, R. W., Lindell, M., & Greene, M. *Evacuation planning in emergency management.* Lexington, Mass.: Heath-Lexington Books, 1981. (b)

Pettigrew, T. *Racially separate or together?* New York: McGraw-Hill, 1971.

Platt, R. The national flood insurance program: Some midstream perspectives. *Journal of the American Institute of Planners,* 1976, *42,* 303–313.

Ponting, R. Rumor control centers: Their emergence and operations. *American Behavioral Scientist,* 1973, *16,* 391–401.

Preusser, H. Der Vulkanausbruch auf Heimaey/Vestmannaeyjar und seien Auswirkungen. *Geographische Rundschau*, 1973, *25*(9), 337–350.

Prince, S. H. *Catastrophe and social change*. New York: Columbia University Press, 1920.

Quarantelli, E. L. The nature and conditions of panic. *American Journal of Sociology*, 1954, *60*, 267–275.

Quarantelli, E. L. The behavior of panic participants, *Sociology and Social Research*, 1957, *41*, 187–194.

Quarantelli, E. L. Images of withdrawal behavior in disasters. *Social Problems*, 1960, *9*(1), 68–79. (a)

Quarantelli, E. L. A note on the protective function of the family in disasters. *Marriage and Family Living*, 1960, *22*, 263–264. (b)

Quarantelli, E. L. Human response in stress situations. In B. M. Halphin (ed.), *Proceedings of the first conference and workshop on fire casualties*. Laurel, Md.: Applied Physics Laboratory, Johns Hopkins University, 1976.

Quarantelli, E. L. Social aspects of disasters and their relevance to pre-disaster planning. *Disasters*, 1977, *1*(1), 98–107.

Quarantelli, E. L. Panic behavior: some empirical observations. In *Human response to tall buildings*. Stroudsburg, Penn.: Dowden, Hutchinson & Ross, 1978.

Quarantelli, E. L. *Evacuation behavior and problems*. Columbus: Ohio State University Disaster Research Center, 1980. (a)

Quarantelli, E. L. *The consequences of disasters for mental health: conflicting views*. Columbus: Ohio State University, Disaster Research Center, 1980. (b)

Quarantelli, E. L., & Dynes, R. Property norms and looting: their patterns in community crisis. *Phylon*, 1970, *31*, 168–182.

Quarantelli, E. L., & Dynes, R. When disaster strikes. *Psychology Today*, 1972, *5*, 67–70.

Quarantelli, E. L., & Dynes, R. Community conflict: its absence and its presence in natural disasters. *Mass Emergencies*, 1976, *1*, 139–152.

Quarantelli, E. L., & Dynes, R. Response to social crisis and disaster. *Annual Review of Sociology*, 1977, *2*, 23–49. (a)

Quarantelli, E. L., & Dynes, R. Response to social crisis and disaster. *Annual Review of Sociology*, 1977, *3*, 23–49. (b)

Quarantelli, E. L., & Taylor, V. *Some views on the warning problem in disasters as suggested by sociological research*. Paper read at the American Meteorological Society Conference on Severe Local Storms, Omaha, Nebraska, 1977.

Quarantelli, E. L. (with B. Baisden & T. Bourdess). *Evacuation behavior and problems: Findings and implications from the research literature* (Miscellaneous Report 27). Columbus: The Ohio State University, Disaster Research Center, 1980.

Raiffa, H. *Decision analysis*. Reading, Mass.: Addison-Wesley, 1968.

Rawlinson, G. *History of Herodotus*. London: John Murray, 1880.

Rees, J. D. Effects of the eruption of Paricutin Volcano on land forms, vegetation, and human occupancy. In P. D. Sheets & D. Grayson (eds.), *Volcanic activity and human ecology*. New York: Academic Press, 1980.

Renzi, M. Negroes and voluntary associations. *Research Reports in the Social Sciences*, 1968, *2*, 63–71.

Regulska, J. *Public awareness programs for natural hazards*. Paper prepared for Hazard Awareness Workshop, Corpus Christi, Texas, March 22–23, 1979.

Reichstag, G. Denschift über die Entwickeling der Schultzgebiete in Afrike und der Südsee, 1906–1907. *Verhandlungen des Reichstages XII*. (Legislaturperidoe I, Vol. 245, Anlagen zu den stenographischen Berichten no. 622, pp. 4117–4126). Berlin: J. Sittenfeld, 1908.

Reilly, M. Personal communication. 1980.

Robinson, D. *The face of disaster*. New York: McGraw-Hill, 1959.

Roen, S. R., Ottenstein, D., Cooper, S., & Burnes, A. Community adaptation as an evaluative concept in community mental health. *Archives of General Psychiatry,* 1966, *15,* 36–44.

Rose, P. I. Race and ethnicity. In Rodney Stark (ed.), *Society today* (2nd ed.). Del Mar, Cal.: CRM Books, 1973.

Rosenfeld, C. Observations on the Mount St. Helens eruption. *American Scientist,* 1980, *68,* 494–509.

Ross, D. The emotional effects of an atomic incident. *Cincinnati Journal of Medicine,* 1952, *33,* 38–41.

Roth, A., & Locke, B. *Continuous community mental health assessment.* Paper read at the 101st meeting of the American Public Health Association, San Francisco, 1973.

Rowe, W. *An anatomy of risk.* New York: Wiley, 1977.

Rubin, C. Disaster mitigation: Challenge to managers. *Public Administration Times,* 1979, *2,* 1–2. (a)

Rubin, C. B. *Natural disaster recovery planning for local public officials.* Columbus, Ohio: Academy for Contemporary Problems, 1979. (b)

Saarinen, T. F. *The relation of hazard awareness to adoption of approved mitigation measures.* Paper preapred for Hazard Awareness Workshop, March 22–23, 1979, Corpus Christi, Texas. Boulder, Colorado: Natural Hazards Research and Applications Information Center, 1979.

Saarinen, T. *Public Response to Mt. St. Helens Volcano hazard warnings.* Washington, D.C.: National Science Foundation, Problem Focused Research, 1980.

Saarinen, T. *Perspectives on increasing hazard awareness.* Boulder: Institute for Behavioral Science, University of Colorado, 1982.

Sandman, P., & Paden, M. At Three Mile Island. *Columbia Journalism Review,* 1979, pp. 43–58.

Savage, P. E. A. Disaster planning. *Injury,* 1971, *3*(1), 49–55.

Schiff. M. Hazard Adjustment. *Environment and Behavior,* 1977, *9,* 233–254.

Schorr, J., & Goldsteen, R. *Public response to a nuclear reactor accident.* Deland, Fla.: Department of Sociology, Stetson University.

Schrag, C. Elements of theoretical analysis in sociology. In L. Gross (ed.), *Sociological theory.* New York: Harper & Row, 1967.

Scott, W. A. Research definitions of mental health and mental illness. *Psychological Bulletin,* 1958, *55*(1), 29–45.

Sheahan, T. Personal Communication. Skagit County Department of Emergency Services, Mt. Vernon, Washington.

Shibutani, T., & Kwan, K. *Ethnic stratification: a comparative approach.* New York: MacMillan, 1965.

State of Idaho. *Natural disaster plan.* Boise: Office of Emergency Planning, State of Idaho, 1979.

Stillar, W. Planning for disasters. *Long Range Planning,* 1975, *8,* 2–7.

Sims, J., & Bauman, D. The tornado threat. *Science,* 1972, *176,* 1386–1392.

Slovic, P., Kunreuther, H., & White, G. Decision processes, rationality and adjustments to natural hazards. In Gilbert White (ed.), *Natural hazards.* New York: Oxford University Press, 1974.

Slovic, P., Lichtenstein, S., & Fischhoff, B. *Images of disaster: Perception and acceptance of risks from nuclear power.* Eugene, Oregon: Decision Research, 1980.

Sotomayor, M. Mexican-American interaction with social systems. *Social Casework,* 1971, *52,* 316–322.

Srole, L., Langner, T., Michael, S., Opler, M., & Rennie, T. *Mental health in the metropolis: The midtown Manhattan study* (Vol. 1). New York: McGraw-Hill, 1962.

Stallings, R. *A description of analysis of the warning systems in the Topeka, Kansas Tornado of June 8, 1966.* Columbus: Disaster Research Center, Ohio State University, 1967.

Stallings, R. *Communications in natural disaster.* Columbus: Ohio State University Disaster Research Center, 1971.

Staples, R. *Introduction to black sociology.* New York: McGraw-Hill, 1976.

Staples, R., & Mirande, A. Racial and cultural variations among american families: A decennial review of the literature on minority families. *Journal of Marriage and the Family,* 1980, *42,* 887–903.

State of California, The Resources Agency. *California Flood Management: An Evacuation of Flood Damage Prevention Programs.* Bulletin 199. Sacramento: The Resources Agency, Department of Water Resources, 1980.

Sterling, J., Drabek, T., & Key, W. *The long-term impact of disaster on the health self-perceptions of victims.* Paper read at meetings of American Sociological Association, Chicago, 1977.

Susser, M. *Community psychiatry: Epidemiologic and social themes.* New York: Random House, 1968.

Sussman, M., & Burchinal, L. Kin family networks. *Marriage and Family Living,* 1962, *24,* 231–240.

Taylor, J., Zurcher, L., & Key, W. *Tornado.* Seattle: University of Washington Press, 1970.

Taylor, J. C. The safe transportation of radioactive material shipping containers including accident and response experience. *Proceedings of the Fifth International Synposium on Packaging and Transportation of Radioactive Materials,* Las Vegas, Nevada, 1978.

Taylor, Sgt. Jon A. Personal Communication to Marjorie R. Greene. Cowlitz County Sheriff's Office, Kelso, Washington, 1980.

Taylor, V. *Delivery of mental health services in disasters.* Columbus: Disaster Research Center, Ohio State University, 1976.

Taylor, V. Good news about disasters. *Psychology today,* 1977, *11,* 93–96.

Terrell, H. S. Wealth accumulation of black and white families. *Journal of Finance,* 1971, *26,* 363–379.

Tierney, K. *Emergent norm theory as theory.* Columbus: Disaster Research Center, Ohio State University, 1978.

Tierney, K. *A primer for preparedness for acute chemical emergencies.* Columbus: Disaster Research Center, Ohio State University, 1980.

Tierney, K., & Baisden, B. *Crisis intervention programs for disaster victims.* Rockville, Md.: National Institute of Mental Health, 1979.

Titchener, J., & Kapp, F. T. Family and character change at Buffalo Creek. *American Journal of Psychiatry,* 1976, *3,* 295–299.

Titmuss, R. *Problems of social policy.* London: HM Stationery Office, 1950.

Todd, D. J. Personal Communication to Marjorie R. Greene. Toutle Fire Department, Toutle, Washington.

Tolsdorf, C. Social networks, supports and coping. *Family Process,* 1976, *15*(4), 407–417.

Tomeh, A. Formal voluntary organizations: participation, correlates and interrelationships. *Sociological Inquiry,* 1973, *43,* 89–122.

Travis, R., & Riebsam, W. Communicating environmental uncertainty. *Journal of Geography,* 1979, *78*(5), 168–172.

Turner, M. B. *Philosophy and the science of behavior.* New York: Appleton-Century-Crofts, 1967.

Turner, R. Collective Behavior. In Robert Faris (ed.), *Handbook of modern sociology.* Chicago: Rand-McNally, 1964.

Turner, R., & Killian, L. *Collective behavior.* Englewood Cliffs, N.J.: Prentice-Hall, 1972.

Turner, R., Nigg, J., Paz, D., & Young, B. *Community response to earthquake threat in southern California.* Los Angeles: University of California at Los Angeles, 1979.

Turner, R., Nigg, J., Paz, D., & Young, B. *Community response to earthquake threat in southern California. Part ten: Summary and recommendations.* Los Angeles: Institute for Social Science Research, University of California, 1981.

Tyhurst, J. S. Psychological and social aspects of civilian disaster. *Canadian Medical Association Journal,* 1957, *76,* 385–393. (a)

Tyhurst, J. S. The role of transition states—including disasters—in mental illness. In National Research Council (ed.), *Symposium on preventive and social psychiatry.* Washington, D.C.: U.S. Government Printing Office, 1957. (b)

Ullman, L., & Krasner, L. *A psychological approach to abnormal behavior.* New York: McGraw-Hill, 1970.

U.S. Department of Housing and Urban Development and Federal Emergency Management Agency. *Evaluation of the economic, social and environmental effects of floodplain regulations* (FIA–8). Washington, D.C.: Office of Policy Development and Research, U.S. Department of HUD and Federal Insurance Administration, FEMA, 1981.

U.S. Nuclear Regulatory Commission. *Report to Congress on Status of Emergency Response Planning for Nuclear Power Plants* (NUREG-0755) Washington, D.C.: Nuclear Regulatory Commission, 1981.

U.S. Senate Hearings. *Disaster assistance Pacific Northwest—Mount Saint Helens eruption.* Washington, D.C.: Committee on Appropriations, 1980.

U.S. Strategic Bombing Survey. *The Effects of Strategic Bombing on German Morale* (Vols. I and II). Washington, D.C.: U.S. Government Printing Office, 1947. (a)

U.S. Strategic Bombing Survey. *The effects of strategic bombing on Japanese morale.* Washington, D.C.: U.S. Government Printing Office, 1947. (b)

Utah State Division of Health, Department of Social Services. *Natural disaster emergency operations plan.* Salt Lake City: Author, 1977.

Vallance, T., & D'Augelli, A. The helpers community: Characteristics of natural helpers. *American Journal of Community Psychology,* 1982, *10*(2), 197–205.

Van Arsdol, M., Sabagh, G., & Alexander, F. Reality and the perception of environmental hazards. *Journal of Health and Social Behavior,* 1964, *5* (Winter), 144–153.

Van den Berghe, P. *Race and racism.* New York: Wiley, 1967.

Vander Zanden, J. *American minority relations.* New York: The Ronald Press, 1966.

Waesche, H., & Peck, D. Volcanoes tell secrets in Hawaii. *Natural History,* 1966, *75* (March), 20–29.

Wallace, A. *Tornado in Worcester.* Washington, D.C.: National Academy of Sciences, 1956. (a)

Wallace, A. *Human behavior in extreme situations.* Washington, D.C.: National Academy of Sciences-National Research Council, 1956. (b)

Wallace, A. Mazeway disintegration. *Human Organization,* 1957, *16* (Summer), 23–27.

Wallace, A. *Culture and personality.* New York: Random House, 1961.

Warrick, R. *Volcano hazard in the United States* (NSF-RA-E-75-012). Boulder: Institute of Behavioral Science, University of Colorado, 1975.

Warrick, R. Volcanoes as hazard. In P. D. Sheets & D. Grayson (eds.), *Volcanic activity and human ecology.* New York: Academic Press, 1979.

Waterstone, M. *Hazard mitigation behavior of urban flood plain residents.* Boulder: Natural Hazards Research and Applications Information Center, 1978.

Watson, E., & Collins, A. Natural helping networks in alleviating family stress. *The Annals,* 1982, *461* (May), 102–112.

Watson, W., & Maxwell, R. *Human aging and dying.* New York: St. Martin's, 1977.

Webber, D. L. Darwin cyclone: An exploration of disaster behaviour. *Australian Journal of Social Issues,* 1976, *11*(1), 54–63.

Weinberg, S. K. *The sociology of mental disorders.* Chicago: Aldine, 1967.

Weissman, M., Sholomskas, D., Pottenger, M., Prusoff, B., & Locke, B. Assessing depressive symptoms in five psychiatric populations. *American Journal of Epidemiology,* 1977, *6*(3), 203–214.

Weller, J., & Quarantelli, E. L. Neglected characteristics of collective behavior. *American Journal of Sociology,* 1973, *79*, 665–685.

Wenger, D. E., Faupel, C. E., & James, T. F. *Disaster beliefs and emergency planning* (Final Report to the National Science Foundation). Newark: University of Delaware Press, 1980.

White, G. Human response to natural hazard. In National Academy of Engineering (ed.), *Perspectives on benefit-risk decision making.* Washington, D.C.: National Academy of Sciences-National Academy of Engineering, 1972.

White, G. *Natural hazards: Local, national and global.* New York: Oxford University Press, 1974.

White, G. *Flood hazard in the United States.* Boulder: University of Colorado Press, 1975.

White, G., & Haas, G. *Assessment of research on natural hazards.* Cambridge: MIT Press, 1975.

White, R. *The abnormal personality.* New York: Ronald Press, 1964.

Whyte, A. V., & Burton, I. *Environmental risk assessment.* New York: Wiley, 1980.

Williams, H. Some functions of communication in crisis. *Human Organization,* 1957, *16,* 15–19.

Williams, H. Human factors in warning and response systems. In H. Grosser (ed.), *The threat of impending disaster.* Cambridge: MIT Press, 1964.

Williams, H., & Fritz, C. The human being in disaster: A research perspective. *The Annals,* 1957, *309,* 42–51.

Wilmer, H. Toward a definition of the therapeutic community. *American Journal of Psychiatry,* 1958, *114,* 824–834.

Wilson, K., & Zurcher, L. Status, inconsistency, and participation in social movements: An application of Goodman's hierarchical modeling. *Sociological Quarterly,* 1976, *17,* 520–533.

Wilson, R. Disaster and mental health. In G. Baker and D. Chapman (eds.), *Man and society in disaster.* New York: Basic Books, 1962.

Windham, G., Posey, E., Ross, P., & Spencer, B. *Reactions to storm threat during Hurricane Eloise.* State College: Mississippi State University, 1977.

Withey, S. Reaction to uncertain threat. In G. Baker & D. Chapman (eds.), *Man and society in disaster.* New York: Basic Books, 1962.

Withey, S. Sequential accommodations to threat. In G. H. Grosser (ed.), *The threat of impending disaster.* Cambridge: MIT Press, 1964.

Wolensky, R., & Miller, E. The everyday versus the disaster role of local officials. *Urban Affairs Quarterly,* 1981, *16,* 483–504.

Working Group on Earthquake Hazards Reduction. *Earthquake hazards reduction: Issues for an implementation plan.* Washington, D.C.: Office of Science and Technology Policy, Executive Office of the President, 1978.

The worst nuclear power plant accident yet. *The Lancet,* April 28, 1979, pp. 909–910.

Wright, C., & Hyman, H. Who belongs to voluntary associations? In W. Glaser and D. Sills (eds.), *The government of associations.* Totowa, N.J.: Bedminster Press, 1966.

Wright, G., & Phillips, L. Cultural variation in Probabilistic thinking: Alternative ways of dealing with uncertainty. *International Journal of Psychology,* 1980, *15*(4), 239–257.

Wright, J., & Rossi, P. *Social science and natural hazards.* Cambridge, Mass.: Abt Books, 1981.

Wyner, A. *Seismic safety planning in California.* Paper read at the Western Political Science Association, San Diego, April, 1981.

Young, C., Giles, D., & Plantz, M. Natural networks: Help-giving and help-seeking in two rural communities. *American Journal of Community Psychology,* 1982, *10*(4), 457–469.

Young, M. The role of the extended family in a disaster. *Human Relations,* 1954, *7,* 383–391.

Zeigler, D., Brunn, S., & Johnson, J. H. Evacuation from a nuclear technological disaster. *The geographical review,* 1981, *71,* 1–16.

Zetterberg, H. L. *On theory and verification in sociology.* Totowa, N.J.: The Bedminster Press, 1966.

Zigler, E., & Phillips, L. Social competence and the process-reactive distinction in psychopathology. *Journal of Abnormal and Social Psychology,* 1962, *65*(2), 215–222.

Zurcher, L. Social psychological functions of ephemeral roles: A disaster work crew. *Human Organization,* 1968, *27,* 281–297.

Author Index

Subject Index